CHAUCER: THE CANTERBURY TALES

LONGMAN CRITICAL READERS

General Editor:

STAN SMITH, Professor of English, University of Dundee

Published titles:

K. M. NEWTON, *George Eliot*

MARY EAGLETON, *Feminist Literary Criticism*

GARY WALLER, *Shakespeare's Comedies*

JOHN DRAKAKIS, *Shakespearean Tragedy*

RICHARD WILSON AND RICHARD DUTTON, *New Historicism and Renaissance Drama*

PETER WIDDOWSON, *D. H. Lawrence*

PETER BROOKER, *Modernism/Postmodernism*

RACHEL BOWLBY, *Virginia Woolf*

FRANCIS MULHERN, *Contemporary Marxist Literary Criticism*

ANNABEL PATTERSON, *John Milton*

CYNTHIA CHASE, *Romanticism*

MICHAEL O'NEILL, *Shelley*

STEPHANIE TRIGG, *Medieval English Poetry*

ANTONY EASTHOPE, *Contemporary Film Theory*

TERRY EAGLETON, *Ideology*

MAUD ELLMANN, *Psychoanalytic Literary Criticism*

ANDREW BENNETT, *Readers and Reading*

MARK CURRIE, *Metafiction*

BREAN HAMMOND, *Pope*

LYN PYKETT, *Reading Fin de Siècle Fictions*

STEVEN CONNOR, *Charles Dickens*

REBECCA STOTT, *Tennyson*

SUSANA ONEGA AND JOSÉ ANGEL GARCÍA LANDA, *Narratology*

BART MOORE-GILBERT, GARETH STANTON AND WILLY MALEY, *Postcolonial Criticism*

ANITA PACHECO, *Early Women Writers*

JOHN DRAKAKIS AND NAOMI CONN LIEBLER, *Tragedy*

ANDREW MICHAEL ROBERTS, *Joseph Conrad*

JOHN LUCAS, *William Blake*

LOIS PARKINSON ZAMORA, *Contemporary American Women Writers*

RICHARD KROLL, *The English Novel, Volume I, 1700 to Fielding*

RICHARD KROLL, *The English Novel, Volume II, Smollett to Austen*

THOMAS HEALY, *Andrew Marvell*

CHRISTINA MALCOLMSON, *Renaissance Poetry*

STEVE ELLIS, *Chaucer: The Canterbury Tales*

CHAUCER: THE CANTERBURY TALES

Edited and Introduced by

STEVE ELLIS

LONGMAN
LONDON AND NEW YORK

Pearson Education Limited
Edinburgh Gate
Harlow, Essex CM20 2JE
England
and Associated Companies throughout the world

*Published in the United States of America
by Addison Wesley Longman Inc., New York*

© Addison Wesley Longman Limited 1998

First published 1998
Second impression 1999

ISBN 0 582 24881-7 Paper
ISBN 0 582 24880-9 Cased

British Library Cataloguing-in-Publication Data

A catalogue record for this book is available from the British Library

Library of Congress Cataloging-in-Publication Data

A catalog entry for this title is available from the Library of Congress

Set by 35 in $9\frac{1}{2}/11\frac{1}{2}$ pt Palatino
Produced by Pearson Education Asia (Pte) Ltd.,
Printed in Singapore (JBW)

Contents

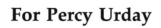

For Percy Urday

General Editors' Preface

The outlines of contemporary critical theory are now often taught as a standard feature of a degree in literary studies. The development of particular theories has seen a thorough transformation of literary criticism. For example, Marxist and Foucauldian theories have revolutionized Shakespeare studies, and 'deconstruction' has led to a complete reassessment of Romantic poetry. Feminist criticism has left scarcely any period of literature unaffected by its searching critiques. Teachers of literary studies can no longer fall back on a standardized, received methodology.

Lecturers and teachers are now urgently looking for guidance in a rapidly changing critical environment. They need help in understanding the latest revisions in literary theory, and especially in grasping the practical effects of the new theories in the form of theoretically sensitized new readings. A number of volumes in the series anthologize important essays on particular theories. However, in order to grasp the full implications and possible uses of particular theories it is essential to see them put to work. This series provides substantial volumes of new readings, presented in an accessible form and with a significant amount of editorial guidance.

Each volume includes a substantial introduction which explores the theoretical issues and conflicts embodied in the essays selected and locates areas of disagreement between positions. The pluralism of theories has to be put on the agenda of literary studies. We can no longer pretend that we all tacitly accept the same practices in literary studies. Neither is a *laissez-faire* attitude any longer tenable. Literature departments need to go beyond the mere toleration of theoretical differences: it is not enough merely to agree to differ; they need actually to 'stage' the differences openly. The volumes in this series all attempt to dramatize the differences, not necessarily with a view to resolving them but in order to foreground the choices presented by different theories or to argue for a particular route through the impasses the differences present.

The theory 'revolution' has had real effects. It has loosened the grip of traditional empiricist and romantic assumptions about language and literature. It is not always clear what is being proposed as the new agenda for literary studies, and indeed the very notion of 'literature' is questioned by the post-structuralist strain in theory. However, the uncertainties and obscurities of contemporary theories appear much less worrying when we see what the best critics have been able to do with them in practice. This series aims to disseminate the best of recent criticism and to show that it is possible to re-read the canonical texts of literature in new and challenging ways.

RAMAN SELDEN AND STAN SMITH

The Publishers and fellow Series Editor regret to record that Raman Selden died after a short illness in May 1991 at the age of fifty-three. Ray Selden was a fine scholar and a lovely man. All those he has worked with will remember him with much affection and respect.

Publisher's Acknowledgements

We are grateful to the following for permission to reproduce copyright material:

Boydell & Brewer Ltd for 'Aspects of Female Piety in the *Prioress's Tale*' by Elizabeth Robertson in *Chaucer's Religious Tales* edited by C. David Benson & Elizabeth Robertson, Copyright © Elizabeth Robertson, 1990; University of California Press and the author, for extracts from 'The Powers of Silence: The Case of the Clerk's Griselda' in *Chaucer and the Fictions of Gender* by Elaine Tuttle Hansen. Copyright © 1992, The Regents of the University of California; Harvard University Press for an extract from 'A Mixed Commonwealth of Style' in *Social Chaucer* by Paul Strohm, Cambridge, MA: Harvard University Press. Copyright © 1989 by the President and Fellows of Harvard College; Johns Hopkins University Press for the article ' "Vanysshed Was This Daunce, He Nyste Where": Alisoun's Absence in *The Wife of Bath's Prologue and Tale*' by Arthur Lindley in *English Literary History* (1992). Copyright © Johns Hopkins University Press; Northern Illinois University for the article 'Signs and/as Origin: Chaucer's *Nun's Priest's Tale*' by Britton J. Harwood from *Style* 20 (Summer, 1986): 189–202; Professor Michael Jones, as Editor of *Nottingham Medieval Studies*, for extracts from the article 'Metafictional Strategies and the Theme of Sexual Power in the *Wife of Bath's* and *Franklin's Tales*' by John Stephens & Marcella Ryan in *Nottingham Medieval Studies* 33 (1989); Pegasus Press for the articles 'Structure as Deconstruction: "Chaucer and Estates Satire" in the *General Prologue*, or Reading Chaucer as a Prologue to the History of Disenchantment' by H. Marshall Leicester Jr, in *Exemplaria* 2 (1990): 241–4, 246–61, and 'The Politics of Discourse in Chaucer's *Knight's Tale*' by Mark A. Sherman in *Exemplaria* 6.1 (1994): 87–105. Copyright © Pegasus Press, University of North Carolina at Asheville, Asheville, NC; The Pennsylvania State University Press for the article 'Umberto Eco, Semiotics, and the *Merchant's Tale*' by Carolyn P. Collette in the *Chaucer Review* 24 (1989–90). Copyright © 1989. The Pennsylvania University Press; Routledge Inc and the author, for the chapter 'Robyn the Miller's Thrifty Work' by Peggy Knapp in *Chaucer and the Social Contest* (1990); The University of Wisconsin Press for extracts from chapter 3 'The Law of Man and Its "Abhomynacions" ' in

Editor's Acknowledgements

I would like to thank my family and colleagues for their customary support, in particular Barbara Rasmussen. I am also deeply grateful to Sarah Bury for her meticulous copy-editing.

STEVE ELLIS

Editions and Abbreviations Used in the Text

Quotations from Chaucer in the Introduction and in the majority of the essays are taken from the *Riverside Chaucer*, 3rd edn, ed. Larry D. Benson et al. (Boston, MA: Houghton Mifflin, 1987; Oxford: Oxford University Press, 1988). Some authors however use the *Works* of Chaucer, ed. F. N. Robinson, 2nd edn (Boston, MA: Houghton Mifflin; London: Oxford University Press, 1957).

The following abbreviations are used in some of the essays:

AnM	*Annuale Medievale*
CE	*College English*
CR or *ChauR*	*Chaucer Review*
EETS	*Early English Text Society*
ELH	*English Literary History*
ELR	*English Literary Renaissance*
ES	*English Studies*
JEGP	*Journal of English and Germanic Philology*
JMRS	*Journal of Medieval and Renaissance Studies*
JNT	*Journal of Narrative Techniques*
Leeds SE	*Leeds Studies in English*
MAE	*Medium Aevum*
MED	*Middle English Dictionary*
MLN	*Modern Language Notes*
MLQ	*Modern Language Quarterly*
MP	*Modern Philology*
MS	*Mediaeval Studies*
NLH	*New Literary History*
PL or *Patr Lat*	*Patrologia ... Latina*, ed. J.-P. Migne, 221 vols (Paris: Migne, 1844–91).
PMLA	*Publications of the Modern Language Association of America*
REL	*Review of English Literature*
SAC	*Studies in the Age of Chaucer*

1 Introduction

I

Chaucer Studies in the 1980s and 1990s have been characterized by a pluralism and self-reflexiveness which make it increasingly difficult to maintain that the culture of the Middle Ages can be retrieved 'as it was' through the mechanisms of scholarship, and is not continually reconstructed through modern reading practices, though as we shall see the idea of the medieval period as a unitary, autonomously existing and objectively specifiable knowledge-bloc (functioning as the antithesis of modernity) has had some success in maintaining itself within the academy. The emerging note in interpretation, however, emphasizes in Thomas Hahn's words that 'all texts and all readings . . . depend for their meaning . . . on the predispositions, interests, and purposes of readers, both in earlier and in current interpretive communities', and indeed Hahn argues that the relationship that should obtain between what he calls the 'premodern text' and the 'postmodern reader' is one in which the latter works with a consciousness of his or her 'situated engagement' within the political and institutional context of the present historical moment.[1] Given that we are now urged to be 'postmodern readers', one dominant note in recent criticism has been not simply the present postmodernization of Chaucer but even the claims that Chaucer himself was actively and purposefully 'postmodern', given that his most celebrated work, the *Canterbury Tales*, can be read as primarily a story about story-telling.

A major impetus to this movement was the publication of Robert M. Jordan's *Chaucer's Poetics and the Modern Reader* in 1987. Chaucer's writing is here continually compared with modern avant-garde fiction and metafiction in its 'self-reflexiveness', its inviting 'primary emphasis on the verbal medium' itself.[2] The most important thing about the *Canterbury Tales* is their combination of, and constant attention to, the different levels of discourse that constitute them, betokening the 'strong authorial consciousness of language as a

1

compositional medium' (p. 133). Such a medley of genres, voices and styles, the complex 'embedding' of one narratorial position within another, the frequency of parody and linguistic play, all this constitutes for Jordan

> a wonderfully flexible and expansive poetics, fundamentally heterodox, open to all modes of discourse, and indifferent to structures of orthodoxy, whether moral, philosophical, aesthetic, or generic. It is this insubordinate attitude that brings Chaucer's poetics into such sympathetic resonance with postmodernism.
>
> (p. 172)

Chaucer therefore becomes peculiarly genial to 'the intellectual and moral fluidity of our time' in its 'aesthetics of uncertainty' (p. 20).

It is ironic that thirty or so years ago the dominant mode of interpretation was to see Chaucer's work as presenting a stable Christian orthodoxy and hierarchy which functioned precisely as an escape from modern relativism. This new Chaucer, however, who is attuned to our own greater 'tolerance', in Jordan's words, towards 'verbal artifice and virtuosity as the artful registration of a shifting, elusive reality' (p. 20) is one example of what Hahn calls a critical 'situated engagement'. Jordan indeed suggests that the fourteenth-century philosophical climate of nominalism, with its increasing interest in the specifics of an empirical knowledge that could be derived from this world and its corresponding scepticism about reason's access to universal truths and categorizations, anticipates the postmodern rejection of universal models of order and rationality promulgated by the Enlightenment (pp. 11–12). The aestheticization of this climate of uncertainty leads to an investment in the manner, rather than the matter, of what writers have to say – to a revived attention to rhetoric, in short – and Jordan is one of several writers who talk about the postmodernity, not only of Chaucer, but of medieval rhetoricians like Geoffrey of Vinsauf who influenced him.[3]

When Jordan talks above of a Chaucerian poetics that is thus both 'indifferent' to structures of orthodoxy and 'insubordinate' in holding this attitude, one notes a slippage between these two adjectives that indicates a contradiction not only in postmodern writing on Chaucer but in theories of the postmodern itself. How far a postmodern rejection of coercive and centralizing 'truths', designated with labels like God, Empire, Mankind, and its attention to voices previously on the margin of such grand narratives – women's writing, postcolonial literature, popular culture – represents an oppositional (or 'insubordinate') politics or an eclecticism in which the particular thrust of each voice is cancelled out in a pluralism that tries to accommodate all, is a question which, as we shall see, has some relevance to interpretation of the *Canterbury Tales*. Lee Patterson has indicated the wariness with which we should treat the postmodernization of Medieval Studies if that is to mean a 'celebration of scepticism' that would equate 'principled commitment' with 'blind dogmatism' and thus lead to 'political self-disenfranchisement'.[4] While welcoming the challenge to centralization noted above, Patterson is aware of how an overriding attention to 'rhetoric' can lead to disengagement from the sphere of social practice – to what he calls 'the erasure of the referent' (p. 89) – and to a dispersal of 'principled commitment' among the interplay of discourses; indifference rather than insubordination, to return to Jordan's terms. Certainly, when a recent follower of Jordan can state quite bluntly: 'in a rhetorical poetics, *what* is said is of far less consequence than *how* it is said' (emphasis in original), we realize the dangers of critical attention being corralled among linguistic effects in this way.[5] It is fair to say, however, that critics anxious to postmodernize Chaucer (including Jordan) have tended to work with a simplified and monolithic definition of 'postmodernism' (which equals, in effect, 'rhetoric') and have either taken for granted or effaced the questions of political effectivity which have led to so much debate among postmodernist theorists themselves, many of whom would question any simple distinction between the 'what' and the 'how' of 'what is said'.[6] The reader is further referred to the essays in this volume, which also tend to resist this distinction strenuously.

In Chaucer's case, the interest in seeing a writer primarily committed to 'rhetoric' is partly a reaction to the prestigious interpretative model of exegetics promulgated in the 1950s and 1960s by D. W. Robertson, Jr, for whom all medieval literature was to be read allegorically in the quest for stable Christian truth beneath the 'veil' of the letter, which was merely a unified doctrine's outer dress; in other words, read in a mode that is exactly opposed by the movement treated above.[7] Reaction to Robertson and his school is plainly signalled by Sheila Delany's book of 1972 on Chaucer's *House of Fame*, with its subtitle *The Poetics of Skeptical Fideism*, a book now seen as something of a landmark in Chaucer Studies in its portrayal of both Chaucer himself and the fourteenth century as experiencing a mood of shift and crisis in which the Robertsonian certainties are being undermined. Although, like Jordan, Delany sees Chaucer in his work as ultimately subscribing to Christian truth, she is more interested in the way he displays a pervading scepticism about the means of accessing or employing that truth in his texts, in matters of moral judgement or in subscription to literary authority; thus his

writings show an 'awareness of coexistent contradictory truths . . .
resulting in the suspension of final rational judgment'.[8] It might be
seen as a short step from here to Jordan's celebration of the 'aesthetics
of uncertainty', but in fact Delany shows some disagreement with the
postmodernist Chaucer she has perhaps started to uncover. While
Chaucer's 'pluralistic impulse' is a welcome challenge, in spite of
Robertson, to the medieval exegetical tradition, and 'generates the
irony and richness of perception that constitute Chaucer's main
appeal' (p. 35), Delany can label such pluralism less flatteringly
'indecisiveness' (p. 119) and can end her book with a warning
against Chaucerian non-commitment and his 'ironic treatment of
intellectual systems'. If a similar pluralism 'causes us to recoil from
the historical future', then the lesson we should finally draw from
Chaucer's work 'is the potential sterility of being unable to choose'
(p. 122). Delany's conclusions thus make a fascinating contrast with
those of some of Chaucer's more wholehearted recent postmodernizers
like Phyllis Portnoy, for whom today, 'in the 90s, where undecidability
is the catch-word, we choose not to make choices. It seems to me that
no-choice is at the same time most modern and most Chaucerian'.[9]

What Delany herself has gone on to 'choose' is to work within the
field of feminism, and her writings have thus paid full attention to
what is said within the Chaucerian text. Indeed, her 1983 essay on the
misogyny of the *Manciple's Tale* has been hailed as 'pav[ing] the way
for a good deal of contemporary feminist criticism of Chaucer' (the
essay makes an interesting contrast with Jordan's examination of the
Manciple's Tale in *Chaucer's Poetics*, which focuses as we might expect
on 'rhetorical' issues, namely the Tale's 'puzzlement over the validity
of man's efforts to capture reality with words' (p. 151)).[10] The
relationship between feminism and postmodernism is troubled and
complicated, given that espousers of both movements have
a common interest in deposing traditional ideals of order and
authority that are obviously patriarchal and in releasing previously
marginalized voices. However, as Patricia Waugh has argued,
many feminists do or should maintain a belief in a (traditional)
'emancipatory politics' with its coefficient beliefs in 'effective human
agency' and in 'historical progress'; a holding, in short, to the
'universal political aims' that the more nihilistic (male) versions
of postmodernism have sought to deny (*Postmodernism*, p. 195).

Many of the following essays will indeed show that there is no
shortage of feminist critics at present going to Chaucer to make his
texts 'work' on behalf of a particular political intervention, rather
than to savour the poetics of pluralism. The accommodation of the
latter to Bakhtin's theories of polyphony and dialogism is another
area of interest for many Chaucerians at the moment, as is the

relation of these theories in turn back to feminism. Before we can resume these debates, however, in the final part of this Introduction, we should consider in some detail the essays themselves. Some of these are extracts from a series of remarkable books produced at the end of the 1980s, and in the first part of the 1990s, which has reinvigorated the field of Chaucer Studies and which forms the nucleus of this collection.

II

The following essays, then, indicate the pluralism I referred to at the outset in that various interpretative strategies drawing on feminist, psychoanalytic, linguistic, anthropological and deconstructive theory are represented, though many pieces individually eschew the favouring of pluralism *per se* that characterizes postmodernist criticism. In making this selection, I have generally chosen pieces that focus on an individual Tale, and have wished to concentrate on those Tales most often read by students, though I have not necessarily opted for pieces that demonstrate the most thoroughgoing application of modern theory. Indeed, for reasons explored below the field of Medieval Studies in general has been resistant to such an application. Some of the most discussed work on Chaucer in recent years – and I will be concentrating for the moment on the studies of Carolyn Dinshaw, Elaine Tuttle Hansen, H. Marshall Leicester Jr, Lee Patterson and Paul Strohm – has however incorporated a modern theoretical perspective, and it is significant not only that each of the above scholars is American but that nearly every piece included in this collection is by an American, for undoubtedly it is in the United States that not only the majority of academics who are propagating 'new' readings of Chaucer are to be found, but also the journals, conferences and various forums in which such readings are advanced and debated.

Two essays that appeared in Arlyn Diamond's and Lee R. Edwards's collection, *The Authority of Experience: Essays in Feminist Criticism* (1977), are often cited as a significant event in Chaucer Studies. Here, under the banner of the opening line from the *Wife of Bath's Prologue*, the modern feminist appraisal of Chaucer's work begins, an appraisal that represents, in the words of Stephanie Trigg, 'probably the most profound critique of and methodological challenge to medieval literary studies' in recent years.[11] Following Lee Patterson, Trigg argues that Medieval Studies as an academic discipline has traditionally tended 'to adopt the authority structures of the dominant medieval institutions of knowledge and doctrine',

leading to the 'powerful interpellation of the medievalist as male,
Christian and, by implication . . . white',[12] an interpellation reinforced
in Chaucer's case by a history of masculinist rhetoric that returns
to him as 'the Father of English Poetry', a no-nonsense (English)
empiricist and, in G. K. Chesterton's phrase, a 'clubable fellow or
a man's man'.[13] Breaking into this male stronghold, whether it
be to rescue the protofeminist poet allegedly confined therein, or
conversely to confirm such a poet's patriarchal allegiances, has been
a rather arduous process, given that it was not until 1989 that the
first full-length feminist evaluation of Chaucer appeared, in Carolyn
Dinshaw's *Chaucer's Sexual Poetics*, though this has rapidly been
followed by the studies (listed in my Bibliography) of Martin, Mann
and notably Hansen, and by many articles in *Exemplaria*, the *Medieval
Feminist Newsletter* and elsewhere.

Already in *The Authority of Experience* the divisions that continue to
characterize feminist writing on Chaucer were evident, with Diamond
arguing that the Wife of Bath is an exercise in misogyny that would
perpetuate the 'nightmare' figure of medieval antifeminism, while
Maureen Fries's essay salutes the Wife in her robust attack on
patriarchy and its medieval institutions, going so far as to label her
'a truly practicing feminist'.[14] Dinshaw is extremely sympathetic to
Chaucer's 'positioning of himself as feminine' in his work, praising
his

> extraordinary and difficult attempts to envisage fully the place of
> the Other in patriarchal society – to imagine even the pleasures
> and pains of a woman's body, be they May's feelings of sexual
> repugnance on her wedding night, the Wife of Bath's delight in
> past sensuality and her rueful awareness of present pain in her
> ribs, or Griselda's resistance to the public exposure of her
> 'wombe' . . .[15]

In occupying this 'feminine' position, Chaucer's work valorizes
'what is devalued in patriarchal culture . . . speaking of and for what
is silenced' (p. 158), a transgressive pursuit that further highlights
'masculine and feminine as positions that can be occupied by either
sex' and that shows Chaucer's alertness to 'the social construction
of gender and to the patriarchal power structures that keep these
gender notions in place' (p. 12). Dinshaw traces how reading,
interpretation and a whole range of cultural practices were
emphatically gendered in the Middle Ages, the 'masculine' associated
with the spirit and the reason, the 'feminine' with the flesh and the
instincts, and thus in one model the masculine with a text's 'deeper',
moral meaning and the feminine with the surface blandishments of

the letter, embellishments which the reader should not be seduced by. Chaucer's texts, however, in their ambiguities and complex modes of narration, resist the practices of 'reading like a man', that is, the attempt to impose 'a single pattern . . . reducing complexity to produce a whole, monolithic structure, thus constraining the feminine' (p. 87). I have included in the following selection Dinshaw's account of the *Man of Law's Tale* from *Chaucer's Sexual Poetics*, in which for Dinshaw Chaucer indicates the inadequacies of a narrator who 'incarnates patriarchal ideology and its expressed system of law' (p. 89) in his self-contradictory attempts to 'constrain the feminine'.

In seeing Chaucer and his work as actively challenging contemporary ideology, Dinshaw follows in the tradition of a critic like David Aers, who stresses that Chaucer should not be seen as a representative male of the Middle Ages (a common perception of him to which we return below), but as a writer in opposition to the dominant institutions of his day in matters such as gender, textual authority, codes of chivalry and so forth. Such institutions are allowed a 'voice' in his work, but one that is challenged and subverted in various ways.[16] However, this position has in turn been challenged, notably by Elaine Tuttle Hansen, whose analysis of the *Clerk's Tale* is included here. For Hansen, though Chaucer's texts do repeatedly occupy the position of the 'feminine', they do so with the greatest reluctance; the fact that 'masculine and feminine [are] positions that can be occupied by either sex' in Dinshaw's words is not a source of liberation but matter for the deepest anxiety, given that patriarchal domination is thereby undermined. Thus for Hansen,

> in the *Canterbury Tales* men loathe, fear, and deny Woman because their efforts to construct masculine identity and discursive authority on the ground of Woman as Other, as properly and stably different, are constantly necessitated and undermined by the experience of both Woman and women as the same . . .[17]

In expressing patriarchy's obsessive fear of Woman encroaching on the domain of the male, Chaucer's writing works above all to re-contain and repress that fear, either through the quest to consolidate the gendered difference of the male protagonists, or through various strategies whereby the 'feminized' male poet himself is able to transcend and thus dismiss this dangerous contagion, or 'infectious feminization', in Hansen's phrase (p. 9).

In her discussion of the *Clerk's Tale* Hansen sees in Griselda not a patriarchal ideal (however nostalgic) of the utterly submissive wife, but a projection of male anxieties about female power. This power is declared not only in Griselda's extraordinary ability to govern Walter's territory in his absence (430–41, what Hansen calls her

7

'unnatural manliness', p. 191; 124 this volume), but also in the very practice of accepting Walter's commands to an extent that finally unnerves and subverts his authority. Griselda becomes something that Walter ultimately 'cannot understand or control', 'a mystery and a threat', a nightmare of female unintelligibility. It is immediately after Griselda shows herself possessed of political judgement 'of so greet equitee' (439) that the text exclusively refocuses on her roles as wife and mother. But in taking the former role to such uncanny lengths she eventually forces Walter to call a halt to a process that she, rather than he, seems increasingly to control in her refusal to be broken by it. In spite of the Clerk's criticisms of Walter's conduct, criticisms that for Dinshaw represent Chaucer's challenge to patriarchy in their questioning of male solidarity, Hansen sees the Clerk as identifying with Walter in various ways and as desperate to affirm his own 'proper maleness' at the end of the Tale (p. 205; 136 this volume). Thus rather than having Chaucer himself exposing the contradictions and injustices of a system of male control, as in Dinshaw's reading of the Man of Law, Hansen sees Chaucer and his texts as incriminated within such a system, with its need to contain and confine that which constantly eludes it: Chaucer's work 'feeds on and cannot escape the specter of Woman's and women's presence, just as it inscribes but cannot guarantee her, and their, absence' (p. 86). In this sense Hansen's main thrust repeats the position of Sheila Delany, for whom Chaucer's portrayal of women does not 'transcend' but rather 'repeats' the elements present in his own culture ('Slaying Python', p. 70).

In Dinshaw's more recent writing on Chaucer there are perhaps signs that her position is coming closer to Hansen's. Thus she ended *Chaucer's Sexual Poetics* with a very upbeat chapter on the Pardoner, the arch-transgressive, the 'not-man, not-woman' (p. 184) who sets the final seal on Chaucer's exposé of the constructedness of gender categories. In her 1995 article 'Chaucer's Queer Touches/A Queer Touches Chaucer', however, she dwells rather more on how the Chaucerian text admits the touch of the transgressive only to recontain it, the kiss of peace that concludes the *Pardoner's Tale* representing a typically Chaucerian reinscription of the norm 'in even greater force' after the queer-ying 'perspective on heteronormativity' that has been opened up by the Tale itself.[18] The queer in Chaucer may 'shake with his touch the heterocultural edifice' (p. 89), and it is still part of Chaucer's position as a 'classic liberal humanist' (p. 90) that he is allowed to do so, but the edifice remains very much intact in Chaucer's work and these touches are '*not* organised into an opposing sexuality' (p. 82 n. 14). In this sense, 'Chaucer's sexual poetics' are now rather less radical.

The antithesis between Dinshaw and Hansen defines the ends of a spectrum of response along which feminist appraisal of Chaucer can be situated, and the debate is represented further in this collection by Elizabeth Robertson's essay on the *Prioress's Tale*. Robertson echoes Hansen's claims that what seem to be examples of female submission can in fact be read as resistance to patriarchy, drawing on the work of critics like Cixous and Irigaray who reclaim positions of female marginality and subordination as 'the very access to power for women'.[19] Unlike Hansen, however, and more like Dinshaw, Robertson sees Chaucer contemplating the case of women with a sympathetic interest, and exploring in his religious Tales ways in which mysticism in particular offers women an escape from the 'subjecthood' of patriarchy. To be sure, Robertson argues that Chaucer is not so much interested in women *per se*, but rather in the way the Christianity they represent is undervalued and oppressed by secularism; Chaucer therefore 'cannot properly be said to have feminist political concerns' (p. 149; 194 this volume). What can be said, however, is that the feminist enterprise has had a far-reaching influence on the type of question critics at present bring to Chaucer, an effect that can be found in many of the following pieces even where the issue of women's role and power is not the principal item on the agenda.

The delay to the feminist investigation of Chaucer noted above is symptomatic of a more general delay, summed up in Faye Walker's statement that 'structural and poststructural critical theories have come late to Chaucer Studies', a situation generally explained with reference to the doughty and purposeful fencing that Medieval Studies erected around itself within the academy in the 1960s and 1970s.[20] It was not simply that the Chaucerian was expected to have an extensive and specialized philological, textual and historical training, but that this training led in many cases to an insistence that the Middle Ages were entirely distanced from the interpretative procedures applicable to post-medieval texts. The key to understanding Chaucer might be either the mastering of the role of the 'medieval reader', who in D. W. Robertson Jr's influential scheme, referred to above, would approach every text in a search for Christian allegory beneath the 'veil' of the letter (the practice of 'reading like a man' deplored by Dinshaw, and, for different reasons, by Patterson in his essay here) or the appreciation in Chaucer of a totalizing Gothic structuring or 'juxtaposition of disparate forms'.[21] This last phrase is Lee Patterson's, as applied to the work of Charles Muscatine, and Patterson offers the fullest diagnosis thus far of the ways in which 'the insistence of institutionalized Medieval Studies upon the otherness of the Middle Ages has perforce contributed to its alienation from the mainstream of literary studies' (*Negotiating the Past*, p. 38).

In Thomas Hahn's words, Patterson's writings on the history of Chaucer criticism amount to 'the most searching, alert, and intelligent self-assessments of medieval scholarship . . . that have yet appeared' (Hahn, 'The Premodern Text', p. 8), and Hahn too attacks institutionalized Chaucer Studies for having been too long the preserve of what he sees as the scholarly connoisseur on the one hand and the dogmatic Christian allegorist on the other; both groups, in their quest for 'autonomous structures' or a 'self-sufficient aesthetic', disguising their nostalgia for a lost medieval wholeness and the readerly acts that create this under a cloak of scholarly 'objectivity' (ibid., pp. 2–5). As we have seen, Hahn outlines a new role for today's reader as one that deliberately brings that reader's own 'situatedness' in modernity into the critical process. The special issue of *Exemplaria* that his essay introduces is entitled *Reconceiving Chaucer: Literary Theory and Historical Interpretation*, and Hahn stresses that this reconception has to be a conscious 'engagement' with the reader's own historical moment, as I began this Introduction by noting (p. 16). The desire to see Chaucer as belonging to 'another' history is itself an historical act now being actively challenged, and it is a tribute to the part played in this process by *Exemplaria* that the first two essays in this present collection are taken from that journal.

The work of Dinshaw, Hansen and Patterson, referred to thus far, shows that the call for a 'situated engagement' has not gone unheeded, and this is further illustrated by Patterson's *Chaucer and the Subject of History* (1991), from which the piece on the *Pardoner's Tale* reprinted here is taken. The book opens with an attack on 1980s individualism, both in Britain (in its Thatcherite version) and in America, and concludes with a lament on 'our inability to think socially, to recognize the social meaning and social consequences of our practices, including our habits of thought'. In this, it plainly continues the earlier attack (in *Negotiating the Past*) on the retreat of medievalists into a self-contained enclave.[22] Chaucer's importance for Patterson is precisely that he was someone who 'thought, and imagined, socially' (p. 423), but without surrendering the concept of the individual, so that in his work human nature is shown as 'at once universal and socially contingent', the poetry being both a 'championing of a sovereign selfhood and . . . [a] critique of it' (pp. 423–4). For Patterson, alarmed about the modern retreat into an individualism that would surrender control of the socio-historical world and about the complete suppression of 'proper' individuality in a world of growing cultural homogeneity, Chaucer's work, which centres on 'the dialectic between the self and history' (p. 155) is an

encouragement for us to 'think socially' without becoming social
clones. The account of the *Pardoner's Tale* reprinted here is taken
from the final chapter of Patterson's book and represents the climax
of his argument. In the Pardoner we see a figure 'fabricated from the
materials of literary convention and contemporary religious culture'
who is struggling at the same time to assert an autonomous selfhood
outside any such cultural construction (p. 423), and it is here that 'the
relationship between the individual and the social, in all its irreducible
complexity, becomes visible' (p. 425). Chaucer's importance to us lies
precisely in our present need to think seriously about this
relationship.

The claims for Chaucer's contemporary relevance made by
Patterson should not obscure the wealth of knowledge his work
displays about medieval literary and historical contexts, and again,
like Dinshaw and Hansen, he is able to combine such areas of
scholarship with modes of analysis deriving from the writings of, for
example, Freud, Lacan and Barthes. Like Dinshaw, however, and like
H. Marshall Leicester Jr and David Aers, and others associated with
propagating 'new' readings of Chaucer, there are limits to Patterson's
theorizing which have led to complaints about an inherent (humanist)
traditionalism in his work. For one thing, by clinging on so tightly to
the idea of a purposeful author conducting his careful ideological
investigations, many of these critics display the curious dualism
of, in Andrew Taylor's words, 'embracing full intentionality and
deconstructive rhetoric almost in the same breath', and thus
'appealing to what Roland Barthes long ago dismissed as the Author-
God'.[23] In this sense, Chaucer is still seen to (at least in part) stand
outside the historical and cultural discourses that constitute all texts
and subjects and to take a divine overview of them, and as Hahn
suggests of Patterson's work, there is little interest in 'forces not
accessible to the self-present consciousness of the individual', and
this places 'beyond consideration those decentering factors that have
been a central concern of feminism, psychoanalysis, and materialism
– the major theoretical positions that have called the subject into
question' (p. 7). As we have seen, Patterson plainly wishes to salvage
the individualistic self while paying due attention to its relationship
of 'irreducible complexity' with those contexts that would decentre
it. For a critic like Hansen, 'Chaucer' and his texts are themselves a
symptom of the inescapable ideological contradictions of his culture,
while the other critics noted above all in one way or another
espouse what Hahn calls a 'conscious activism by individuals in
a coherent, idealistic program [which] sketches out a one-person,
one-text renovation of history' (p. 7). The blending of traditional
and innovative perspectives in Patterson's work reflects his

ambivalent relationship to the postmodern situation, pointed out above (p. 3).

H. Marshall Leicester Jr's study *The Disenchanted Self: Representing the Subject in the Canterbury Tales* (1990) goes in some ways further down the road towards 'calling the subject into question' in Hahn's phrase. Leicester's essay on the *General Prologue* included here is taken from the journal *Exemplaria* (as a self-contained piece) rather than from his book, though it overlaps a good deal with the material of his final chapter. He argues that the way the *General Prologue* has been put together shows us 'structure as deconstruction', in that what gradually emerges for the reader is what Leicester calls a 'disenchanted' picture of selfhood. Thus the world comes to be seen as

> a tissue of institutions rather than of 'natures' . . . the subject is not a thing, like a rock, but a position or a site through which various forces pass, the continually constructed and reconstructed vector-product of all the agencies in play at the subject site – unconscious desire, concealed or mystified material and social power, the structures of language, and even . . . consciousness itself.[24]

The *General Prologue* is thus the dramatization of the narrator's increasing awareness that the individuals he assembles are in fact 'subjects', constituted by the various structures and material forces described above; what had been thought to be a divinely ordained pattern of society is similarly re-presented as the subject of political agency. In both cases we have a process of 'disenchantment': the transcendental power, be it God or the individual, is demystified, reformulated as historical construct. Thus the sanctioned model of the 'three estates' pattern of society, with which the *Prologue* opens, is gradually undermined by a structure that answers to the narrator's 'own social concerns' (p. 252; 32 this volume); that which was thought to be other-originated is materialized as a product of secular and ideological agency.

For Leicester, Chaucer's *General Prologue* can be read as not simply prefacing the *Canterbury Tales*, but as 'a prologue to the history of disenchantment', to quote from his essay's subtitle. The realization of the 'perennial' fact of the ideological and demystified construction of our world, which Leicester sees as the 'radical implication of poststructuralism', is adumbrated in the *Prologue*, though today we have an extensive and sophisticated equipment for analysing and understanding it in modern theory, as Chaucer did not (p. 259; 40 this volume). Leicester's emphasis on the 'perennial' has drawn attacks from those who see his work as ahistoricist, even though he attempts to forestall such objections in his essay: what is needed, according to one such critic, is a 'reconstruction of the conventions of reading and writing of earlier periods', an 'historically informed critique of cultural institutions rather than one which universalizes problems of agency and meaning as if these were always more or less the same'.[25] It is ironic that in Leicester's attacks on what he sees as the overweening arrogance of the institution of modern theory in claiming to originate readings of past works in which a deconstructive intent is already there, he opens himself to the attack that in positing Chaucer as any kind of deconstructionist he performs an 'appropriation' of Chaucer 'by an alien, homogenizing and thoroughly imperialistic tradition', and one that pays little regard to 'the discursive specificity of other traditions, cultures and texts'.[26] Although I have found Leicester's essay a stimulating and useful piece to use at the outset of teaching courses on the *Canterbury Tales*, it does illustrate the dangers of eclecticism: its application of deconstruction is not likely to please cultural materialists, while its salvaging of the author-function, and of authorial intent as categories which remain in something of a mystified way outside the procedures of 'disenchantment' offends deconstructionists. In 'Chaucer Our Derridean Contemporary?' Andrew Taylor talks (though in a not unsympathetic way) of the difficulties many medievalists, including Leicester, seem to have in adopting a fully deconstructive approach to their subject, and of their frequent desire 'to serve two masters, Chaucer and Derrida' (p. 475). I have, however, included one piece in this collection (and they are not easy to find) which makes a more thoroughgoing use of Derrida's work, particularly *Of Grammatology* – that by Britton J. Harwood on the *Nun's Priest's Tale*.

Leicester's argument that the *General Prologue*'s unfolding reveals that a social order supposedly divinely sanctioned is, in fact, the product of 'concealed or mystified material and social power' is taken forward by the second piece in this collection, where Mark Sherman writes on the *Knight's Tale*. It is apparent that when Theseus talks of 'the faire cheyne of love' that governs the universe at the end of the Tale (2988), and of the order and stability that underlie what might seem to be a world of random brutality, this teaching is at odds with what the reader sees of the callous behaviour of the gods who govern human affairs. In other words, ideas of design and control here seem plainly humanly originated, though there is a long history of critical debate over what the Tale is thereby showing, running from the approval of Theseus's stoical quest for civilized values in a dark and hostile universe to attacks on his disguising his own quest for absolutist power under a metaphysical sanction. This last position, developed by critics like Terry Jones and Hansen, is also taken by Sherman, who extends the consideration of order and repression from political to psychological and narrative fields.[27] From Theseus's conquest, or 'erasure', of 'Femenye' at the start of the Tale (859–74), to his construction of the lists where Palamon and Arcite are to fight on the very site of the lawless grove where they intended their private battle (1862), Sherman interprets Theseus's quest for order as synonymous with the exclusion of categories defined as 'other', be these represented by women, the realm of the natural world or the erotic. This 'centripetal power politics' (p. 100; 53 this volume) is replicated in the Knight's own mode of narration, particularly in his frequent use of *occupatio*, the device whereby reference is made to what the Tale is not going to tell. In this, Sherman argues, the Knight is excluding or marginalizing other narratives which 'could potentially contradict the one he's telling' (p. 94; 48 this volume), but the Knight's and Theseus's twin modes of exclusion only serve to empower that which is repressed in both cases. As with Hansen's work therefore, Sherman reads the *Knight's Tale* as an account of the anxieties rather than the strengths of patriarchal chivalry, anxieties which are linked in Lacanian terms to that which is relegated to the 'imaginary' order in Theseus's quest to gain control over the symbolic, the realm of public signification (pp. 100–1; 53 this volume).[28]

The *General Prologue* opens with a portrait of traditional authority in the Knight, both a literal and metaphorical father, and the Tale he tells, the first on the pilgrimage, also attempts to assert authority in the ways outlined above. The Knight's attempts to control discourse, or to rein it within a unitary narrative are, in fact, antipathetic to the enterprise of the *Canterbury Tales* as a whole, as Sherman argues, given that the *Tales* represent a divergent collection of speakers often in conflict with one another. If the *Tales* begin with a father they also end with one, or rather, two; first, another figure of traditional authority in the Parson, and then the overriding Father to whom the final prayer of the 'Retraction' is addressed. The proliferation of 'voices' occupying the space between these poles of paternal authority has led many critics in recent years to make use of Bakhtinian concepts of polyphony and dialogism in discussing the *Tales*. A Bakhtin-informed analysis of the 'carnivalesque' discourse of the *Miller's Tale*, for example, is as old as Alfred David's *The Strumpet Muse* of 1976, but it is again only in the last ten years that Bakhtin has become a common reference in Chaucer criticism.[29] Two of the pieces included here, those by Peggy Knapp and Paul Strohm, make use of Bakhtin's work, and Knapp's analysis of the *Miller's Tale* as a thoroughgoing act of opposition to the Knight's talks of its version of a 'ritual of misrule' to challenge aristocratic modes of order, and of the way that the 'heteroglot' nature of fabliau discourse is 'corrosive of the high, straightforward genres' of which the Knight's philosophical romance is an example.[30] Knapp, however, supplements her use of Bakhtin with a tracing of the Oedipal elements in the *Miller's Tale* that are directed against the law of paternal authority set up by the Knight, and Freud's work in *Jokes and Their Relation to the Unconscious* is also used to explain how the fabliau mode is able to retrieve on a communal level pleasure that is repressed by the 'civilized' codes exemplified in the *Knight's Tale* (pp. 41–4; 72–5 this volume).

Although many commentators would agree on the oppositional relationship of these first two Tales, on levels that are social, linguistic, psychological, philosophical and so forth, and although such an opposition is promised by the Miller's express intention to 'quite' what the Knight has said (3127), of late feminist critics have begun to insist on their underlying sameness. There is indeed an element of this in Knapp herself (p. 35; 66 this volume), but it is taken further by Karma Lochrie and Elaine Hansen. For the latter, in telling these Tales, 'knight and peasant talk to each other across their differences' (*Chaucer and the Fictions of Gender*, p. 209), that common talk representing a marginalization of and violence towards woman in which she becomes merely a site for male rivalries. Lochrie argues that the distinction between adultery and cuckoldry is crucial in understanding the *Miller's Tale*, the latter involving sexual pleasure with a woman as a kind of by-product of the challenge to outwit and better another man,[31] and Hansen has also suggested that the entire 'misdirected kiss' episode and Absolon's brutal desire for revenge on Alison represents the male fear of castration and the need to punish woman for provoking that fear (pp. 230–1). For Hansen, the 'normal' response of ribald laughter the Tale has prompted is truly remarkable; as she says, 'what is odd about this tale is not its innocence, but the modern critical insistence on its innocence' (p. 225). Lochrie notes that to read the *Miller's Tale* as an example of uncomplicated carnivalesque 'play', as for example Jon Cook has done, 'fails to account for the complicity of carnival and fabliau in medieval politics, particularly where gender is concerned' (p. 302), a point also made by Faye Walker ('Making Trouble', p. 587).[32]

I have included in this collection of essays as the final piece a short extract from Paul Strohm's *Social Chaucer* (1989), a piece that attempts an overview of Chaucer's project in the *Tales* as a whole. Strohm argues that the *Tales* are 'polyphonic' in ways outlined in Bakhtin's work on the novels of Dostoevsky, that is, they embrace 'separate and distinctive voices as a means of asserting social difference'.[33] For

Strohm, 'Chaucer's commitment to polyvocality' is a 'socially significant gesture' because his work as a 'commonwealth of "mixed style" ' thereby represents 'the idea of the natural state as a socially heterogeneous body that recognizes the diverse interests and serves the collective good of all' (pp. 168–9; 227–8 this volume). Chaucer was alert to the new social patterns and pressures of his day, the *Tales* showing themselves receptive to the voices of 'previously excluded or underacknowledged ranks and groups' such as women and the mercantile and professional interests (p. 157), and in spite of the authority figures who open and close the *Tales*, Strohm argues that the work as a whole displays a 'generally antihierarchical and communal thrust' in which the various voices maintain a polyphonic equality (p. 163). To be sure, Strohm is aware that in writing for a predominantly *gentil* audience Chaucer has to set limits to this plurality, and in particular the absence in the *Tales* of any real opportunity for the voice of the peasant-labourer to emerge signals the limits to Chaucer's social thinking (pp. 172–4). Even so, Strohm is clearly sympathetic to the new note of social openness and conciliation he finds in Chaucer, and his book ends on the assertion that the *Tales* allow 'readers in posterity a continuing opportunity to refresh their own belief in social possibility' (p. 182).

III

Strohm's claims for Chaucer's relevance to our contemporary social thinking have struck some critics as offering too benign a model of 'social Chaucer' and of underestimating the extent of his social alienation and pessimism.[34] Others, myself included, find much that is persuasive in Strohm's reading but would argue that it represents a collusion between poet and critic that threatens to efface many of the issues concerning authority and gender raised by other critics in the essays included here (Strohm's 'Preface' is quite clear about the respect he accords Chaucer as a social thinker, pp. xii–xiii). Although Strohm talks at several points in his piece about the 'competing' nature of the *Tales*'s voices, about their 'ultimate irreconcilability' and, quoting Bakhtin, about the 'unceasing ... quarrel' between them (pp. 166–8; 225–8 this volume), he sees the Chaucerian form that embraces them as itself an act of conciliation:

> the socially creative form of the *Canterbury Tales* permits a relatively untroubled contemplation of extreme difference, a degree of difference that could not be acknowledged in the social sphere without danger to the participants.
>
> (p. 172; 231 this volume)

This serene contemplation of difference bespeaks perhaps Strohm's own office in the mid-1990s as one of the trustees of the vast and vastly plural New Chaucer Society, with its own need to recognize a diverse spectrum of often contentious voices, and it is true that the Society does in fact hold together as a community, just as (it can be maintained) Chaucer's pilgrimage-party does. But an emphasis on the *Tales* as conciliation can pay too little attention to the issues raised in the polemic their voices do introduce, with the effect that letting them speak becomes more important than listening to what they are actually saying.[35] This collection of essays, though gathered together within the pages of a book to represent its own type of speech-community, does I think show that some readers (particularly women readers) go to the *Tales* and come away from them rather less 'untroubled' by the differences therein, differences which continue to demand voicing in our own day. Strohm's interest in Bakhtin's polyvocality is a rather partial one, ignoring as it does the governing principle of Bakhtin's sense of social difference in the Middle Ages in its neglect of the genre of the carnivalesque, that voice of the 'folk' whereby what Bakhtin calls the 'dogmatic and hostile' mode of 'gloomy official seriousness' promulgated by authoritarian and patriarchal institutions like the Church is actively and constantly challenged (*Problems of Dostoevsky's Poetics*, p. 160). Bakhtin's commitment to this carnivalesque challenge to official culture becomes diluted in Strohm's (and arguably Chaucer's) emphasis that *all* voices represent a 'partial truth': 'just as no claims are permitted to stand unchallenged, so is no claim . . . presented to us as devoid of any truth at all' (p. 171; 231 this volume). If the *Tales* do conduct this liberal gentrification of dialogism, then we are back with something like the postmodern emphasis on reading Chaucer as a celebrator of a 'difference' that, in Linda Hutcheon's words, 'suggests multiplicity, heterogeneity, plurality, rather than binary opposition and exclusion' (*A Poetics of Postmodernism*, p. 61). This position would thus seem to downplay any reading of Chaucer's work as (for example) supporting (or attacking) patriarchy's exclusion of women. To repeat the motto Elaine Hansen uses at the start of her essay here, 'to take a stand would be to upset the beautiful balance of the game'.

The final piece in the collection I wish to discuss, Arthur Lindley's on the Wife of Bath, brings some of these issues to a head in its approach to a text that has always generated enormous controversy. The piece is valuable not only in the vigour of its argument, but also because it gives at the outset a brief overview of many of the different ways in which the Wife and her Prologue and Tale have been interpreted – feminist, Lacanian, cultural-materialist and so forth. It does this though in order to dismiss them under its opening rubric, 'there is no single key'.[36] However, a politicized reading of the Wife of Bath will want to make that text 'work' on behalf of a particular discourse and a particular intervention, and Lindley, in insisting on the absence of the single key, emphatically sets one up himself in the form of keylessness, a reading that polices the text's availability to other forms of interpretation. The procedure is reminiscent in Hutcheon's words again of certain postmodernists' 'master-narrativizing of our suspicion of master narratives' (p. xiii). Thus the text of the Wife of Bath becomes in Lindley's eyes 'an authoritative warning about the dangers of authority' (p. 18; 116 this volume); in other words an open text that might permit a range of readings but only to eschew them on the grounds of their inevitable partiality. Only readings that recognize their own non-authoritativeness are permitted in this highly authoritative reading.

Moreover, Lindley himself ends up by offering a more traditional 'key' to the text. By insisting on the Wife as a 'metafictional puzzle' (p. 3; 103 this volume), or pure textual effect, he is able to question her representational value as woman for a feminist reading, for example (p. 4; 104 this volume) – 'there is no Alisoun' (p. 3; 103 this volume). But his insistence on Alisoun as an absence, a 'nothing' in effect, ultimately brings us to a heavily moralizing reading in which she is recuperated beyond gender as a representation of evil, aligned with traditional medieval ideas of the satanic: 'evil is not-being' (p. 15; 114 this volume). By the end of his essay, he has in fact performed a kind of feminist intervention in suggesting that Chaucer's recycling of a text out of the various materials of medieval antifeminism is his own 'intricately ironized protest at the silencing of women in the official culture of which he was a part' (p. 17; 116 this volume). But this is a by-product of a deeper issue for Chaucer: beyond the medieval erasure of women lies a depiction of evil as the erasure of 'being' itself.

Lindley's final sentence, 'we create the Alisoun we see, Chaucer's Alisoun is an absence' (p. 18; 116 this volume), takes us back to the present widespread consciousness of 'meaning' as an ineluctably readerly act, the note sounded at the outset of this Introduction. It is an aspect of the 'magisterially subversive' (p. 17; 116 this volume) quality of Chaucer in Lindley's eyes that he creates in the Wife of Bath a teasing *tabula rasa* on which the reader can only depict his or her own aspirations, prejudices and fantasies, be these the desire to see woman as 'evil' or for that matter woman as victim; and yet Lindley's final distinction between 'our' Alisoun and 'Chaucer' 's Alisoun (the latter representing satanic non-being) emphatically reinscribes a 'correct' and finalized interpretation, summoning authorial intent, that the essay as a whole has supposedly ruled out.

Lindley's conclusion that the Wife of Bath is 'a sustained demonstration of the incompleteness of all texts and of the dangers of that necessary imaginative act we perform to complete them' (p. 18; 116 this volume) would elicit much agreement today, even though, as we have seen, he is more aware of the 'dangers' of others' readings than of his own. Any act of reading is a 'necessary' fiction; the question then arises how far a consciousness of this might paralyse some interpretative procedures, especially those wishing to 'claim' texts for a specific political affiliation. One could hardly have a more diverse interpretation of the Pardoner and his Tale, for example, than that offered by Jordan on the one hand (anticipating Lindley in his 'absentist' formulations) – 'there is no person here, only a composed text, a text whose colliding realms of discourse betray a strong authorial consciousness of language as a compositional medium . . .', and so forth (*Chaucerian Poetics*, p. 133) – and on the other by Steven F. Kruger, very much interested in the 'person' of the Pardoner and in claiming him as part of a gay tradition contesting 'dominant heterosexual paradigms'.[37] As Kruger puts it, 'we – gay men and lesbians, queers, anti-heterosexist critics and historians – can read the text *against* what might have been the homophobic intentions of its author, celebrating rather than condemning the Pardoner and his disruption of the heterosexual constructions of dominant medieval culture' (p. 137). And we can also read it against the arguably no less insidious intentions the postmodernization of Chaucer has started to claim, that is those of an author primarily and even obsessively concerned with 'rhetorical' effects. That such effects are inherently subversive or 'transgressive' is frequently claimed: 'the polysemic and polyphonic nature of the *Canterbury Tales* and of works of postmodernists such as Joyce and Pynchon can make a powerful point regarding the imposition of impoverishing univocal meanings in the process of reading literature'.[38] But when such a 'univocal meaning' works on behalf of a marginalized history, as in Kruger's desire to retrieve or 'claim' the Pardoner within Chaucer's text as a 'self' that postmodernism would erase, we can justifiably ask which reading is the more transgressive.[39]

There is one quotation from the *Tales* which has to end this Introduction, that describing the pilgrims' reactions to the *Miller's Tale*: 'Diverse folk diversely they seyde, / But for the moore part they loughe and pleyde' (3857–58). It is hoped that the reader will find a stimulating diversity of reaction to Chaucer's *Tales* in the essays that follow, but also one that promotes a sense of problematic and argument-generating difference rather than a too ready conciliation. One may not find too many writers in this collection 'laughing and playing' over Chaucer, but I hope the sense of varied engagement is an adequate and exciting compensation.

Notes

1. THOMAS HAHN, 'The Premodern Text and the Postmodern Reader', *Exemplaria*, 2 (1990), 14, 16.

2. ROBERT M. JORDAN, *Chaucer's Poetics and the Modern Reader* (Berkeley: University of California Press, 1987), p. 16.

3. See the articles by Andreas, Booker and Portnoy referred to later in this Introduction.

4. LEE PATTERSON, 'On the Margin: Postmodernism, Ironic History, and Medieval Studies', *Speculum*, 65 (1990), 90.

5. JAMES R. ANDREAS, ' "Wordes Betwene": The Rhetoric of the Canterbury Links', *Chaucer Review*, 29 (1994), 48.

6. Helpful discussions of postmodernist issues can be found in PETER BROOKER, ed., *Modernism/Postmodernism*, Longman Critical Readers (London: Longman, 1992); STEVEN CONNOR, *Postmodernist Culture: An Introduction to Theories of the Contemporary* (Oxford: Blackwell, 1989); LINDA HUTCHEON, *A Poetics of Postmodernism: History, Theory, Fiction* (London: Routledge, 1988); and PATRICIA WAUGH, ed., *Postmodernism: A Reader* (London: Edward Arnold, 1992).

7. See D. W. ROBERTSON, Jr, *A Preface to Chaucer: Studies in Medieval Perspectives* (Princeton, NJ: Princeton University Press, 1963).

8. SHEILA DELANY, *Chaucer's House of Fame: The Poetics of Skeptical Fideism* (1972; rpt. Gainesville: University Press of Florida, 1994), p. 1.

9. PHYLLIS PORTNOY, 'Beyond the Gothic Cathedral: Post-Modern Reflections in the *Canterbury Tales*', *Chaucer Review*, 28 (1994), 291.

10. SHEILA DELANY, 'Slaying Python: Marriage and Misogyny in a Chaucerian Text', in *Writing Woman: Women Writers and Women in Literature, Medieval to Modern* (New York: Schocken, 1983), pp. 47–75. The comment on Delany's essay is from STEPHANIE TRIGG's Introduction to *Medieval English Poetry*, Longman Critical Readers (London: Longman, 1993), p. 17.

11. ARLYN DIAMOND and LEE R. EDWARDS, eds, *The Authority of Experience: Essays in Feminist Criticism* (Amherst: University of Massachusetts Press, 1977); TRIGG, p. 8.

12. TRIGG, p. 11; PATTERSON, 'Critical Historicism and Medieval Studies', Introduction to *Literary Practice and Social Change in Britain, 1380–1530*, ed. Lee Patterson (Berkeley: University of California Press, 1990), p. 3.

13. G. K. CHESTERTON, *Chaucer* (London: Faber, 1932), p. 205.

14. ARLYN DIAMOND, 'Chaucer's Women and Women's Chaucer', in Diamond and Edwards, *Authority of Experience*, p. 70; MAUREEN FRIES, ' "Slydynge of Corage": Chaucer's Criseyde as Feminist and Victim', in ibid., p. 59.

15. CAROLYN DINSHAW, *Chaucer's Sexual Poetics* (Madison: University of Wisconsin Press, 1989), p. 10.

16. See DAVID AERS, *Chaucer, Langland and the Creative Imagination* (London: Routledge and Kegan Paul, 1980) and *Chaucer* (Brighton: Harvester, 1986).

17. ELAINE TUTTLE HANSEN, *Chaucer and the Fictions of Gender* (Berkeley: University of California Press, 1992), p. 240.

18. CAROLYN DINSHAW, 'Chaucer's Queer Touches/A Queer Touches Chaucer', *Exemplaria*, 7 (1995), 90.

19. ELIZABETH ROBERTSON, 'Aspects of Female Piety in the "Prioress's Tale" ', in *Chaucer's Religious Tales*, ed. C. David Benson and Elizabeth Robertson (Cambridge: D. S. Brewer, 1990), pp. 148–9; 193 this volume.

20. FAYE WALKER, 'Making Trouble: Postmodern Theory With/In Chaucer Studies', *Style*, 26 (1992), 582.

21. LEE PATTERSON, *Negotiating the Past: The Historical Understanding of Medieval Literature* (Madison: University of Wisconsin Press, 1987), p. 25.

22. LEE PATTERSON, *Chaucer and the Subject of History* (London: Routledge, 1991), p. 424.

23. ANDREW TAYLOR, 'Chaucer Our Derridean Contemporary?', *Exemplaria*, 5 (1993), 476, 477; see ROLAND BARTHES, 'The Death of the Author', in *Image – Music – Text*, ed. and trans. Stephen Heath (London: Fontana, 1977), p. 146.

24. H. MARSHALL LEICESTER, Jr, 'Structure as Deconstruction: "Chaucer and Estates Satire" in the *General Prologue*, or Reading Chaucer as a Prologue to the History of Disenchantment', *Exemplaria*, 2 (1990), 243; 25 this volume. See also his *The Disenchanted Self: Representing the Subject in the Canterbury Tales* (Berkeley: University of California Press, 1990), esp. pp. 383–417.

25. VICTORIA KAHN, 'Intention, Interpretation, and the Limits of Meaning: A Response to A. C. Spearing and H. Marshall Leicester, Jr', *Exemplaria*, 2 (1990), 284.

26. DAVID AERS, 'Medievalists and Deconstruction: *An Exemplum*', in *From Medieval to Medievalism*, ed. John Simons (London: Macmillan, 1992), p. 36.

27. MARK A. SHERMAN, 'The Politics of Discourse in Chaucer's *Knight's Tale*', *Exemplaria*, 6 (1994), 87–114. See also TERRY JONES, *Chaucer's Knight: The Portrait of a Medieval Mercenary* (London: Weidenfeld and Nicolson, 1980) and HANSEN, *Chaucer and the Fictions of Gender*, pp. 208–23.

28. For basic introductions to the work of Lacan, see TERRY EAGLETON, *Literary Theory: An Introduction* (Oxford: Blackwell, 1983), chapter 5; MAUD ELLMANN, Introduction to *Psychoanalytic Literary Criticism*, Longman Critical Readers (London: Longman, 1994); and ELIZABETH WRIGHT, *Psychoanalytic Criticism: Theory in Practice* (1984; rpt. London: Routledge, 1989), chapter 7.

29. ALFRED DAVID, *The Strumpet Muse: Art and Morals in Chaucer's Poetry* (Bloomington: Indiana University Press, 1976), pp. 90–107. Further examples of Bakhtinian approaches to Chaucer are listed in my Bibliography.

30. PEGGY KNAPP, *Chaucer and the Social Contest* (London: Routledge, 1990), pp. 36, 41; 66, 72 this volume.

31. KARMA LOCHRIE, 'Women's "Pryvetees" and Fabliau Politics in the *Miller's Tale*', *Exemplaria*, 6 (1994), 288–9.

32. See JON COOK, 'Carnival and the *Canterbury Tales*: "Only equals may laugh" (Herzen)', in *Medieval Literature: Criticism, Ideology and History*, ed. David Aers

(New York: St Martin's Press, 1986), esp. pp. 181–3. Bakhtin's concept of the carnivalesque is fully set out in MIKHAIL BAKHTIN, *Rabelais and His World*, trans. Helene Iswolsky (Bloomington: Indiana University Press, 1984).

33. PAUL STROHM, *Social Chaucer* (Cambridge, MA: Harvard University Press, 1989), p. 168; 228 this volume. See MIKHAIL BAKHTIN, *Problems of Dostoevsky's Poetics*, ed. and trans. Caryl Emerson, introd. Wayne C. Booth (Manchester: Manchester University Press, 1984).

34. See, for example, DEREK PEARSALL, *The Life of Geoffrey Chaucer* (Oxford: Blackwell, 1992), p. 247n.

35. Problems with the 'conciliatory' mode of interpreting Bakhtin are examined in LYNNE PEARCE, *Reading Dialogics* (London: Edward Arnold, 1994), pp. 12–15, 80–111.

36. ARTHUR LINDLEY, ' "Vanysshed Was This Daunce, He Nyste Where": Alisoun's Absence in the *Wife of Bath's Prologue and Tale*', *ELH*, 59 (1992), 1; 100 this volume.

37. STEVEN F. KRUGER, 'Claiming the Pardoner: Toward a Gay Reading of Chaucer's *Pardoner's Tale*', *Exemplaria*, 6 (1994), 137.

38. M. KEITH BOOKER, 'Postmodernism in Medieval England: Chaucer, Pynchon, Joyce, and the Poetics of Fission', *Exemplaria*, 2 (1990), 589.

39. Relevant to this debate is Patricia Waugh's discussion of 'the postmodern concept of language games, dissensus and dispersal' as 'often naively appropriated by an avant-garde desire to conflate artistic textual disruption with political subversion', and her desire that feminists retain 'the goals of agency, personal autonomy, self-expression and self-determination' as necessary political ideals. See WAUGH, *Postmodernism*, pp. 193–9.

2 Structure as Deconstruction: 'Chaucer and Estates Satire' in the *General Prologue*, or Reading Chaucer as a Prologue to the History of Disenchantment*

H. MARSHALL LEICESTER, JR

Leicester reads the *General Prologue* not as the traditionally conceived gallery of neutrally observed 'portraits', but as the psychological self-revelation of a narrator undergoing a progressive crisis of 'disenchantment', here defined as the realization that the social hierarchy is not divinely planned but originates in human desires for order and classification. As this recognition takes hold, the narrator's increasingly moralizing tone in the *Prologue* testifies to a desperate need for certainty that is forced, reluctantly, to confront its own agency and motivation; Chaucer's interest in staging a coming to consciousness of such disenchantment, while focusing on the narrator, extends to many of the pilgrims also, seen as inhabitants of a particularly 'disenchanted epoch' at the end of the fourteenth century. The acknowledgement that the narrator actively *creates* what he had set out simply to transcribe, and that by extension the supposed objective 'truths' of our world are ideologically originated, are what leads Leicester to claim Chaucer as a deconstructionist *avant la lettre*. For more on Leicester's piece, see my Introduction, pp. 12–13.

For some time now I've been interested in using structuralist and poststructuralist theory to read Chaucer, though I should say at once that I'm not very interested in seeing these texts as instances or examples of the theory's doctrines. I try to make use of the light thrown on Chaucer's practice by the methods developed in the work of Barthes, Derrida, Foucault, Lacan and others, but only insofar as those methods illuminate the text's representation of such things as the relationships between writing and speech, language and subjectivity. As I see it, the problem is to acknowledge the radical force of the poststructuralist critique of traditional, historically oriented positivism, while avoiding the totalizing tendencies that

---

* Reprinted from *Exemplaria*, 2 (1990), 241–61.

have sometimes crept into poststructuralist practice. One discounts as a matter of course the extreme historicist positions that disallow certain kinds of ironic reading on the grounds that 'they couldn't have thought that then', since nothing requires that the textual phenomena that psychoanalytic or deconstructive reading draws on be construed as conscious or intended. But to assume too readily that such effects are always *un*intended still gives too much credit to the assumptions of positivist reading. Such an assumption can play down the real trouble contemporary methods ought to cause, and can actually make the naturalization of those methods too easy.

Structuralist and poststructuralist perspectives have been enormously powerful in evoking the deep structures of desire, language, and institutional power that move through and constrain individual texts and subjects, and thus have provided a corrective to the 'naturalistic' assumptions of historicism. But, as Michel de Certeau and others have pointed out, analyses like those of Foucault and Althusser have often concentrated so intensively on what texts and historical actors 'are really doing' as opposed to 'what they thought they were doing', as to open themselves to the accusation of portraying historical agents as what Anthony Giddens calls 'cultural dopes'.[1]

From this point of view both the older and the newer methods seem to me to agree too readily that 'they couldn't have thought that then': they share a bias toward discounting the agency of texts and subjects, and privileging institutional power and constraint, thereby in effect reducing agency to structure. The older methods might do this by showing how the structures of allegorical interpretation discursively formulated by St Augustine and others are replicated in Chaucer's text without going on to consider how those structures are deployed and work there. The newer methods might trace the ways medieval texts qua texts undo the meanings they simultaneously affirm as if this process had no immediate historical effect at the level of the agent, but was an unnoticed perennial feature of textuality that has only come to be understood in our own time. Too easy an assimilation of modern perspectives can keep them from making enough of a difference in the way we read, and too uncritical an acceptance of at least some of the ways those methods have been used can make every deconstruction look the same. I want neither old readings dressed up in new language nor old texts reduced to modern themes, and in what follows I'd like to suggest one route, based in my own work, for converting these avoidances into a positive program.

One thing the various forms of contemporary theory and reading – for three, Lacanian psychoanalysis, Foucauldian genealogy and Derridean deconstruction – have in common is what I call disenchantment. I take the term, with some adjustments, from Max Weber, who gives it a technical meaning that focuses directly on the active relation of subjects to institutions, and therefore serves my particular turn. In the sense Weber gives it, disenchantment is a function of the process of intellectualization and rationalization of society and the world, the awareness that in dealing with them

> . . . There are no mysterious processes that come into play, but rather . . . one can, in principle, master all things by calculation. This means that the world is disenchanted. One need no longer have recourse to magical means, in order to master or implore the spirits, as did the savage, for whom such mysterious powers existed. Technical means and calculations perform the service.[2]

In order to make best use of the term for my purposes it is necessary to disengage it, at least initially, from the developmental/ historical context of the rise of a scientific world-view that leads Weber to adopt the vocabulary of calculation and technics and to focus instead on the more general issue of human agency. From this perspective, disenchantment means the perception that what had been thought to be other-originated, the product of transcendent forces not directly susceptible of human tampering and subversion, is in fact humanly originated and the product of human creation.

At the social level, disenchantment is thus the perception, as in Foucault, that what had been taken to be 'natural', 'the way things are', 'what everybody knows' is actually institutional, an epistemic construction, knowledge/power. In its extreme form, as in Foucault, it is the suspicion or even the conviction that the category of transcendence itself is a human construction, that there are only institutions. A fully disenchanted social perspective constitutes the world as a tissue of institutions rather than of 'natures', and therefore tends to see experience and social existence as an encounter between conflicting interpretations rather than as the passive reception of pre-existing meanings.

At the level of the individual, disenchantment is the familiar modern perception that the subject is not a thing, like a rock, but a position or a site through which various forces pass, the continually constructed and reconstructed vector-product of all the agencies in play at the subject site – unconscious desire, concealed or mystified material and social power, the structures of language, and even (though it is sometimes a bit neglected) consciousness itself. The subject of disenchantment is a construct, something human beings have made, albeit largely unconsciously, and made in time, historically. A disenchanted view of subjectivity like Lacan's (especially in the more recent feminist inflections of it) focuses on the so-called 'split subject' as it is constituted in the relations of language and desire, and therefore provides a way of allowing the unconscious, sexuality and gender to figure in an account of the subject without requiring us to regard them as immutable biological facts. They are instead the 'discourse of the Other', that is, constructions that are imposed on the subject when it enters into the larger social construct of language.[3]

Finally, at least for now, a disenchanted perspective on discourse itself, such as deconstruction, registers (by undoing it, as the name suggests) the constructed character of any meaning whatever, by showing that meaning is never an immanent property of things but always a way of reading, something done to a text by human agents rather than derived by them from it.

My aim here is not to do a deconstruction or a genealogy or a psychoanalysis of Chaucer – there isn't time anyway, to say the least – but rather to try to suggest how one Chaucerian text, the *General Prologue* to the *Canterbury Tales*, actively encourages the taking of such perspectives on itself, by representing them. The *content* of these disciplinary discourses is of variable usefulness depending on the particular interpretive situation, the character of a text and what's wanted from it. The reason I've trotted out even these brief potted commonplaces is that I wanted to single out the common thread of disenchantment that runs through modern theory in order to argue that it also runs through Chaucer's poem. As deconstruction proposes, and as is obvious anyway, disenchantment itself is no more a property of things or of culture than any other interpretive procedure: it is a way of reading. In theory, as they say, anybody can do it any time, which is to say that medieval people could do it – in theory – as well as moderns, and one of the things I find most useful about the modern discourses I've enumerated (and a number of others as well) is that they supply a complex and sophisticated rhetoric of disenchanted reading. They supply a repertoire of moves whose analogues in medieval, and specifically Chaucerian, *practice* are easier to ferret out because of the discursive thoroughness and suggestive richness of the examples of Derrida, Lacan, Foucault and the rest.

. . .

The *General Prologue* . . . is, as Jill Mann demonstrated conclusively a few years ago, an estates satire, that is, a deployment of a culturally sanctioned scheme of social classification. The poem is one of a class of medieval treatments of the orders, or estates, of society, a scheme that, in its oldest and simplest form, divides society into Clergy, who see to its spiritual needs, Knights, who take care of its temporal order and defense, and Ploughmen, who feed it. In their more historically developed forms, these works generally list the various members of society according to some form of the traditional scheme of the estates, and comment on their abuses – themselves generally quite stereotyped. Though she notes that Chaucer shows a typical freedom in the selection of the particular estates he presents, Mann proves that he 'does cover the elements of social anatomization made familiar by estates literature', as a means 'to suggest society as a whole by way of [a] representative company of individuals'.[4] The traditional classification provides Chaucer with a conceptual framework, shared with his audience, for organizing his observations of individuals in society, an underlying structure of common assumptions about the kind of thing society is and the way it is put together.

One of the most valuable features of Mann's book is the attention she pays to Chaucer's unique treatment of the estates form itself. The *General Prologue* is not, she argues, merely an example of estates satire, but an alteration and revision of estates techniques producing a different, perhaps one might say a more 'modern', image of society. As she shows, Chaucer consistently displaces or complicates the relatively straightforward moral judgments of traditional estates literature in favor of the more ambiguous details of the immediate social impression his pilgrims make. Where we are never in doubt about what we are to think of the monks or friars or townsmen in other estates satires, we are almost always unsure of exactly how good or bad their counterparts in the *General Prologue* are. This produces what Mann describes as the effect of an estates satire from which the purpose of moral classification has been removed, and at least the suggestion of a view of society as constituted more by the behavior and performances of individuals and groups than by an a priori scheme. Chaucer, she says, 'ironically substitut[es] for the traditional moral view of social structure a vision of a world where morality becomes as specialized to the individual as his work-life'.[5]

Though I agree with all of this, Mann's way of formulating and presenting her case does seem to me to go at once too far and not far enough. Too far, in that her unquestionably valid insights are applied too broadly and generally to all the portraits and the *Prologue* as a whole; and not far enough, in that in practice she neglects the ways the poem actively challenges not only the traditional assumptions of moral classification in general but those of estates satire in particular. Both of these difficulties seem to me to stem from a neglect of the poem's structure, and especially of its *sequence*.

The question of sequence is especially important because it is explicitly posed by the poem. The *General Prologue* presents itself, on first reading, as the record of an experience: the experience of the speaker in putting together the *matere* of memory, as Donald R. Howard has shown,[6] so as to give it to us *re*-ordered 'accordaunt to resoun'.[7] This is the task he undertakes *now*, in the present of narrating, 'whil I have tyme and space, / Er that I ferther in this tale pace' (I.35–36), at some time after the pilgrimage itself was completed. The 'experience' is, of course, a fiction, the textual representation of a fictional 'I' addressing a fictional audience in order 'To telle yow al the condicioun / Of ech of hem' (I.38–39). It is a fiction of *performance*, the logocentric illusion, as we say nowadays, of a performer who unfolds his meaning to us as he speaks, but it is no less consistently presented for all that. The poem keeps us aware of this fictional or virtual now of audience address from its beginning to its end, when 'now is tyme to yow for to telle . . . al the remenaunt of oure pilgrimage' (I.720–24). The rational ordering of the pilgrims is thus so to speak a *project* the narrator proposes at the outset of the *General Prologue*, and one we watch him enact as the poem unfolds.

If the ordering of the pilgrims is a project of the narrator's, it is not initially one that seems difficult or challenging to him or to us. Like the famous opening sentence, with its effortless progression from the impersonal cosmic eros of seasonal change through vegetable growth and animal (or at least avian) sexuality to the *amor spiritualis* that drove St Thomas, the presentation of the pilgrims in the first half of the *Prologue* is a richly embroidered and elegantly varied expression of 'what everybody knows' about the shape of society.[8] The progression of portraits from the Knight through the Wife of Bath is consistently though complexly structured on the time-honored model of the Three Estates that I alluded to earlier. The tally of the pilgrims begins with a pre-eminent representative of the estate of *milites*, and pauses for a moment to list the Knight's hierarchically ordered entourage – his son the Squire and his servant the Yeoman – before passing on to the second group, the three members of the regular clergy. As Mann notes,[9] it would be more 'correct' in conventional estates terms to place the clerical figures first, and this suggests that the estates organization is modified by hierarchical considerations of another sort: the Knight is in some sense the highest ranking pilgrim. This does not, however, affect the overall organization in estates terms. With the clerical figures too there is room for flexibility and play – the Prioress's entourage is also listed briefly at the end of her portrait. But here, as with the treatment of the Five Guildsmen as a single unit, the choice to stress the portrait as more basic than the

individual person by brushing past the Second Nun and the
Nun's Priest(s) points to the importance of estates classification over
individuality as such. In any case, the basic structural outline is clear:
three religious presented in the order of official rank, Prioress, Monk
as monastery official ('kepere of the celle' – I.172), and ordinary Friar.
This grouping is followed by the inevitably more miscellaneous list
of the pilgrims of the third estate, which by the late Middle Ages had
become a kind of catchall category that included all who were not
knights or clergy, and which is itself variously carved up by other
estates satires. The first part of the poem, viewed from a certain
distance, displays a complex articulation of interrelated hierarchical
schemata within a basic triadic structure, which is continued through
the Wife of Bath's portrait, at least in the sense that the portrait
groupings continue to be divisible by three in ways that can be made
to make sense. The 'triad' Franklin, Five Guildsmen, Cook, for
instance, outlines a modern, citified, bureaucratic and competitive
parallel – Knight of the Shire, burgesses who aspire to rank,
proletarian craftsman in the temporary hire of his betters – to the
more traditional and naturalized socio-moral hierarchy of the first
triad, Knight, Squire, Yeoman, bound together by ties of blood
and homage.

If there are problems with the order I have sketched so far, and
there are, they are not allowed to emerge in the unfolding of the
poem for some time. Like the opening sentence, the order of the
pilgrims in the first half of the *General Prologue*, rooted as it is in
conventional and collective norms, reflects 'what everybody knows'
about the exfoliation of natural and spiritual energies in springtime
and about the relation of these energies to the shape of society and
its estates. This is perhaps one reason why the portraits in this part
of the poem exhibit the relatively relaxed tone and the lack of overt
moralization that Mann notes. These descriptions draw easily on the
shared framework of assumptions in whose name our representative
the narrator speaks. That the kind of loving the Squire currently
practices is more closely allied to the energies of the animal soul than
to the rational love of *ecclesia* and *res publica* his father embodies need
not be spelled out. It is carried in the implications of the image that
links him to the sleeplessly amorous birds of the first eighteen lines,
'He sleep namoore than dooth a nyghtyngale' (I.98) – birds who are
themselves balanced between the immanent 'gravitational' love that
moves the sun and the other stars through the round of the seasons,
and the focused and rational divine love that calls to and through the
saint. Similarly, our common expectation that any literary friar will
be a bad one makes it unnecessary for the narrator to condemn the

pilgrim Friar explicitly. One reason the Friar's portrait is the longest in the *Prologue* is the extreme popularity and ubiquity of anti-fraternal satire in the fourteenth century: there is a very rich fund of conventional material to draw on, and the narrator-poet can count on this tacitly shared background to enforce his ironies.[10]

The precise placing of these pilgrims does create some difficulties, however, and, as I want to insist, these difficulties are experienced by the speaker, and experienced progressively. An overview of the pilgrims of the third estate reveals an increasing strain between what the poet's common culture tells him he ought to be able to say about people ('what everybody knows') and what his actual experience of trying to describe them provides. It is preeminently in this section of the poem, for example, that technical and scientific jargon and the language of craft become conspicuous, with the effects Mann notes: the felt absence of more widely applicable and less specialized role-definitions, and a sense of the disjunction between the moral and professional spheres that tends to stress the fundamentally amoral character of professional expertise: think of the Shipman's navigational skill, which appears to make him a more efficient pirate, or the doctor's learning, whose tag, 'He was a verray, parfit praktisour' (I.422), calls attention to the difference between his *skills* and the Knight's *virtues* (cf. I.72). Details of dress and appearance become less informative. The end of the Man of Law's portrait with its abrupt dismissal, 'Of his array telle I no lenger tale' (I.330), stresses how little we can learn about him from his off-duty dress, especially compared to the amount of symbolic information about character carried by the estates uniform of the Knight with his armor-stained 'gypon', or of the Friar with his double-worsted semicope. The same indefiniteness characterizes such things as the Cook's mormel, the name of the Shipman's barge, the *Maudelayne* (what would that mean if it meant?) and most of the details of the Wife of Bath's portrait: her deafness, her complicated love-life, her big hat. The Wife's portrait is the culmination in the poem of the progressive tendency of particular qualities of individuals to shift their area of reference from the exemplary to the idiosyncratic. The often-noted 'excellence' of each pilgrim becomes more and more rooted in the existential being and activity of the individual, and less and less in his or her representative character as the symbol of a larger group. The individual's place in a hierarchy becomes less important than his or her performances; consider again the difference between a 'verray, parfit gentil knyght' and a 'verray, parfit praktisour'. These are persons whose stories you would have to tell to understand them – or who would have to tell their stories. This is overtly recognized in the Wife's portrait, the only place in the portraits that refers beyond them to the tale-telling to come:

Housbondes at chirche dore she hadde fyve,
Withouten oother compaignye in youthe –
But therof nedeth nat to speke as nowthe.

(I.460–62)

'What everybody knows' is not enough to account for the Wife either
morally or socially, and the promise of more to come points to the
narrator's awareness that she will have to do it herself later.

It seems to me to be no accident that the portrait of the highly
idealized and morally transparent Parson occurs at just this point,
forming the strongest possible contrast to the ambiguities of the
Wife of Bath. Even more significant, however, is the fact that now
the organizing principle of the poem as a whole changes. After the
closely linked Parson-Plowman grouping, the final five pilgrims are
bunched together and announced in advance as completing the tally:

Ther was also a REVE and a MILLERE,
A SOMNOUR, and a PARDONER also,
A MAUNCIPLE, and myself – ther were namo.

(I.542–44)

As opposed to the complex complementarity and hierarchy of the
ordering of the portraits in the first half, we are here presented
with rather simple oppositions: two against five, bad against good.
The rhetorical and other evidence for a structural division here is
too extensive to cite, but one piece of it will forward the current
discussion. If the initial organization of the poem is indeed that of the
Three Estates, we obviously do well to ask why the Parson's portrait
is not included with the second, clerical, triad, why it interrupts the
account of the third estate (to which all the remaining pilgrims in the
list belong) instead. In the sort of sequential or prospective reading
I am urging here, the question does not arise until we reach the
Parson's portrait itself, but it certainly does arise then. The effect is to
make the initial three-estates ordering, *in retrospect*, look much more
selective and *ad hoc* than it did at first, much more the product of
tacit choices and decisions on the part of the narrator who now alters
and abandons it.

The two most striking features of the final sequence of seven
portraits from the Parson through the Pardoner are, first, a drive
to ultimate moral clarification that I will call 'apocalyptic', in the
etymological sense of the word as an unveiling (and more or less in
the sense that Bloomfield called *Piers Plowman* a fourteenth-century
apocalypse), a stripping away of surface complexity to reveal the
fundamental truth beneath it, and second, the conspicuous emergence

of the narrator as the source of this drive. The effect of the insertion
of the Parson-Plowman dyad is to provide a golden 'ensample'
against which not only the remaining pilgrims but the previous
ones – the Parson's portrait contains a number of 'snybbing' critical
references to previous portraits such as those of the Monk and Friar
– are measured and found wanting. Besides the animal imagery
cited by Mann,[11] which is itself susceptible of typological and
physiognomical interpretation *in malo*, as Curry, Robertson and
others have shown, there are other patterns that cut across the
last portraits and produce the effect of a uniformly wicked and
worsening world: The Miller, whose badness is qualified by the
energy of his animal spirits, carries a sword and buckler. The more
sinister-sounding Reeve, who does not just defraud a few village
yokels but undermines a whole manor from lord to laborers, carries
a *'rusty* blade' (I.618), while the Summoner's failure to sustain and
defend ecclesiastical order is pinned down by the allegory of his
armory: 'A bokeleer hadde he maad hym of a cake' (I.668). Read
across the portraits, and, once again, against the image of hierarchy
and vigilant order embodied in the first triad, where the Yeoman
keeps the Knight's weapons 'harneised wel' (I.114) for use at need,
the symbolic progression of weapons implies that as evil becomes
more spiritual and intense its outward signs become clearer and
more concrete emblems of the inner state, and that such progressive
evils are increasingly revealed as demonic parodies of the good. The
Summoner and the Pardoner, in particular, have the *privatio boni*
theory of evil written all over them.

At the same time, the narrator moves forward out of the relatively
anonymous 'felaweshipe' of what everybody knows and into a
position of isolated prominence, as he takes a God's-eye-view more
akin, perhaps, to the Parson's. He says 'I' more often, he addresses us
oftener and more overtly, frequently breaking off description to do
so, he warns and exhorts and judges: 'Wel I woot he lyed right in
dede' (I.659), he says of the Summoner. The effect is well represented
by the Manciple's portrait, which is, notoriously, not about the
Manciple but about the lawyers he works for. As the speaker moves
toward the end of the portrait he idealizes those lawyers more and
more, stressing the power for social good bound up in them 'And
able for to helpen al a shire' (I.584), and then managing to suggest
that it is somehow the Manciple's fault that they don't: 'And yet
this Manciple sette hir aller cappe' (I.586). Because the speaker
so conspicuously wrenches us away from the Manciple, he calls
attention to himself and his own social concerns. For this reason
among others, all this apocalyptic processing registers, I think, as
a failure of vision on the narrator's part. In sequence and in context,

it looks like a reaction to the complexities and uncertainties of classification and judgment generated by the enterprise of the first half of the *Prologue*, a retreat to simpler and more rigorous standards of moral classification which, precisely because its psychological motives emerge so clearly, also looks like name-calling, a product less of objective appraisal of the pilgrims in question than of the speaker's own wishes and fears about the evils of society. The pattern of this psychology is fairly precisely that of a certain sort of disenchantment, since it is focused on the ways human agents like the Manciple and the Summoner manipulate and subvert what should be a transcendent and stable order, and it is marked by nostalgia for what it knows has been lost. The Summoner is an actively disenchanted cynic, whose perversion of what ought to be the Justice of God is accompanied by an articulate conviction that it is only the justice of men as corrupt as himself: ' "Purs is the ercedekenes helle," seyde he' (I.658). If the speaker protests this blatant assertion, he seems nonetheless to agree that it is all too often all too true, as the Pardoner's portrait affirms even more strongly:

> But with thise relikes, whan that he fond
> A povre person dwellynge upon lond,
> Upon a day he gat hym moore moneye
> Than that the person gat in monthes tweye;
> And thus, with feyned flaterye and japes,
> He made the person and the peple his apes.

> (I.701–6)

The narrator of the *General Prologue* does not simply use categories to make neutral descriptions; the unfolding of the performance makes clear that he has attitudes toward the descriptions he makes and the things he describes. The pervasive symbolic processing of the end of the portrait gallery shows that there is more at stake for him here than the features and foibles of individuals. By the end of the *Prologue* the pilgrims are being made, aggressively, to stand for estates as images of the state of society. Once again it seems no accident, in retrospect, that the tale of the pilgrims ends with the Pardoner, the darkest example and the most trenchant spokesman of an attitude the speaker here comes close to sharing.

This reading of the narrator's psychology is the more convincing, at least to me, because of the character of the passage that immediately follows the portraits. An address that begins with a straightforward statement of what has been achieved: 'Now have I toold you soothly, in a clause . . .', becomes more and more tentative and apologetic as it proceeds, and more and more nervous about the *effect* not only of what remains to say, but of what has already been said:

> But first I pray yow, of youre curteisye,
> That ye n'arette it nat my vileynye,
> Thogh that I pleynly speke in this mateere,
> To telle yow hire wordes and hire cheere,
> Ne thogh I speke hir wordes proprely.
> For this ye knowen al so wel as I:
> Whoso shal telle a tale after a man,
> He moot reherce as ny as evere he kan
> Everich a word, if it be in his charge,
> Al speke he never so rudeliche and large,
> Or ellis he moot telle his tale untrewe,
> Or feyne thyng, or fynde wordes newe.
> He may nat spare, althogh he were his brother;
> He moot as wel seye o word as another.
> Crist spak hymself ful brode in hooly writ,
> And wel ye woot no vileynye is it.
> Eek Plato seith, whoso kan hym rede,
> The wordes moote be cosyn to the dede.
>
> (I.725–42)

The passage is dogged by the speaker's repetitions of the attempt to deny responsibility for the descriptions of the pilgrims he is about to give, and haunted by his sense that the denials are not convincing because he is too clearly responsible for the descriptions he has already given. He ends oddly, after a discussion of the tales that are to come, where one might have expected him to begin: with an apology for having failed to order the pilgrims correctly, and this peculiarity suggests what is really on his mind:[12]

> Also I prey yow to foryeve it me,
> Al have I nat set folk in hir degree,
> Here in this tale, as that they sholde stonde.
>
> (I.743–45)

In strong contrast to the atmosphere of shared understandings and common agreements he projected at the beginning of the prologue, the speaker here appears nervously isolated, as if surrounded by an audience of Millers, Manciples, Reeves, Summoners and Pardoners, whose accusation of 'vileynye' he might well have some cause to anticipate.

What seems to *happen* in the performance represented in the *General Prologue* is that two rather different procedures of classifying the pilgrims, procedures which I have called hierarchical and apocalyptic, and which seem to correspond in emphasis to the classificatory and the moralizing impulses respectively in estates satire, are successively adopted and then discarded by the speaker. In the final movement of the poem, he turns to the pilgrims themselves, in part as a way of getting himself off the hook. The movement of the *General Prologue* is within two versions of 'resoun', understood, as it can be in Middle English, as a translation of Latin *ratio*.[13] The distinction I have in mind is between on the one hand 'underlying cause', the reasons in things that are patterned on the *rationes seminales* in the mind of God, the basic 'rational' structure of reality, and on the other hand 'account', 'argument', and especially 'opinion', as with the Merchant: 'His resons he spak ful solempnely, / Sownynge alwey th'encrees of his wynnyng' (I.274–75). The poem goes from an account 'accordaunt to resoun' that seems to want to claim the first definition, to the moment when the Knight begins his tale, 'As was resoun, / By foreward and by composicioun' (I.847–48) – that is, according to an explicitly man-made, *ad hoc* and open-ended *ratio* or plan, the tale-telling project, which will require, not the activity of the narrator, but of the pilgrims themselves in telling their tales on the one hand, and of the reader in putting together and evaluating the various performances on the other. This movement is paralleled by a cognate shift in the meaning of the word 'tale' from the force it has in 'Er that I ferther in this tale pace' at the beginning to the force it takes on contextually in the apology quoted just above. In the first instance, the primary meaning would seem to be 'tally, reckoning', in the sense of a completed list or account, which is also one of the primary meanings of *ratio*. By the time the end of the portrait gallery is reached, however, the developed sense of the speaker's contribution to the way the list has unfolded lets the meanings of 'Canterbury tale' – that is, traveler's tale, whopper, and more generally, 'fiction, story', such as the pilgrims will tell – speak out. These transformations of 'tale' and 'resoun' have in common the disenchanted view that they enforce of the enterprise of the poem and of its speaker. What is stressed by the poem's representation of itself as a prospective unfolding is the human use of available systems of classification to create rather than to discover the order of society. It is precisely the dramatized failure of the original 'project' of the poem that makes the estates conventions applied to the pilgrims emerge as constitutive institutional processes put in play by the personal and ideological interests that act through the subject, rather than simply neutral and objective descriptions of what was there to begin with.

I began by saying that the *General Prologue* actively challenges the traditional assumptions of estates satire. It does so, however, in the mode of deconstruction: by enacting or miming the traditional classifications themselves in such a way as gradually to bring out the tensions and contradictions that underlie and constitute them. The stalking horse of this enterprise is the performing narrator, who appears to find himself enmeshed in those tensions, bedeviled by the various impasses that lead to what I take to be a central theme of the *General Prologue*, the question of just what it means to judge and classify one's fellows. If he feels and fears that he may have falsified the pilgrims in describing them, the corollary is that the poem is indeed a performance in exactly the way that the tales are. It is the self-presentation of a speaker, as much or more the poet's portrait as an account of the other characters, who must now be expected to present themselves in their tales.

It is one thing to have such an experience, but it is quite another to write it down. In particular, it is something more and different to make *a written representation of a failed performance*. If the aim is to give a satisfactory account of the pilgrims, one might start over on a different plan, or, having learned one's lesson, discard the *Prologue*. But to read the poem prospectively as a fictional performance – a reading it initially encourages – is finally to be made aware of the inadequacies of that mode of reading, and this I take to be one of the aims of the representation. From this point of view, what the poem is criticizing, in estates satire and elsewhere, is the notion that having heard what you say (as, in the fiction, the narrator has, though we have not), I know what you mean and who you are – the familiar logocentric supposition that would make of the *General Prologue* a version of Derrida's characterization of Hegel's preface to the *Phenomenology of Mind*: something you write last and put first, something meant, in an odd way, to do away with the need for the work itself.[14] What replaces this notion, what moves into the gap created by the undoing of definitive classification and interpretation, is the notion of reading and rereading, or to put it another way, the replacement of the poem as performance by the poem as text. The *General Prologue* ends, in a typically deconstructive move, with an act of *différance*, a deferring of the meaning of the pilgrims and the pilgrimage as something different from what the poem as performance achieved. The deferral is what makes the difference, and makes difference possible, because it frees up the *General Prologue* itself to be reread as a piece of writing, in all sorts of new conjunctions with the tales.

That's a sketch of the *General Prologue* as what might be called a practical deconstruction. A similar set of moves can be made with respect to the way the psychoanalytic themes of desire, gender and the paternal Law are represented in the poem. The disenchanted perspective on its own unfolding that characterizes the end of the

General Prologue is potentially psychoanalytic, in a loose sense, insofar as it focuses on a representation, not of the objective reality of others, but of the undeclared (or, again loosely, unconscious) motives that lie behind a particular attempt to classify them. An interrogation of the poem in terms of the sorts of motives psychoanalysis is interested in reveals some interesting patterns.

The *General Prologue* begins in an atmosphere of official hierarchy, plenitude and male power (*vertu*, from 'vir-tus', maleness) that are quite specifically associated with phallic assertion in the opening lines, which contain, one might say, a very *gendered* representation of what April does to March to get the world moving in spring:

Whan that Aprill with his shoures soote
The droghte of March hath perced to the roote
And bathed every veyne in swich licour
Of which vertu engendred is the flour. . . .

(I.1–4)

In line with this opening, the first portrait, the Knight's, gives us the image of a powerful patriarch, worthy and virtuous. He is a victorious fighter, a defender of the Church, and the legitimate father of a squire who will succeed legitimately to the paternal estate, just the sort of person to justify the speaker's tacit faith in the links between authority, determinate transmissible meaning, and male gender-dominance. By the time those assumptions have been put in question by the anomalies of the third estate and the breakdown of hierarchy associated with them, it seems more than fortuitously appropriate that the boundaries of the third estate, and of the project to order the poem hierarchically, should be marked by a woman, and a markedly competitive, combative and threatening one at that. The vibrancy of the details in the Wife of Bath's portrait only stresses their lack of coherence in traditional terms, and the aggressiveness of her challenge to tradition. The Wife certainly raises the *questions* that sexuality and the feminine put to the standard patriarchal hierarchies, the questions of the relations between sensual love, 'felaweshipe', marriage, *amor dei* and *remedia amoris*, but these relations, as she will remind us in her prologue and tale, are matters of controversy.

Just as it seems to me no accident that the Parson's portrait, which is a fairly strident reaffirmation of male authority as well as of ideal Christian order, follows the Wife's and initiates the last phase of the portraits, it seems even less of one that the gallery ends in an atmosphere of divine order undermined by human abuses, of active disenchantment, and with the Pardoner, the one pilgrim who is – I use the word I didn't quite use of the Wife because the text demands it here – lacking the phallus, the embodiment of the not-masculine, castrated: 'I trowe he were a geldyng or a mare' (I.691).

That will have to do as a suggestion of the direction this sort of interpretation can take. Since the central problem of all psychoanalytic reading, as it seems to me, is the question of who is conscious of what when, I'll just say here that I didn't pull this perspective on the *General Prologue* out of a hat, or even out of modern theoretical interests. The observations I've just made about the poem were guided by a retrospective re-reading of the tales back into the *General Prologue*, more or less in the way the *Prologue* itself demands. The disenchanted suspicion about motives that psychoanalysis shares with Chaucer extends to a suspicion about the constructed character of gender, and especially of the links between gender and authority – that is, of the phallus. Both the Wife's and the Pardoner's tales are quite directly *about* those links and quite critical of them – so, for that matter, though in a more indirect way, is the Knight's. All three pilgrims follow the lead of the *General Prologue* into what I would call practical psychoanalysis.

Finally, the *General Prologue* is and encourages a form of practical genealogy insofar as it conspicuously displaces itself at its end from its own prologality and directs us back to its 'real' origin in the tales, to which, as I argued above, it finally presents itself not as a beginning but as a response, and a defective one at that. More generally, the poem enacts, or rather represents, the coming to consciousness of the problematic character of what begins as the relatively unreflective practical activity of classifying people, and it presents that coming to consciousness as an awakening to disenchantment. Further, if the speaker of the *General Prologue* encounters his own disenchantment in the confrontation of his own agency, what he has contributed to the supposedly neutral enterprise of description, he does so in a society that he increasingly recognizes as itself disenchanted, and it is in following *his* lead that I find the *General Prologue* carrying me into an historical reading of its own genealogy.

There are many gross features of the fourteenth century in Western Europe and in England that suggest that it is a disenchanted epoch, many of whose inhabitants have become not only practically but quite consciously and discursively aware of the extent to which matters previously held to be established and maintained by God have actually been humanly produced and then ascribed to divine agency. This used to be quite a traditional reading of the period before the piety of Robertsonian reading overtook us. One might mention in passing the Great Schism, Lollardy, the Peasants' Revolt, the depositions of Edward II at the beginning of the century and of Richard II in Chaucer's lifetime at its end, as examples of the collapse of traditional structures of authority beneath the weight put on them by active and often articulately critical human agents such as caesarian clergy, Lollards, revolutionary peasants and over-mighty barons, anti-papal political theorists, etc. I do not intend, however, to argue an 'historical' justification of this sort for reading Chaucer in this way here, as if the presence of a certain institutional setting were the historical 'cause' of my reading or of the poet's writing. As I have suggested, I think Chaucer's text is among the best primary evidence we have for this reading of the fourteenth century as its genealogy, that it is what best supports such an *interpretation* of the relevant 'facts' of the period. The *General Prologue* directs a reading of its age as one in which not only the structures of the Church (e.g., pardoning) but gender roles and estates, such as wives and knighthood, and, more generally, subjectivity itself, have been deeply affected by a pervasive disenchanted scrutiny. My way of arriving at this view of the period through the analysis of voicing in Chaucer's texts puts a new twist on it, by allowing me to show not only that these things are going on, but that the actors involved are not simply undergoing but enacting and producing them, often with a high degree of awareness of what is happening and what they are doing about it. Chaucer, on the evidence of the text, would seem to have been such a disenchanted agent or he could not have portrayed the pilgrims as he does. More important for such an historical view, however, is the fact my ongoing reading seeks to establish, which is that the poet's text portrays so many of the pilgrims, and such central ones for the work as a whole, as themselves disenchanted, the sufferers and agents of a culture whose cover is blown.

But I don't want to stop even at this, as if modern theory were only relevant to late and transitional periods in a given cultural sequence, because that allows some remnant of the assumption that disenchantment is the product of some Hegelian, developmental, period-historical self-consciousness or Zeitgeist. The more radical implication of poststructuralism that I want to have make a difference in our reading is that the problems of meaning and agency, the insistence of the human construction of the world, are as perennial as the insistence of the letter in the unconscious: there is *différance* as soon as there is language, that is, primordially. There was never a golden age, and there is no time when naive consciousness holds sway unproblematically, because there is no time without practice and the *de facto* disenchantment of practical consciousness.

That disenchantment is primordial and perennial does not mean that nothing changes, that there is no such thing as history. What changes are the institutional structures that disenchantment, whether unconscious, discursive, or practical, works with or against, and the story of the specific ways in which practice has undone specific institutional arrangements over time is what would constitute the history of disenchantment. One example of such historical change can be found in a crucial difference between us and the Middle Ages: it is that we have an institutionalized *discourse* of disenchantment and they didn't. That institution is precisely the set of discursive practices called modern theory, and it is their simultaneous connection with and difference from medieval practices that constitutes the influence of modern theory on my work. The use of modern theory is in our practice: if we accept that there may be some times that are more explicitly and discursively, more *institutionally* disenchanted than others, I've argued that there can be no time when disenchantment is absent, and the discourses of disenchantment, modern theory, ought to make it easier – or so I've been arguing – to detect it wherever it occurs. We don't yet know what a history of disenchantment in the Middle Ages would look like, but with modern theory we have, I hope, better tools than ever for finding out.

Notes

1. See, especially for Foucault, MICHEL DE CERTEAU's two essays in his *Heterologies: Discourse on the Other*, trans. Brian Massumi, Theory and History of Literature 17 (Minneapolis: University of Minnesota Press, 1986): 'The Black Sun of Language: Foucault', 171–84, and 'Micro-Techniques and Panoptic Discourse: A Quid Pro Quo', 185–92. ANTHONY GIDDENS, *Central Problems in Social Theory: Action, Structure and Contradiction in Social Theory* (Berkeley: University of California Press, 1979).

2. MAX WEBER, 'Science As a Vocation', in *From Max Weber: Essays in Sociology*, ed. and trans. H. H. Gerth and C. Wright Mills (New York: Oxford University Press, 1946), 139.

3. See especially *Feminine Sexuality: Jacques Lacan and the École Freudienne*, ed. Juliet Mitchell and Jacqueline Rose (New York: Norton, 1982).

4. JILL MANN, *Chaucer and Medieval Estates Satire: The Literature of Social Classes and the General Prologue to the 'Canterbury Tales'* (Cambridge: Cambridge University Press, 1973), 4, 5.

5. MANN, xi.

6. DONALD R. HOWARD, *The Idea of the 'Canterbury Tales'* (Berkeley: University of California Press, 1976), 134–58.

7. All citations of Chaucer's poetry are from *The Riverside Chaucer*, 3rd edn, gen. ed. Larry D. Benson (Cambridge, MA: Houghton Mifflin, 1987) by fragment and line numbers; here, I.37.

8. I here follow the fine discussion of ARTHUR W. HOFFMAN, 'Chaucer's Prologue to Pilgrimage: The Two Voices', *ELH* 21 (1954), 1–16.

9. MANN, 6.

10. See Muriel Bowden, *A Commentary on the 'General Prologue' to the 'Canterbury Tales'*, 2nd edn (New York: Macmillan, 1967), 119–45.

11. Mann, 194–5.

12. Laura Kendrick notices the changing tone of this apology, *Chaucerian Play: Comedy and Control in the 'Canterbury Tales'* (Berkeley: University of California Press, 1988), 144–5.

13. See the excellent account of *ratio* and its medieval uses in Richard McKeon, *Selections From the Medieval Philosophers* (New York: Scribners, 1930), 2: 488–90.

14. Jacques Derrida, 'Outwork, prefacing', in *Dissemination*, trans. Barbara Johnson (Chicago: University of Chicago Press, 1981), 3–59.

3 The Politics of Discourse in Chaucer's *Knight's Tale**

MARK A. SHERMAN

As opposed to the 'disenchantment' that characterizes Leicester's reading of the *General Prologue* (see previous piece), Sherman notes in the Knight's narration a resolute attempt to maintain chivalric ideals of order, an order, however, that can only function by marginalizing and eliding that which is seen as 'other' to it, in particular women and the realm of the erotic. The Knight's favourite rhetorical device of *occupatio* (by which reference is made to that which the narrative is *not* going to discuss) acknowledges and effaces a variety of what Sherman calls 'countercoherent narratives' that remain to threaten the chivalric project; Theseus's desire to purge the narrative's 'erotic restlessness' in fact contests the pro-creative force out of which the entire *Canterbury Tales* spring, as indicated in the *General Prologue*'s opening lines, and though this force may be driven underground at several points in the *Knight's Tale* it bursts out anew in later Tales that will challenge the Knight's. The Tale is, however, internally challenged at various places, though the attempt is made at silencing such challenges; one such instance (discussed in the final few pages of Sherman's original article but omitted here because of space constraints) relates to Theseus's slay-ing of the Minotaur and the crucial assistance offered by Ariadne, a narrative of female intervention that has to be suppressed because of the Knight's 'misogynistic anxiety'. For further discussion of the piece, see my Introduction, pp. 13–14.

Mitius inveni quam te genus omne ferarum;
credita non ulli quam tibi peius eram.

(*Heroides* 10.1–2)

Much is at stake when the tale-telling game of the *Canterbury Tales* begins. As the *General Prologue* wends its way, the comparatively

---

* Reprinted from *Exemplaria*, 6 (1994), 87–105.

static, externalized portraiture of the individual pilgrims is abandoned in order to make possible their transformation into the dynamic community of interchangeable, subjective auditors and orators which will characterize the remainder of the *Tales*. Consistent with the needs of the pilgrimage fiction, this movement is paralleled by the progress of pilgrims out from the contained venue of their initial assembly and 'forward' in the Tabard and onto the road to Canterbury. Simultaneously, the poet who constructed these images for his audience and who contextualized as part of the seasonal round the desire of 'folk to goon on pilgrimages' yields the floor, so to speak, to a more immediate governor in the figure of Harry Bailly. Harry, we are told, is 'A semely man . . . / For to been a marchal in an halle',[1] leaving room for the suggestion that, despite his *ad hoc* administrative and critical authority, in this new mobile context he is as out of his element as he is out of his hall.

Whether or not one cares to follow Talbot Donaldson's suggestion that Harry Bailly rigged the cut to insure that the Knight tells his tale first,[2] the narrator's comment which prompts Donaldson's suspicion (I.835–49; especially 844–45) and the passage immediately preceding it wherein the Host established himself as 'social manager' of the game are indications that Harry, at least, believes such a company is incapable of adequate self-governance and furthermore that he wishes to contain any pilgrim who might be 'rebel to [his] juggement' (I.833). A portion of such rebelliousness is inherent in the increasing degree of subjectivity that a narrator acquires in performance, when she or he either confirms or resists the categorizations that contribute to the *General Prologue* and the expectations that Harry has as an auditor. Things threaten to fall apart, and on the level of fictional performance Harry assumes his role is to ensure that the internal logic of a tale-telling competition doesn't subvert the ideological context in which he would have the game played.

The poem, in one sense, then, begins by establishing a dialectic of containment and release, but does so in a manner encouraging an understanding of that dialectic as something which varies in character as it inhabits different spheres. To be sure, the erotic natural activity opening the *General Prologue* is one manifestation of this model, yet that very force seems to carry a different set of consequences when inscribed under the rubric of Christianity and realized in the practice of pilgrimage. Granted, the impetus may be the same in both worlds, but whereas in the former it is free to follow its natural course and so participate in the great cycle of creation, in the latter, despite the fact that it continues to be the primary motivation, the erotic impulse must be sublimated lest it undermine the deterministic ideological hierarchies on which certain social and religious practices depend.[3]

Clearly, the 'struggle between noble designs and chaos' which Charles Muscatine saw as the fundamental concern of the *Knight's Tale*[4] has its precedent in the *General Prologue*, and a reader might wonder whether the Knight doesn't take his cue from Harry when, given the circumstances, he selects what would be the most appropriate of his 'olde stories'. Questions remain, however, concerning the particular discursive 'level' at which the anxiety about chaos might be situated, what its origins are, into what recesses of the fiction it penetrates, whether it succeeds in establishing any sort of order, and what the ramifications are for the poetic project undertaken in the *Canterbury Tales*. Furthermore, we might ask, what exactly are the architectonics of such 'noble designs' as the Knight's, and to what end are they directed? Is the phrase to critics what Lee Patterson suggests the term *honor* is to chivalry – 'a shorthand for motives that would not bear further inspection'?[5] I think we might attempt to answer these questions by examining the *Knight's Tale* as an individual performance which provides insight into the concerns of its pilgrim narrator and attempts to establish within its own fiction a narrative and political paradigm that the remaining pilgrim performers must either ratify or contradict. Simply stated, the Knight's greatest foe is not Islam, but rather whatever might be identified with eros and the stories through which its complexities, constructive as well as destructive, would be better understood.

When the Knight begins his tale he introduces the legendary Theseus, Duke of Athens, returning home from a military campaign during which he has successfully 'conquered al the regne of Femenye' (I.866). Though an important pretext for the ordered world of the Knight's tale, this conquest of both a place and, more specifically, the political power there, is external to the narrative from the very start and is deemed to have no place within the tale because it is a *fait accompli*, a deferred history best understood, we are led to believe, by the conqueror who writes it. From the outset of the tale, both 'Femenye' and its 'regne' have been dismissed as possible subjects of the ensuing narrative, the now safely married Amazon queen Hippolyta and her sister Emelye being brought home as the ornamental spoils of war.

An important task begun immediately in the *Knight's Tale* is the erasure of *Femenye* (a word which happens to disappear twenty lines into the tale) through a series of representations and deliberate *non*-representations. In seeing this process through, the Knight engenders and privileges immutable categories of subjectivity and objectivity which he would in turn impose upon his audience. What motivates the Knight's telling and the order it transcribes is a basic fact of which we are reminded by Fredric Jameson:

> [T]he concept of good and evil is a positional one that coincides with categories of Otherness. Evil thus, as Nietzsche taught us, continues to characterize whatever is radically different from me, whatever by virtue of precisely that difference seems to constitute a real and urgent threat to my own existence. So from the earliest times, the stranger from another tribe, the 'barbarian' who speaks an incomprehensible language and follows 'outlandish' customs, but also the woman whose biological difference stimulates fantasies of castration and devoration . . . are some of the archetypal figures of the Other, about whom the essential point to be made is not so much that he is feared because he is evil; rather he is evil *because* he is Other, alien, different, strange, unclean, and unfamiliar.[6]

The construction of this binary opposition embodies for the Knight an epistemological order into which one must be inscribed or suffer obliteration, as befalls the history of Femenye. In the tale the primary agent of this ideology is Theseus, and through him the Knight reveals much about himself, with the result that the fictive worlds inside and outside the tale mirror one another, the image reversal grounded perhaps only in the difference he, a Christian knight, attributes to pagan antiquity.[7]

In his recent examination of the *Knight's Tale* Patterson contends that the self-consciousness which would make such a deliberate agenda possible in the narrative is indicative of a 'crisis of chivalric identity' arising from the contemporary politico-economic situation. 'The *Knight's Tale*', he writes, 'represents a paradox: an act of self-conscious narration by a man whose social ideology precludes self-consciousness.'[8] This ought not to suggest, however, that the Knight's narration constitutes a transgression of chivalric ideology or that it evinces anything like Leicester's Weberian 'disenchantment' wherein what were once thought to be transcendent forces are discovered to be the product of human institutions.[9] On the contrary, the Knight's character, long held by readers to be that of 'a verray, parfit, gentil knyght', is indeed the epitome of Christian chivalry, adhering faithfully to its tenets and agenda, anticipating opposition even if only in the denial that any threat exists, and diligently, possibly blindly working as a matter of course to insure chivalry's ideological ascendence, futile though that might be. Perhaps what Patterson identifies as self-consciousness is more properly this internal mustering of resources in an individual so completely bound ideologically. The Knight's self-consciousness in this case would not be subversive but exemplary, and his discursive agenda, as Chaucer represents it, is geared toward militantly institutionalizing the transcendent ideal of Christian orthodoxy.

Chivalric self-consciousness, then, in adhering uncritically to the hegemonic ideology of the class producing it, becomes the privileged mode of subjectivity which allocates the otherness of Femenye to whoever would occupy a position outside its rule. This is essentially the process of feminization functioning in the tale, and it is not enacted on women exclusively, though it is through femaleness and the women in the tale that such associations are forged. Femenye becomes a pejorative identification for any Other figured in opposition to the reign of Theseus, and must be expanded to include Palamon, Arcite, and of course Thebes. Though Femenye, as a noun, betokens the fact of sexual difference, in the final analysis it is purely a matter of one's position relative to a given power structure. Outside the tale, the Knight's iron-handed rhetoric would similarly define the competition among the pilgrims, and this unspoken agenda is manifest in the relation of the pilgrim narrator to his audience.[10] Moreover, I suggest that Femenye is situated as the repressed voice of an historical perspective ultimately antagonistic to the providential scheme the tale nominates to rule the Canterbury pilgrimage. The unexpected result, however, is that after its erasure Femenye is ubiquitous within the tale and becomes equated with the erotic force which initiates the pilgrimage and enables the tale-telling competition to continue fairly and openly after the Knight has told his 'noble storie'.

As a narrator the Knight relies heavily on his arsenal of rhetorical devices, a practice which Stephen Knight sees as an indication of the high and eloquent style formally suited to a noble tale.[11] And this is true, I think, so far as genre and estate are coterminous, but not privileged, in the *Tales*. Among these devices the Knight exhibits an unnerving predilection for *occupatio*, the first instance of which is his immediate declaration that the conquest of Femenye is a tale too long to recount (I.875). He uses the technique as a means of paring down the ancillary narratives that would otherwise variegate the master narrative he is in the process of constructing. (Those narratives, a corpus of 'olde bookes' discarded as they are recalled, comprise the epic upon which the Knight's decorous and ambitious romance depends.) *Occupatio* is for the Knight a way of occupying the textual space which would be devoted to some other narrative thread which he has decided is extraneous. *Occupatio* is also a means of shaping the consciousness of his audience by neglecting those other paths toward which the narrative seems to direct us, thereby making his tale a series of narrative roads not taken. The Knight, as Winthrop Wetherbee has written, is a figure who has a powerful professional investment in the optimistic, 'romance' version of his story, and whose suppression of historical and psychological reality, though largely unwitting, is also to a certain extent a deliberate, political gesture.[12]

The technique is, in short, a gentle way of laying siege to an audience in a manner more subtle than those techniques we can imagine were well honed 'In Gernade at the seege . . . / Of Algezir' (I.56–57).[13] More subtle, perhaps, but equally effective.

The Knight's approach to story-telling is evidence that narrative to him is the most effective means of establishing order, at least within the civilian sector. But there is also a certain desperation underscoring his tale, which is in many ways a last-ditch attempt to lend coherence to what he fears will become an amorphous, contradictory body of narrative material; the tale is his means by which to impose order on a seemingly unruly world threatening to go its own way. We will recall that after his first use of *occupatio* the Knight returns to his story by confessing: 'I have, God woot, a large feeld to ere, / And wayke been the oxen in my plough' (I.886–87). More than just a modesty topos, the comment registers the Knight's aspirations and an uncertainty that his means will achieve his desired end. And in a nostalgic pause before the grande mêlée of the tournament he turns to his audience of pilgrims as though seeking reassurance that the centerpiece of his story is still ideologically relevant, his finger having been so long away from the English pulse:[14]

> For if ther fille tomorwe swich a cas,
> Ye knowen wel that every lusty knyght
> That loveth paramours and hath his myght,
> Were it in Engelond or elleswhere,
> They wolde, hir thankes, wilnen to be there –
> To fighte for a lady, benedicitee!
> It were a lusty sighte for to see.

$$(I.2110–16)$$

The Knight's rhetoric, however, like the world in general, might prove equally indifferent toward the desires of its master because each instance of *occupatio* also signifies a countercoherent narrative running through the tale.[15] Indeed, the Knight's ornament functions similarly to those rhetorical techniques of abbreviation about which Geoffrey of Vinsauf says the effect is to enable an observation of 'what is said through what is left unsaid . . . so that through the perception of the mind, many can be seen in one'.[16] This paradoxical technique acquires a kind of surplus significance by heightening the reader's awareness of excluded narratives to such a degree that the unsaid exerts greater narrative force than the said, that the utterance stands in the shadow of what it obfuscates. The Knight's mistaken assumption, however, is that the oblique allusions he employs in his *occupationes* will be evidence for his audience that he is aware of these other stories, is willing to provide a glimpse of them, that doing so is a gesture of reassurance that we all value the same 'Trouthe and honour, fredom and curtesie' (I.46), and that we all read the same stories in the same way. Through such an assurance he is attempting to bring under his control the many tales which could potentially contradict the one he's telling. Employed in this fashion, therefore, *occupatio* becomes, as Stephen Knight has also written, 'a rhetorical device . . . of deliberately negative impact'.[17] But the spoken word once uttered is not easily retrieved; hence the capacity for a circumvented narrative, like that of the conquest of Femenye and the marriage of Theseus to Hippolyta, or, more generally, the history of Theseus the masculine chivalric hero and love, to underwrite the tale and become, in a way, its allegorical referent. This is to say that what is passed by in the first of the Knight's *occupationes*, the account of

> . . . the grete bataille for the nones
> Bitwixen Atthenes and Amazones;
> And how asseged was Ypolita,
> The faire, hardy queene of Scithia;
> And of the feste that was at hir weddynge;
> And of the tempest at hir hoom-comynge

(I.879–84)

remains in fact an ongoing struggle and a primary scene of resistance to the Knight's ideological, narrative agenda.

The tempest in question, which is evidently Chaucer's invention, having no source in either Statius or Boccaccio, need not be understood as a hazard to travel or a turbulent popular response to Theseus's return but as the continued resistance of the Amazons taken in bondage, played out domestically, even in the romance micronarrative of Palamon and Arcite.[18] And as the discourse of this micronarrative would suggest, it is the speaker's intention that we see the world in small; that is, from within restrictive parameters and with little or no access to other narrative structures. Thebes is not so devastated in the first part of the tale that Arcite cannot return to all his wealth in the second. Though we are told that the city was 'rente adoun bothe wall and sparre and rafter' (I.990), it is clearly Thebes which most threatens Athens at the tale's end. Why should we think less of Femenye? Precisely because of its numerous truncations and diversions, the tale must be read from its very beginning with an eye for what is *not* articulated and is in fact blatantly suppressed.

Between the first instance of *occupatio*, where the tale's prehistory is deferred, and Theseus's confrontation with the Argive widows there are a scant twenty-one lines. Yet a crucial transition is begun herein when Theseus hears the women's lamentation, and chides:

> 'What folk been ye, that at myn homcomynge
> Perturben so my feste with criynge?'
> Quod Theseus. 'Have ye so greet envye
> Of myn honour, that thus compleyne and crye?'
>
> (I.905–8)

More than a mere quotation, this transition of the speaking voice from outside to inside the story reduces the perspective so that what was earlier 'their' homecoming and wedding becomes 'mine': 'myn homcomynge', 'my feste', 'myn honour'. What was originally one tale which happened to be about Theseus among myriad others now focuses on its central subject to the exclusion of all else. Contrary to the possibility that the Knight might be establishing a basic difference between himself and his protagonist, this transition is a way of delimiting his audience's sensibilities through a reorientation which entrenches the available point of view within the chivalric perspective shared by the Knight and his proxy in the tale, a maneuver which would define all meaning in the story according to the activities of this central figure. In other words, the *Knight's Tale* suffers from the cult of its own heroism in a poem which would displace that idea. Precisely because of the Knight's performative context, however, that totalizing perspective becomes its own undoing.[19]

An additional significance of this encounter with the widows, despite Theseus's pledge to amend the wrongs done to them, resides in the reconfiguration of Femenye initiated by his questioning. Femenye is no longer perceived as a nation of defiant female warriors but as supplicant widows; that is, women who, unlike Hippolyta, desire and need husbands, and authoritarian husbands in particular – the Amazons are transformed into the sort of clients every romance knight is looking for. Rather than see the event as a magnanimous gesture on the part of Theseus, I suggest that the imperious effects of this meeting not be underestimated, because it is a moment which sets the stage for the tale to come and indicates how subtly the Knight's martial rhetoric works.

The scene might best be visualized as a kind of historic tableau threatening to reveal its kinship with mythography at any moment, because, the reality of Theseus as mythic character notwithstanding, the Knight himself is in the process of presenting Athenian mythology as a model for understanding history. Flanked by two extremes of defeated womanhood, the duke maintains his control over the categorization of otherness. The reconfiguration of Femenye here is accomplished through an identification of two radically different groups of women, not under the sign of their common anatomy, but by their common defeat and dependence now on the whim of the conqueror. The fact that they are females is coincidental and merely the mark of their condition, military defeat (which itself denotes to the Knight a kind of castration) now determines their identity. Consequently, the differentiation *within* otherness is so thoroughly erased that when Theseus acquiesces to the request of the Argive widows, the Knight quietly juxtaposes the magnanimous 'honour' of his champion against what will be for the remainder of the tale the image of a supplicant Femenye. And as if to seal the obliteration of the Amazons, once Theseus turns toward Thebes and sends Hippolyta to Athens, her name, like that of Femenye, is never mentioned again.

David Anderson also sees this episode as a turning point in the tale, but believes that it marks the duke's change of heart, and that the transition is emblematized by the temple of Clementia which provides a suitably auspicious setting for the encounter. He proposes that 'The temple of Clemency, as the only feature on the civic landscape, stands in metonymy for Athens itself'.[20] However, that temple is emphatically *outside* Athens, and Athens itself is nowhere to be seen. Consequently, Theseus as tyrant and opposed to the temple metonymically comes to represent the city. Furthermore, the temple is a venue chosen by the Argive women, not by Theseus (I.927–30), and they have waited there two full weeks, so the temple represents their desires rather than the duke's inclination. Ironically consistent with Anderson's fourteenth-century glossators and book twelve of the *Thebaid*, by downplaying Statius's lengthy description of the temple and moving it out from the center of Athens the Knight casts his Clemency a bit too literally as the *ignotus deus*, the unknown god – that is, a god unknown in the tale. This Theseus proves as he rides off to Thebes where, as Leicester notes, disposing of one heap of corpses he creates another.[21]

Rather than argue for the duke's change of heart we might better see this episode as an extraordinary example of the ability of the powerful to adapt his methods to the immediate situation, something which the Knight himself is compelled to do, having returned from his professional tour only the day before. Any clemency, far from being a selfless act of compassion, is not so much a change of heart for Theseus as it is a way of reaffirming the 'honour' which the widows threatened. Anderson notes also the suggestion of a pilgrimage as the *Thebaid* ends with the Argive widows journeying to Athens.[22] It would seem no mere coincidence, then, if one of those palimpsestic referents constantly shadowing the tale is the context of its narrator's performance, that the Knight introduces his protagonist in a scene which is reminiscent of his meeting at the Tabard the night before: a Knight returning home from the wars encountering a group of pilgrims. As Theseus is to the widows, therefore, so is the Knight to his fellow travelers – accommodating but in charge, but perhaps not really one of them at all. And in that discursive sphere resides the movement to feminize the audience of pilgrims. I suggest as a rule of thumb, therefore, that we not be taken in by the *Knight's Tale* solely on the grounds that it has a degree of sentimental appeal and because it is the first (and perhaps the last) noble story on the Canterbury pilgrimage. The nobility attending the tale is no absolute, pre-existent, or transcendent quality, but something the tale attempts to construct.

Before Theseus returns from the carnage at Thebes, there is an incident recorded which is of equal importance to the occupation of Femenye. It is more significant, in fact, than the battle itself and subsequent looting, and certainly more so than the funerary clamor of the lamenting widows which the Knight deems as also 'to long for to devyse' (I.994). This is of course the discovery of Palamon and Arcite amid a heap of corpses.

> Two yonge knyghtes liggynge by and by,
> Bothe in oon armes, wrought ful richely
> Of whiche two Arcita highte that oon,
> And that other knight highte Palamon.
> Nat fully quyke, ne fully dede they were
> But by hir cote-armures and by hir gere
> The heraudes knewe hem best in special
> As they that weren of the blood roial
> Of Thebes, and of sustren two yborn.
>
> (I.1011–19)

Though we are given their names, the two young knights are undifferentiated other than by class. Either one could be Palamon or Arcite. They are not only lying side by side, but they bear the same arms, are born of two equally generalized sisters, and, most important, are neither alive nor dead. They are, as Pirandello might put it, two characters in search of an author, or two signifiers in search of signifieds, but ultimately two signifiers signifying each other and so signifying nothing (unless it were signification itself).

Yet their very insignificance makes them the perfect actors for what
is to follow. Neither should the importance of their mothers, the
'sustren two', be overlooked, because they are analogous to the
defeated Amazon sisters, thereby making Palamon and Arcite, as
they are pulled from the pile of corpses, the symbolic offspring of
Hyppolita and Emelye insofar as the two young Theban knights now
represent the principle of opposition to Theseus's rule – Femenye
refigured yet once more – until they too are subsumed into it.[23]

Palamon and Arcite wake from the death they experience on the
fields of Thebes only to find themselves born into Theseus's prison.
This is a narrative turn which thematically renders the tale's political
structure and its highly internalized, centripetal movement: attending
the cousins' eventual differentiation (accomplished only as a result of
their gazing on Emelye) is the fact of their inscription into the duke's
symbolic order. Indeed, Theseus's rule in the tale is so pervasive that,
even when they have escaped physical bondage, Palamon and Arcite
are compelled to uphold his order. This imperative is apparent not
only in their absurd conformity to ritual as they fight in the grove,
but also in the fact that when they are discovered Palamon hastily
asks for death – a moment marking the transition of a desire for the
forbidden into a desire for the prescribed, the awkwardness of which
is revealed in Palamon's apologetic confession that both he and his
cousin are 'encombred of oure owene lyves' (I.1718).

His reaction is that of a child who has been caught in violation
of paternal decree. Upon his discovery, what becomes the burden
of Palamon's own life is his imminent dispossession, that he will be
written out of the world he has lived in for the past seven years, and
he desperately offers his own life in return for reinstatement. He'll do
anything to bear again the mark of social inscription, as he proves
when he reveals Arcite's identity and offers *his* life as well. (One
can only imagine the expression on Philostrate's face at Palamon's
magnanimity!) The cousins' dilemma is that they are now subject to
Theseus's censuring paternal gaze for having replicated his order
out of his sight. They are in essence usurpers. But ever since their
'rebirth' into the tower, all of their desires have been located within
the compass of Theseus's governance, so that their threat to usurp is
only the last vestige of a Theban identity. To be taken back into the
father's order they must repeat their covert performance under his
scrutiny as a public acknowledgment of his power and admit that
they desire nothing which is not of his providence. Actually this
has been the case all along, or at least since they first laid eyes on
Emelye, because her appearance in the garden punctuates a radical
and sudden transformation from Amazon warrior to courtly damsel,

another of the Knight's subtle erasures.[24] Since they were plucked from the *taas* the cousins haven't desired a thing that wasn't prescribed; they merely failed to recognize the fact.

The centripetal power politics, which account for these maneuverings in the first two parts of the tale, are relevant to the problems surrounding history and its inscription in that the manipulation of the historical record, and consequently how that record is understood, is dependent upon controlling the system of representation, the symbolic order, within which the record is produced, displayed, and interpreted. The prominent role of oration and oratory denote the tale's devotion to what Lacan has called 'the world of words that creates the world of things'.[25] Far from believing that history is a means of reclaiming an original truth, the Knight is well aware of the power residing in representation to form an understanding of the world, and it is this awareness which informs his ideological and rhetorical agenda.

The theater built for the tournament which will reinstate Palamon and Arcite after their year of exile is, we are told, of an equitably circular configuration (I.1891–92), so equitable that the multitude of spectators is at an even advantage. However, the archetypal spectator is the architect himself, and so it stands to reason that the structure would display his magnanimous image, particularly when he, like Narcissus, gazes at his own reflection. The elaborate edifice of the theater, then, is foremost an external projection of his own mind. To consider the theater in this light is to stress the literal implications of the otherwise formulaic hyperbole which the Knight uses to praise the theater: 'swich a place / Was noon in erthe, *as in so litel space*' (I.1895–96, my italics). The antagonism between the space in question and what occupies it, what is represented there, puts the Knight in the position of confessing that his construct exceeds the limitations of reference to a physical theater and draws attention to the very space occupied by the tale, cultivating an interdependence between the various levels of the narration to produce the sort of palimpsestic textuality that Craig Owens contends is 'the paradigm for the allegorical work' where one story is always read in another.[26]

The circuit of the theater, however, with its oratories to Mars, Venus, and Diana, also has a built-in triangle of adversity which inscribes within that equitable circle the overt purpose of the tournament: the elimination of at least one of the triangle's three points, perhaps two. The contest, then, is not so much over Emelye as flesh and blood but as imaginary (and) woman; it is the inscription of an advanced phase of the struggle for the domination of the symbolic (with all that those Lacanian terms imply).[27]

Even within the reality of the tale the theater is an illusion which exceeds authorial intention to become a figure of the space of polysemous allegorical representation. The theater, as opposed to the garden or the grove, is the authorized scene of Theseus's desire in addition to being a tribute to his order. The elaborate mechanism of the tale – in particular the building of the theater and the tournament performed therein – is constructed, as I proposed above, as an allegorical psychomachia of Theseus's conquest of Femenye, a space in which to represent the drama of his, and the Knight's, general anxiety and animosity toward women, love, and the threat he locates in the imaginary and in discursive liberty: in short, the reality of history as he would not write it.

As evidence that the tale has a good deal in common with psychomachic allegory we might also consider the matter of Palamon and Arcite's insignificance outside the duke's order combined with the fact that, almost in a nod to personification allegory, each fights under one of the colors that comprise Theseus's banner: Arcite under the martial red, Palamon under venerean white. Robert Blanch and Julian Wasserman have commented on this very issue, suggesting that the chromatic iconography in the *Knight's Tale* encourages a reading of the narrative as one which moves toward a resolution of tension and into an ideal harmony emblematic of Theseus's 'neo-platonic oneness'.[28] Yet if Palamon and Arcite are introduced in part one as bearing identical arms, a symbol of 'oneness' to which the tale eventually returns, that oneness is singularly unable to transcend the order of its inscription because Palamon and Arcite are commanded to play out a conflict *within* that order until, as Theseus himself decreed, 'Ye shul noon oother ende with me maken, / That oon of yow ne shal be deed or taken' (I.1865–66). Far from an ameliorating process of psychic integration, the *Knight's Tale* moves only toward a disintegration of difference, an infernal downward spiral passed off as the sublime. It should then come as no surprise that the tale's divine scheme is executed by a 'furie infernal' (I.2684) because the fact of the matter is that Theseus's Athens is a hellish place.

However, even as a symbol the theater in which this performance occurs was not created *ex nihilo*, as the beginning of part three informs us. Within the fiction, it is comprised of marble and stone, but as an image of the text it is constructed of that earlier scene in the tale when Palamon and Arcite are discovered in the grove. The theater is the grove redivivus. Both locations afford a spectacle of conflicting desires, the only difference being that one location is prescribed, the other forbidden – and both scenes revisit the garden in which Emelye first appears. Leicester has written that the garden (I.1033–55) marks a new concentration on nature (including human nature, in line with the interest of romance in the seasonal rhythms of generation) and on psychological experience. . . . This description, a set piece unlike anything in the poem that precedes it, concentrates on natural, seasonal energy and its general effects though it is scarcely a realistic description of nature. . . . The lady's individuality is of little importance to the forces being described here – so little, in fact, that she is assimilated to the season, made its embodiment and one of its effects, like the lily and the rose. Indeed, as it proceeds, the description increasingly sublimates and chastens the erotic restlessness it conveys at its beginning.[29]

He is correct, I believe, but for the omission of one important point. While, as a set piece, the description of the garden has no precedent in the *tale*, it does have an important pre-text in the *poem*, that is in the *Canterbury Tales*, in the hierogamic opening of the *General Prologue*, to which the language of Leicester's analysis alludes. Although the Knight's appropriation of the *General Prologue* seems literally or 'dramatically' absurd (How can he have read something written after the fact of his telling? Maybe the pilgrim Chaucer was working on it at the Tabard?) it is textually incontrovertible.

> Er it were day, as was hir wone to do,
> She was arisen and al redy dight,
> For May wole have no slogardie anyght.
> The sesoun priketh every gentle herte,
> And maketh it out of his slep to sterte,
> And seith 'Arys, and do thyn observaunce.'
>
> (I.1040–45)

> . . . the yonge sonne
> Hath in the Ram his half cours yronne,
> And smale foweles maken melodye,
> That slepen al the nyght with open ye
> (So priketh hem nature in hir corages),
> Thanne longen folk to goon on pilgrimages
>
> (I.7–12)

The significance of this gambit is that the Knight himself assumes the responsibility of chastening the erotic restlessness from which the entire *Canterbury Tales* is born, and with which Emelye (i.e., Femenye) is clearly associated. The allegorization of Emelye as the Spring, in which she is rendered almost in the style of Botticelli, performs an important function in the process of rarefication the female body undergoes in the *Knight's Tale*, and is the product of a misguided (neo)Platonism which understood platonic love 'only in the narrow, popular sense in which it means a complete disengagement from earthly passions'.[30]

If this is the Knight's response to the fiction which has created him, then it is surely the objective of his tale not only to chasten but to purge that erotic restlessness for the sake of stability, which he does, I would argue, *by constructing the theater on the very site of the grove*.[31] Arcite goes there a-maying, Palamon there initiates his revenge on Arcite, and Theseus heads in that direction to slay, suggestively, the 'greet herte' (I.1675). The convergence of these three locations into one is further confirmed by the translation of Arcite and Palamon's conflict,[32] as I mentioned earlier, and by the fact that while he is standing in the midst of the grove Theseus unequivocally states 'The lystes shal I maken *in this place*' (I.1862, my italics).

My suggestion is of course completely at odds with the very explicit clearing of the grove after Arcite's death – if we impose the limitations of realist narratives on the tale. But then we would have to accept the infernal fury which causes his death, as well as the counsel and strife among the Olympians (themselves allegorical parallels to the human theatrics below) as conforming to realist narrative practice as well. The imposition of that sort of convention on an allegory is, to say the least, unwarranted. The elaborate machinations which accomplish this rhetorical superimposition of performances onto a single space have as their objective, as I have argued, the inscription of an illicit desire into the official order in an effort to eradicate not only the fact of its illegitimacy but the desire itself. This reading is upheld by the basic plot of the tale, the purpose of which is to displace eros for the expedient stability of the patriarchal marriage contract. In much the same way, the clearing of the grove for Arcite's funeral pyre drives away the wood nymphs and fauns (I.2925–28), or, as the Wife of Bath later notes, the arrival of the friars has made sightings of elves and fairies a thing of the past.

One should not overlook the possibility that the Wife's introduction to her tale serves as a commentary on this scene, for she explicitly states that

> In th'olde dayes of the Kyng Arthour,
> Of which that Britons speken greet honour,
> Al was this land fulfild of fayerye.
> The elf-queene, with hir joly compaignye,
> Daunced ful ofte in many a grene mede.
> This was the olde opinion, as I rede;

I speke of manye hundred yeres ago.
But now kan no man se none elves mo.

(III.857–64)

Undoubtedly, the Wife's criticisms are not reserved for the
Friar alone, because her appropriation of this motif (which the
Knight introduces to the *Tales,* and which he yokes to the subject
of marriage) is a deliberate reversal of the Knight's efforts to chasten
the primal erotic scene. And as her tale demonstrates, there is a clear
opposition between chivalry and faerie. In contradistinction to the
Wife's argument, the cumulative effect of the Knight's deforestation,
which ultimately superimposes Arcite's funeral pyre onto the garden,
is to cast the place of sexual desire as the place of death.

Yet the Knight is not so vulgar a tactician that he would frighten
away young grooms, his potential heirs, thereby jeopardizing the
massive power based in patriarchal marriage. Even the *demande
d'amour* which summarizes the predicament of the two young knights
at the end of part one seems just the sort of cliff-hanging conundrum
which can only be resolved in marriage. The Knight's romance
capitalizes on this dilemma to inculcate a paradigm of desire not
only for the characters in his tale but for his auditors as well. By
obliterating the erotic threat posed by Femenye he is able to portray
marriage as a diplomatic necessity, and he does so in the same
smooth, offhand manner as his protagonist, which, among other
things, has led Richard Neuse to characterize the duke as a 'brilliant
political opportunist' exhibiting 'many of the characteristics of the
Renaissance machiavel'.[33] The Knight ingeniously delivers this
polemical *coup de grâce* of Theseus as if it were an afterthought, and
not a terribly important matter:

Thanne *semed me* ther was a parlement
At Atthenes, upon *certein* pointz and caas;
Among the whiche pointz yspoken was,
To have with *certein* countrees alliaunce,
And have fully of Thebans obeisaunce.

(I.2970–74, my italics)

Like a raptor circling lazily above his prey unnoticed, the Knight
speaks nonchalantly until he seizes on the point with deadly
certainty. Within that easy delivery he clearly distinguishes between
relationships of alliance and obedience, the latter reserved for Thebes
as it is for Femenye. . . .

Notes

1. All citations of Chaucer's poetry are taken from *The Riverside Chaucer*, 3d edn, ed. LARRY D. BENSON, et al. (Boston, MA: Houghton Mifflin, 1987), by fragment and line numbers; here I.751–52.

2. E. T. DONALDSON, *Chaucer's Poetry: An Anthology for the Modern Reader* (New York: Ronald, 1975), 1061.

3. I might mention here that pilgrimage, insofar as it is, in Edith and Victor Turner's words, a 'liminoid phenomenon', is necessarily the site of instability, and consequently the object of piqued scrutiny. See EDITH and VICTOR TURNER, *Image and Pilgrimage in Christian Culture: Anthropological Perspectives* (New York: Columbia University Press, 1978); VICTOR TURNER, 'Betwixt and Between: The Liminal Period in Rites de Passage' in *The Forest of Symbols: Aspects of Ndembu Ritual* (Ithaca, NY: Cornell University Press, 1967); also JONATHAN SUMPTION, *Pilgrimage: An Image of Medieval Religion* (Totowa, NJ: Rowan & Littlefield, 1976).

4. C. MUSCATINE, *Chaucer and the French Tradition: A Study in Style and Meaning* (Berkeley: University of California Press, 1957), 181.

5. L. PATTERSON, *Chaucer and the Subject of History* (Madison: University of Wisconsin Press, 1991), 174. DAVID AERS, *Chaucer, Langland and the Creative Imagination* (London: Routledge & Kegan Paul, 1980), comments similarly that if in the *Knight's Tale* Theseus is intended as a representative of order, 'then Chaucer is leading us to see we should never celebrate abstractions such as "order" but inquire about the kind of order and its specific human content' (p. 177).

6. F. JAMESON, *The Political Unconscious: Narrative as a Socially Symbolic Act* (Ithaca, NY: Cornell University Press, 1981), 115.

7. The identification of the Knight with Theseus has been considered most recently by H. MARSHALL LEICESTER, *The Disenchanted Self: Representing the Subject in the 'Canterbury Tales'* (Berkeley: University of California Press, 1990), 4–5 and part 3, 'The Institution of the Subject: A Reading of the *Knight's Tale*', esp. 370. His view of the role of Femenye is quite different from mine, and he argues for the Knight's identification with the situation of the women in the tale, what he calls the Knight's 'bisexuality' (pp. 293–4). I might comment here that the Knight's own contingent on the pilgrimage is a suspiciously homosocial group which seems the product of a kind of chivalric parthenogenesis, causing one to wonder: did the Squire have a mother?

    The implications of David Anderson's commentary on the Augustinian economy of history which informs the *Knight's Tale* seem particularly relevant to the oppositional scheme I've proposed, particularly insofar as Augustine's model contributes to the pathologization of recursivity in the tale. See DAVID ANDERSON, *Before the Knight's Tale: Imitation of Classical Epic in Boccaccio's 'Teseida'* (Philadelphia: University of Pennsylvania Press, 1988), 167 and 216–17. However, I must disagree with his suggestion that the competition among the pilgrims replicates '"Babylonian" forces of division'.

8. PATTERSON, *Chaucer and the Subject of History*, 39.

9. LEICESTER, *Disenchanted Self*, 26–7.

10. On this matter Patterson's point is well made, I think, that the crisis in chivalric identity is evident only because on pilgrimage the Knight finds himself in 'unstable territory where questions are asked', to which he

responds with 'the same kinds of suppressions and elisions that enabled chivalry to function' (*Chaucer and the Subject of History*, 168–9).

11. S. KNIGHT, *Rymyng Craftily: Meaning in Chaucer's Poetry* (Oxford: Blackwell, 1974), 136 ff.

12. W. WETHERBEE, 'Romance and Epic in Chaucer's *Knight's Tale*', *Exemplaria*, 2 (1990), 305.

13. See TERRY JONES, *Chaucer's Knight: The Portrait of a Medieval Mercenary* (Baton Rouge: Louisiana State University Press, 1980), 59–63, for a summary of that 'long-drawn-out affair' and how it compares to other struggles with the Moors. For a more benign interpretation of the Knight's motives, see KURT OLSSON, '*Securitas* and Chaucer's Knight', *SAC*, 9 (1987), who holds that the Knight 'works to create order and unity by a rhetoric that uniquely builds on shared perception' (p. 127).

14. JONES, *Chaucer's Knight*, writes, 'by Chaucer's day tournaments tended to be grand ornamental affairs rather than mere blood-baths. The mêlée in which all the participants took to the field at once, like a miniature battle, had long since been replaced by elaborate jousts which generally featured single combat' (p. 179).

15. See MIEKE BAL, *Death and Dissymetry: The Politics of Coherence in the Book of Judges* (Chicago: University of Chicago Press, 1988), 5, 37, 254, and *passim*, whose central point about narrative coherence and the influence it has on historiography is that coherence is an exclusionary process, one of obliteration, which cannot help but privilege one reading/inscription over another. And particularly in Judges, coherence is the means and product of a masculine cultural and narrative domination.

16. 'Prudentia docti / In dictis non dicta notet . . . / Mentis ut intuitu multae videantur in una' (lines 702–3 and 706) in ERNEST GALLO (trans.), *The 'Poetria Nova' and its Sources in Early Rhetorical Doctrine* (The Hague: Mouton, 1971), 51. Geoffrey mentions *occupatio* only briefly as an illustration of *figurae verborum* (line 1164), but the correlation I'm making to techniques of abbreviation ought to stand, particularly considering the use of *occupatio* in the *Knight's Tale*.

17. S. KNIGHT, *Geoffrey Chaucer* (Oxford: Blackwell, 1986), 89. On the other hand, ROBERT W. HANNING, ' "The Struggle Between Noble Designs and Chaos": The Literary Tradition of Chaucer's *Knight's Tale*', in Geoffrey Chaucer's *'The Knight's Tale'*, ed. Harold Bloom (New York: Chelsea House, 1988), 69–89 (originally published in *The Literary Review*, 23 [1980]), sees *occupatio* as an 'emblem of the hard choices and discipline of art' (p. 79), and finds that the Knight 'makes us painfully aware of his difficulties as an amateur storyteller' (p. 70). Yet I find it difficult to fathom that an old and well-travelled campaigner would not also be an accomplished storyteller. . . .

18. See VINCENT J. DIMARCO's note to I.884 in *The Riverside Chaucer* that Curry, *MLN*, 36 (1921), 272–4; Wagner, *MLN*, 50 (1935), 296; Parr, *PMLA*, 60 (1945), 315 argue that the meaning of *tempest*, like Boccaccio's *tomolto*, implies the activity of a crowd. This, however, seems at odds with the account of the separate arrivals of Theseus and the women; when he does return, it is more as a military conqueror than as a newlywed. ELAINE TUTTLE HANSEN, *Chaucer and the Fictions of Gender* (Berkeley: University of California Press, 1992), however, considers the possibility that 'The tempest might well allude to the untold story of stormy early days in Theseus and Hippolyta's marriage; in any naturalistic account, the transformation of an Amazonian queen into a

proper wife for an Athenian king would probably be difficult and protracted' (p. 218).

By *micronarrative* I mean what in some contexts might be called an inset narrative, a kind of allegorical and allegorizing subset of a larger discursive project which can serve either to delimit or expand thematic significance.

19. Cf. Patterson, *Chaucer and the Subject of History*, 202.

20. D. Anderson, 'The Fourth Temple of the Knight's Tale: Athenian Clemency and Chaucer's Theseus', *SAC*, Proceedings 2 (1986), 117. Concerning the *Thebaid*, Wetherbee, 'Romance and Epic', commenting on the 'quasi-Christian cult of compassion centered on the Athenian altar of Clementia' (p. 308), observes that Clementia, unlike most other pagan deities, 'offers a sort of amnesty, a release from the burden of history. In her presence . . . the effects of authoritarian power are rendered null and void' (p. 309). I am suggesting that what happens at the temple in the *Knight's Tale* has little to do with clemency and makes history a greater burden for those who must bear its consequences.

21. Leicester, *Disenchanted Self*, 229.

22. Anderson, 'The Fourth Temple', 115.

23. Anderson, *Before the Knight's Tale*, 207–12, ingeniously decodes a submerged genealogy identifying Palamon as the son of Polynices and Antigone. But this might be an excessively literal reading, which inordinately concentrates on Thebes. This is not, however, to dispute the fact that Palamon and Arcite are in any of several senses the tale's equivalents to the sons of Oedipus.

24. Leicester, *Disenchanted Self*, sees this as a rebirth from 'epic to romance, from heroic combat and the cries of the vanquished to the flowering of springtime and lovers' groans. Political issues appear to fade away, and war becomes something undertaken, if at all, in the service of love' (p. 231).

25. Jacques Lacan, 'The function and field of speech and language in psychoanalysis', in *Écrits: A Selection*, trans. Alan Sheridan (New York: Norton, 1977), 65.

26. C. Owens, 'The Allegorical Impulse: Toward a Theory of Postmodernism', in *Art After Modernism: Rethinking Representation*, ed. Brian Wallis (New York: New Museum of Contemporary Art, 1984), 205. Rosemond Tuve has demonstrated a similar dynamic at work in *entrelacement*, where a primary narrative performs the double duty of relating a vicarious or off-stage development. See Rosemond Tuve, *Allegorical Imagery: Some Medieval Books and Their Posterity* (Princeton, NJ: Princeton University Press, 1966), 363.

27. I am following Teresa L. Ebert's politicization of Lacan's orders wherein she sees 'the symbolic as the site of social struggle over signification in which opposing significations are repressed and relegated to the imaginary, which is the space for what the symbolic excludes. The imaginary is thus the arena of desire – the repressed and unattainable wish for what the subject loses upon joining the symbolic order.' Teresa L. Ebert, 'The Romance of Patriarchy: Ideology, Subjectivity, and Postmodern Feminist Cultural Theory', *Cultural Critique*, 10 (1988), 25.

28. R. Wasserman and J. Blanch, 'White and Red in the Knight's Tale: Chaucer's Manipulation of a Convention', in *Chaucer in the Eighties*, ed. Wasserman and Blanch (Syracuse, NY: Syracuse University Press, 1986), 175–91.

29. Leicester, *Disenchanted Self*, 231–32.

30. EDGAR WIND, *Pagan Mysteries in the Renaissance* (New York: Norton, 1968),
     124–5. Wind's comment is appropriately from his discussion of Botticelli's
     Primavera, according to which it appears the Knight understands only half of
     the concept he employs.

31. See LEICESTER, *Disenchanted Self*, 274 and 352 ff. on the *proximity* of the theater
     and grove. ANDERSON, 'Fourth Temple', notes that the three oratories are
     'constructed in the walls of a "theater" which is built around the site of a
     grove' (p. 117).

32. There is even a reiteration of the text to heighten the identification of the two
     performance spaces when Palamon and Arcite are compared to a lion and a
     tiger, respectively. The simile in the theater, as one might expect, is the more
     elaborate. In the grove,

     > Thou myghtest wene that this Palamon
     > In his fightyng were a wood leon,
     > And as a crueel tigre was Arcite.

     (I.1655–57)

     In the theater,

     > Ther nas no tygre in the vale of Galgopheye,
     > Whan that her whelp is stole whan it is lite,
     > So crueel on the hunte as is Arcite
     > For jelous herte upon this Palamon.
     > Ne in Belmarye ther nys so fel leon,
     > That hunted is, or for his hunger wood,
     > Ne of his praye desireth so the blood,
     > As Palamon to sleen his foo Arcite.

     (I.2626–33)

33. R. NEUSE, 'The Knight: The First Mover in Chaucer's Human Comedy', in
     Geoffrey Chaucer: A Critical Anthology, ed. J. A. Burrow (Baltimore, MD:
     Penguin, 1969), 52.

4 Robyn the Miller's Thrifty Work*

PEGGY KNAPP

Knapp concentrates on the adversarial relationship between the
Miller's Tale and the *Knight's*, suggesting that the challenge to
the dominant discourse of the latter works through the former's
'internal persuasiveness', in particular through the 'psychical conformity' among individuals that jokes, according to Freud, produce. In the *Miller's Tale*, the son-figure Nicholas is able to use
patriarchal systems of obedience (to biblical injunctions) against
the 'father' of the Tale himself, John, and more generally against
the whole paternal order represented by the Knight and his telling.
Knapp locates the Tale within a climate of medieval nominalism
sceptical about authoritative truth-claims such as those advanced
by the Knight. For more on nominalism and on Knapp's piece, see
my Introduction, pp. 2, 14–15.

'Lat us werken thriftily'

(Harry Bailly)

Robyn the Miller is not one of those readers who notes the fragility
of the Knight's telling; he interprets the Knight's long, elevated story
as dominant ideology encoded in dominant discourse plain and
simple. And, of course, he objects to it violently on those grounds,
disputing the Host's governance as the first step in disputing the
rightness of the Knight's supposition of orderly governance in the
world. His unruly protest provides a marked contrast with the
Knight's 'wys' and 'obedient' (I.851) yielding to the temporary social
rules of the 'compaignye ... by aventure yfalle / In felaweshipe'
(I.24–26). If a person's story is 'a symbolic meditation on the destiny
of the community', as Fredric Jameson has claimed, it is easy to see
why Robyn opposes every facet of what he takes to be the Knight's
image of the world.[1] The Miller's tale is a second, a reactive, rather

---

* Reprinted from PEGGY KNAPP, *Chaucer and the Social Contest* (New York and
London: Routledge, 1990), pp. 32–44, 146–7.

than a founding gesture. Its structure, characterization, and language have their fullest force in point by point contrast to the Knight's. The Miller, therefore, begins the counterpoint between the various voices of the *Canterbury Tales*, for the fiction as a whole is not (and could not be) a direct image of the fourteenth-century world, but of an image of fourteenth-century languages, each associated with a social and philosophical view of that world.

The Miller's voice is raised at an inappropriate time – his turn would not come for a long time if degree were considered. Harry Bailly tries to stop Robyn so the *compaignye* can work 'thriftily', 'thrift' in Middle English meaning both propriety and prosperity. But Robyn's extravagant 'Pilates voys' is too loud to be ignored, for playing roaring villains was a great attention-getter, as his Absolon knows. He swears, tearing God's body in just the way the Pardoner and Parson will both condemn later. Furthermore, he is drunk, he knows it by his sound, and when a man is drunk, the Knight has said, he knows he has a house but not where it is. The Miller does not know, or will not acknowledge, where his voice belongs in this tale-telling; he is in every way an affront to hegemony. Yet his tale depends for its subversion on the authorized discourses of the Middle Ages as surely as the Knight's does for its very different effects. The *Canterbury Tales* continually creates new voices and meanings, but not out of nothing; there are already languages – social, philosophical, rhetorical – through which its dialogues are carried on.

Fathers and sons

The Knight's fatherly version of the dominant discourse is quite resilient, in spite of the wear and tear inflicted on it in the course of its re-tellings, so Robyn has his work cut out for him if he means to counter it through the internal persuasiveness of his own vision. Bakhtin describes the internally persuasive as that which is 'denied all privilege, backed up by no authority at all'.[2] Although Bakhtin notes that it is 'interwoven with everyday life', tales like the Miller's may not be seen as merely the welling up of unmediated experience. Such tales bear a more problematic relation than that to both everyday experience and common language: depending on both for some of their force, but not exclusively based on either, they are products of a 'denaturing literary act', as R. Howard Bloch puts it.[3] It is not that the Knight's story is artificial and the Miller's realistic – both are fabulous (examples of Cicero's rhetorical figure *fabula*, which neither is nor seems to be true[4]) but in different systems of convention. The Knight's characters answer to the exaggerated demands of aristocratic styles, the Miller's to equally exaggerated intricacies of fabliau plotting. The fabliaux, like other forms, participate in a linguistic discourse; this particular fabliau depends more heavily on linguistic effects than most.

Moreover, discourses produce knowledge. The knowledge produced by the patristic tradition, for example, is always ready for a revolt like the Miller's. Its overarching system of types and antitypes can account ahead of time for the challenge Robyn offered through his behavior and even his physical characteristics. Reading through the exegetical tradition, as D. W. Robertson does, the Miller is recognizable as a sinner through his bagpipe playing[5] and his wrestling (p. 243), as well as his drunkenness and improper language. His created characters are equally predictable. The brilliance of his Alison's 'realistic characterization' must be seen from the exegetical vantage point as neither realistic nor suggestive of a specific character (any more than the Wife of Bath's); she is merely 'a manifestation of *woman*' as the object of lust (p. 249). Jealous husbands like John are icons of avarice (p. 369), and Absolon is 'vainglory' (p. 385). Patristic reading of texts and the world is perhaps the specifically Christian result the orderliness of the *Knight's Tale* pointed only dimly toward. It, being fully authorized, does not need to be internally persuasive.

The knowledge produced by the Miller suggests Michel Foucault's 'subjugated knowledge', 'blocs of historical knowledge which were present but disguised within the body of functionalist and systematizing theory'.[6] An attempt to resuscitate the 'subjugated knowledges' of the *Miller's Tale* or to account for the persuasiveness of its internally persuasive discourse discourages seeing it as merely naive 'realism' and enables us to do justice to both the witty intelligence of the tale and its potential social force.

The dominant discourse is at work in the Miller's tale, but to altogether different ends than in the Knight's. Robyn understands the ideological point of his predecessor's story well enough. He sees in it the way fathers (Theseus and Egeus) and The Father control discourse in order to bring sons, the unruly, passionate Palamon and Arcite, into conformity with it. The Knight has been candid about this lesson, since he presents Theseus as controlling his domain both discursively (through his eloquence) and socially (through rule, his direct power over life and death). It is a critical commonplace that the Miller's tale requites the Knight's by replicating its formula – a woman under the guardianship of an older man sought by two young lovers – but debasing its tone and direction. I am arguing more than that. I think that Robyn is replacing a story ultimately referable to the authoritative discourse of Statius and Boethius, with a story in the same form which rests on a subjugated, but internally persuasive discourse and makes an entirely different point about the power of the Father to control the sons. There is an Oedipal edge to his endeavor, a feature not uncommon in fabliaux, as Bloch argues.[7] I take this Oedipal contention to be not merely local (a response to the Knight himself) or even merely social (a response to *degree* on the pilgrimage), but philosophical as well.

In choosing and telling his tale, Robyn rejects all three of the authorizing features the Knight's story had made use of. The 'whilom' of his tale is a continuing present – he makes no attempt to elevate his characters above the everyday life of contemporary Oxford. He rejects and ridicules the chivalrous patriarchal stance of the Knight toward women and the aura of noble birth which surrounds his tale. In the *Miller's Tale* 'swynkyng' shows – John may be seen building tubs, Absolon swinging his 'sencer', Nicholas calculating with his astrolabe and augrym stones, and Gerveys smithing 'shaar and kultour' – and of course also 'swyvyng'.

The Knight's distanced, respectful language about women is one of Robyn's early satiric targets. The Knight asserts Emelye's beauty through a stylized code based on light, at once courtly and faintly sacramental:

> I noot wher she be womman or goddesse,
> But Venus it is soothly, as I gesse.
>
> (I.1101–2)

Alison's, in contrast, is concretely rendered through her likeness to desirable items in the everyday world:

> As any wezele hir body gent and smal
>
> (I.3234)

> She was ful moore blisful on to see
> Than is the newe pere-jonette tree,
> And softer than the wolle is of a wether.
>
> (I.3247–49)

> Wynsynge she was as is a joly colt,
>
> (I.3263)

> She was a prymerole, a piggesnye,
> For any lord to leggen in his bedde,
> Or yet for any good yeman to wedde.
>
> (I.3268–70)

What is being invoked here is, in Bakhtin's phrase, the 'everyday rounds of our consciousness' (p. 345), especially those usually called 'lower'. Chaucer seems to have deliberately emphasized the lower, scatological force of his nearest analogue (the Flemish version) of the 'misdirected kiss' story, especially in enlarging Alison's active role in the joke.[8] The reader who appreciates the force of Emelye's beauty must align him or herself with the abstractly expressed system of worth already approved in medieval culture. To appreciate Alison's appeal, however, is to refer to the domain of experience: sights in the ordinary world, the odors of pears and apples, pleasantly soft tactile sensations, and sex itself – 'for any lord to leggen in his bedde' (I.3269).

This closeness to everyday life seems to obligate the Miller to treat Alison's actions and preferences as fully as those of his male characters – no 'folwen alle the favour of Fortune' (I.2682) for Alison. She makes up her own mind 'atte laste' to grant her love to *hende* Nicholas, and she thinks up the way Absolon will kiss her through the window. Her sexual nature is not ignored, as Emelye's is, nor is it denied, like Custance's (II.708–16). I would not want to overrate the gender equality the tale allows us to impute to the Miller, for surely here, as in the *Knight's Tale*, the woman is most essentially a prize competed for by the men. Nonetheless, the hearty this-worldliness of the tale prevents the hypocrisy of patriarchy's protection of women from dangers its own social formation creates. For Robyn, women are to some extent responsible for the world, chaotic as it is.

Where even Palamon and Arcite's unruliness is linked with aristocratic conventions (those of courtly love, a secondary target for the Miller's irony), Nicholas and Absolon, in different ways, act out the basic appetitiveness of lust and desire for power. In social terms, what is portrayed in both the Knight's and Miller's tales is competition and disorder among young men, those not yet married or incorporated into the guilds and professions. Such groups were a source of anxiety to the populus, especially when they formed a large proportion of the men in a village (as must have been the case in Oxenford). Theseus recognizes the threat posed by Arcite and Palamon's quarrel, but transforms it into a public spectacle, a lawful, and perhaps socially instructive, tournament, allowing good governance to win the day. The Miller does no such thing.

In medieval France, such young men celebrated a ritual of misrule which Natalie Zemon Davis argues allowed them to learn the social conscience of the community by becoming its 'raucous voice' in charivaris.[9] In the Athens the Knight creates, we may be seeing an analogous case of the competition of the young used for public edification. England had similar rites of misrule and charivaris which might be explained in similar ways. Nicholas and Robyn (and perhaps Absolon too) are aware of the 'gross disparity in age between the bride and groom' in John's household, such disparity often being the occasion for charivaris. But in the Miller's story, of course, the young men are not engaging in a traditional form of social ridicule which could clear the air by expressing loud disapproval (Davis, p. 107), but a private, self-interested reaction to the inappropriate marriage of delightful Alison to a man not likely to keep her sexual interest.

The *Knight's Tale* treats the taming of the young by positing their cooptation, their adoption of the self-restrained behaviors, the patience, the meekness in the face of 'necessity' which is the counsel of the dominant ideology. The *Miller's Tale* posits just the opposite: the triumph of the uninitiate, their successful embarrassment of the 'rich gnof' who legally possesses what they both want: Alison. An eighteenth-century eruption of this kind – younger, poorer men acting out a ritualized violation of their landlord's household – is discussed by Robert Darnton in *The Great Cat Massacre*. Darnton writes that the young men, in this case apprentices to a printer, made their 'sedition' meaningful 'by playing with the themes of their culture',[10] just as Nicholas achieves his victory (short-lived though it may be) by using in a distorted way the dominant discourse of obedience to biblical injunctions which his life is an attempt to discount or circumvent. The aggressiveness of the *Miller's Tale* is aimed at unmasking the serene universal assurance that informs the *Knight's*. Perhaps it is not going too far to see the Miller's deliberately debased, not-easily-recognized image of the Knight himself in the good-hearted, conservative, gullible John the Carpenter. The Reeve thinks himself Robyn's satiric target, and in a surface reading he is, but the tale at its deepest reaches is stalking bigger game.

The ideology of Robyn's discourse

The Miller's reply to the Knight uses genre to make an ideological point. This fabliau is, according to Charles Muscatine, 'so completely realized that the genre is virtually made philosophical'.[11] I agree with Muscatine's argument that the philosophical point of the genre is 'the sovereignty of animal nature' (although I prefer to say 'the compelling nature of material conditions, including natural appetites') and will not replicate his excellent marshaling of the evidence that the details of the story are arranged to create 'an extraordinary solidity' for the physical, 'real' world.[12] The tale begins, therefore, with a literal and 'realist' notion of language, something like some of the passages in the *Knight's Tale* which attempt internal persuasiveness.

But the Miller quickly swerves toward a nominalist mode in both plot and language, making his telling philosophically significant in a more extended sense as well, since it opposes the Knight's in the matter of how language is fitted to the world.

The protagonists of the *Knight's Tale* enact a thinly plotted, thickly decorated, fiction. They act, but their actions do not count for very much. The mere fact that critics have waged such a convoluted debate about whether Arcite and Palamon differ at all should make the point that the center of the tale is not the individual men, but the ordered, and order-replicating, world in which their story moves.

In the *Miller's Tale* the opposite is true. The plot is intricate and careful, yet surprising. The characters, individually, plan for what they want, and, at least temporarily, they get it. The story moves forward because of the cooperation and interference of one person's planning with another's. First, Nicholas successfully tricks John into separating himself from his wife for the night, but his plot eventually results in John's noisy response to the cry 'Water'. Second, John, misled about the flood, plans to save himself and his wife. Note that Robyn does not suppress the likeable traits John shows here: his concern for Nicholas, his desire to save Alison, his willingness to endure discomfort to abide by what he thinks is the law ('This ordinance is seyde' [3592]). Third, Absolon, who plans to be kissed for his serenade, is at first frustrated and humiliated, but later successfully revenged, although not on his intended victim. His stratagem has no connection in his own plot with Noah's flood – it is pure happenstance that *his* victim's need to quench fire with water intersects with *Nicholas's* victim's obsession with water. The tale is built neither on a predictable 'faire cheyne of love' which binds 'the fyr, the eyr, the water, and the lond / In certeyne boundes' (2991–93) or the orderly moral assignment of rewards and punishments which was predicated on it.[13]

The element of surprise which provides the Miller's triumphant humor is based on split-second timing. Here again the contrast with the Knight's plotting is telling. In the *Knight's Tale*, time expands to create a sense of epic scope, years – not always specified as to how many – pass between one event and the next. For example, 'By process and by lengthe of certeyn yeres', grief for Arcite faded and the parliament which decided on Emelye's marriage to Palamon was convened (2967). The *Miller's Tale* takes close note of time and measures it in days, hours, and minutes, rather than years. Beyond the obvious reduction in magnitude this attention to small units of time indicates, it also points to a growing awareness of time in the towns and cities of the fourteenth century, the era in which the hour, as Jacques Le Goff notes, came to have its 'mathematical sense, the twenty-fourth part of the day'.[14] The new time sense was important for manufacturing and trade more than for agriculture, for towns more than rural estates, for makers of their wealth (like millers and carpenters) than for inheritors of landed wealth.

The very basis of the Miller's story is thus entrepreneurial and nominalist, in contrast with the aristocratic, philosophically realist Knight's. This story is not referable to a universal system, but to the ungoverned desires and talents of Nicholas and Absolon. Yet this nominalist point is made by refashioning some conventional languages: Nicholas's management (or mismanagement) of Christian and astrological lore and the courtly idiom with which the Miller surrounds Absolon. A several-sided dialogue is thus heard throughout the tale.

The *Tale* should also be called nominalist because words – signifiers – are irreverently pried loose from what they signify. No guaranteeing order is assumed to prevail to keep everything in place. The story proceeds because Nicholas, in his con of the carpenter, plays fast and loose with the faith the dominant discourse had placed in the revelatory power of words.

As it concerns Absolon, the humor cuts two ways. Absolon is trying to fulfill the dictates of a code of love, no matter how silly his attempts actually sound, so he sweetens his breath and sends gifts to speed his suit along. The humor in his presentation is the result of his 'success', his incorporation of the courtesies which elevate Absolon himself and Alison to lover and beloved lady, and ought to insure his acceptance. He is reaching for a definition of courtship which, though still seeking sexual consummation, is finicky about noticing the body – he himself was 'somdeel squaymous of fartyng'. The trouble is that Alison is not. The other half of this joke is that she responds to the direct, unrule-bound approach of Nicholas. The prize in this competition does not go to the patient, self-restrained suitor (whose self-restraint is of course on a far lower and less serious plane than Arcite and Palamon's), but to the one who seizes the main chance.

The concern of the story with astrology makes several points. By suggesting for Nicholas a student's keen interest in the subject, the Miller is referring to a discourse which did, as Keith Thomas points out, prove a likely locus for intellectual curiosity, the 'desire to reduce things to order'.[15] Nicholas, like Aurelius's brother's friend in the *Franklin's Tale*, is one of those learners who has both an intellectual fascination and a practical application for this science. At the same time, John is being characterized as favored to be let into the circle of those who can see into these recessed corners of learning, since in England 'astrology was primarily the concern of Court, nobility and

Church' (Thomas, p. 301). His quick, secondhand glimpse into this facet of 'Goddes privetee' makes yet another point about the social hierarchies of the *Miller's Tale*. John is richer than Nicholas, but his access to this privileged discourse can only come through his poorer boarder. This advantage is, of course, just what Nicholas is both counting on and hoping to prove by his trick:

> A clerk hadde litherly biset his whyle,
> But if he koude a carpenter bigyle.

> (3299–300)

A further irony for us, which may have been a commonplace in Chaucer's day as well, concerns William Lily's assertion (1675) that Noah's flood could not have been foretold astrologically, since only events with natural causes could be predicted, and the flood was the result of God's direct intervention (quoted by Thomas, p. 336). If fourteenth-century astrologers shared this viewpoint, Chaucer would be stressing Nicholas's misrepresentation of one of the discourses of his day, as he reshaped it for his own purposes.

When he relies on Christian discursive forms, Nicholas is equally convincing to John. He powerfully calls up both the apocalyptically destructive powers of water and the calm of the cleansed state which will follow the destruction. It makes sense, then, that the climax of the tale comes when the word 'water', linked with the non-linguistic sound of Nicholas's thunderous fart, is made to function in two competing schemes simultaneously. In Nicholas's trick, the predictive power of science, in this case astrology, and the sacred power of scripture (the Noah story) are used cynically to authorize a scam completely of Nicholas's own manufacture.

But in his vivid description of the world after the flood, Nicholas almost goes too far in imitating the dominant discourse in its idyllic mode.

> Whan that the grete shour is goon away,
> Thanne shaltou swymme as myrie, I undertake,
> As doth the white doke after hire drake.

> (3574–76)

Allowing Nicholas to create such a persuasive picture of the new world for the credulous John, Robyn risks calling up support for the orderly and familiar vision of perfection promised by the dominant discourse. The white duck passage is too close to its biblical antecedent, too idyllic, too winning, to be entirely subordinated to Nicholas's selfish intention to con John. It glancingly evokes a

cleansed, shimmering world familiar to religious piety, even while
the counter-movement is clearly in the reader's mind: isn't this a
clever joke? It might be taken to show Nicholas's linguistic force
touching him, briefly, too deeply, an effect of the language he uses
that he cannot fully command, as Derrida puts it.[16]

This episode contains a remarkable play of intertextual forces.
Nicholas is conning John into sleeping apart from Alison to make
way for his planned adultery. His persuasion, however, is based on
another text, the biblical description of the flood. The whole scam
relies on John's belief in the truth of the Bible, which in turn rests on
its pervasiveness and authority in his culture (for John is a simple
and unoriginal man). Yet from Nicholas's angle, the Bible story of
God's punishment for sin cannot be taken as truth; if it were, the
chance he takes with his blasphemy would be too great. The whole
interdependence of text upon text here is a complicated version of
the style of literary borrowing in which the one member of the
narrative audience (John) believes the flood story to be true while
another (Nicholas) does not. The authorial audience probably
assumes its truth, but the Miller does not ratify their belief by
including God's punishment of Nicholas or even want to remind
them of it so strongly that they renounce their pleasure in his antics.[17]

On the social level, though, the Miller's story works directly
against the clergy. In allowing Nicholas to succeed at his stratagem,
at least temporarily, he depicts clerical learning as a cynical
exploitation of the Word with which the religious estate is
entrusted.[18] Nicholas is not afraid of the consequences of diverting
authorized discourses – biblical and astrological – to his own ends,
and the Miller supports his recklessness through the outcome of the
tale. For Nicholas and Robyn the power *of* the word to direct nature
through magic or myth is replaced by power *over* the word, like that
exercised by Odysseus in the Polyphemus episode when he abandons
his 'real' name and adopts the name 'Nobody' (in Greek 'Udeis'), a
name sounding like his own, to effect his escape. In Max Horkheimer
and Theodor Adorno's discussion of enlightenment, the link is made
between this abandonment of an animistic world through rationality
and a movement toward nominalism.[19] Nicholas seized the power of
the word through cunning (and 'cunning is defiance in a rational
form' [Bakhtin, p. 59]), and Robyn the Miller allowed him to get
away with it. Like pretty Alison, authoritative language allowed itself
to be appropriated by a resourceful ('hende') young man who will
not recognize the 'authority already fused to' the system he distorts
for his own ends.

Nicholas takes a chance when he manipulates language this way
(one might say he links himself with Odysseus and other trickster

figures), but he does not suffer the 'scalded towte' which is his
punishment because an orderly universe stands behind authorized
language in which it is expressed. He suffers because another willful
young man had *another* scheme going, and was not so stupid as to
be trickable the same way twice. Nicholas should have trusted the
stability of language less, not more. The very real world of the hot
colter and his singed ass produced his automatic call for 'Water'
and made him forget both the elaborate fiction he had invented
concerning water and his own habitual control of language. He is
vulnerable to unpredictable accidents and the machinations of his
rivals in this chaotic world, but the moral order neither punishes
him nor rewards John's generous concern for Alison or regard for
the law.

The allusiveness of Robyn's telling to the Knight's is both
philosophically nominalist and socially scornful. It continually
distorts and mocks the solemnity of the Knight's sober formulations.
The line in which the Knight phrases his melancholy description of
Arcite's grave, 'Allone, withouten any compaignye' (I.2779), appears
unchanged to describe Nicholas's strategically private bachelor pad.
The featured term 'queynte' in Emelye's temple scene (in which she
prays to Diana to protect her maidenhood [I.2333]) is employed
obscenely in the description of Alison's 'wooing' (I.3275–76), first to
mean quaint and then cunt, and later, in the phrase 'queynte cast'
to mean both at once (I.3605). The narrator's voice is as unafraid
as Nicholas's to reappropriate language for its own cunning and
irreverent uses. It is equally important to note that the signifiers
Robyn exploits *already have* the double edge that allows his outrageous
linguistic alchemy, suggesting the possibility for dialogic discourse in
this society.

The languages of wit

The reception of the *Miller's Tale* is that of a joke. Bakhtin argues
that 'comic familiarity' is itself corrosive of the high, straightforward
genres, both because of its implied reference to everyday life and its
'contradictory and heteroglot' language (p. 55), but does not explain
how comic familiarity achieves its effects. Because dominant discourse
purports to convey the 'natural' workings of society, it normally blocks
direct, conscious attacks on its hegemony. Sigmund Freud turned to
largely unconscious mechanisms to explore jokes as psychic and
social phenomena.

Robyn's joke looks both obscene and tendentious in Freud's system
of classification in *Jokes and Their Relation to the Unconscious*.[20] The

Miller forces the company, perhaps especially the Knight and Harry Bailly, who had offended him by their deference to the hierarchical world, to see disorder and sex graphically. He embarrasses the women and affronts the men, as the narrator acknowledges in his advice to 'chese another tale' and his defense of himself for including this one, lest he should 'falsen som of [his] mateere', (I.3177, 3175). The Knight had carefully banished Emelye's sexual nature from his telling, although the sexual possession of her is the motive force for the contest between the two young men. He also hides it in the description of the temple of Venus, through his allegorized paintings and iconic statue of Venus herself. The Miller forces the physical into the center of his picture and into the consciousness of his hearers:

And prively he caughte hire by the queynte . . .

(I.3276)

And heeld hire harde by the haunchebones

(I.3279)

These lines are an affront to the Knight and Host in that they force the company to laugh (all but Osewold the Reeve), thereby making a common bond on the Miller's own turf, since 'laughing over the same jokes is evidence of far-reaching psychical conformity' (Freud, p. 151). But the company in fact does not normally share that ground – that is why Robyn's joke is such a *tour de force*. The Miller *creates* the common ground which allows the company to laugh together, and he does so in the awed hush which followed the *Knight's Tale*, a mood inhospitable to the 'state of feeling' he wishes his joke to induce (Freud, p. 145). How is Robyn able to produce 'psychical conformity' among such sondry folk? And why is his tale taken as funny rather than insulting by everyone but Osewold?

The *Miller's Tale* is on one level merely an example of the 'cheerful humor' which 'those who work' find in obscene jokes – it is on this level that Osewold sees himself as its victim. Told to a public which shared his suppositions about sex and society, Robyn's joke would be an everyday matter of shared humor among men and (possibly) seductiveness toward women. In the aftermath of the universally admired *Knight's Tale*, the Miller's story becomes instead a campaign in a philosophical and social struggle to establish a common understanding about life within the company. When the pilgrims laugh, Robyn has won at least tolerance, and perhaps a measure of acceptance, for his point of view. Since his discourse has no institutional authority fused to it, he must have accomplished this feat by creating internal persuasiveness.

As an attack on the Knight's philosophical pretention and social coyness about sex, the *Miller's Tale* uses the two techniques Freud mentions specifically: degradation, exposing 'dependence on bodily needs', and unmasking, uncovering 'the physical demands lying behind the claim of mental love' (Freud, p. 222). Robyn strips the authoritative discourse of its exalted status by pointing out what he takes to be the common needs of all people – John's ungovernable curiosity about Nicholas, both suitors' sexual appetites, Alison's desire for a young lover, Nicholas's getting up 'for to pisse', and the like.

These are, of course, exactly the features the Knight leaves out of his telling, especially by devising the attenuated time-scheme which keeps the young man in his story waiting until middle age to 'attain the love' of Emelye. In arranging his telling this way, of course, the Knight is not speaking merely idiosyncratically 'for himself', but on behalf of a philosophical tradition which asserts the lower and peripheral nature of the physical realm superintended by Fortune to the concerns of life. The other aristocratic tradition he invokes – courtly love – also allows the suppression of the everyday realities of loving in favor of the extravagant gestures of courtship – the return from exile and the tournament – offered by Arcite and Palamon. Such mental and social games are associated with the upper social echelons, Robyn's technique implies, but those exalted and authoritative types none the less laugh at his story because something in them finds his discourse internally persuasive.

Jokes 'evade restrictions and open sources of pleasure that have become inaccessible' because of our 'high' level of civilization (Freud, p. 103). They allow the teller's obscene, hostile, or cynical thoughts, normally kept repressed, to be expressed and shared so as to enlist support among listeners. The listeners, who might take offense at argument or invective because of *their* proprieties, are bribed by the pleasure in wit afforded by the joke. The joke liberates pleasure by getting rid of inhibitions, protecting the pleasure from the criticism of reason by being 'nonsense' without losing the pointedness of 'sense' (Freud, pp. 134, 131). If the Miller is indeed registering a protest against the Knight's philosophical and social conservatism, his tale is a perfect vehicle, both for masking the hostility in his rejoinder and for providing pleasure to the company. Direct argument could not have afforded such pleasure and could not, presumably, have won him the prize for story-telling. That is one sense in which the Miller has been thrifty (economical) in serving his own cause, though unthrifty (improper) in terms of the dominant ideology.

Another sense of Robyn's thrift is the brevity of his tale. Brevity, as everyone since Polonius knows, is the soul of wit. According to

Freud, wit entails a psychic shortcut. Something is used where it is unexpected, but not unfamiliar; something repeated or rediscovered saves the psychic energy of introducing new subject matter (Freud, p. 124). The economy of the *Miller's Tale* is the strongest feature of its wit, for the single word 'water' brings to a climax the two plots being worked out simultaneously.[21] Water has figured centrally in Nicholas's plot against John. The water Nicholas needs later to cool his burning behind is a comic economy in that it suddenly links the two plots just when the audience had nearly forgotten the first.[22] In its degradation of Nicholas's flight of imagination about water, the tale associates him with the comic type of Icarus, another high flier who gets wet.

When Harry Bailly admonishes Robyn to 'werken thriftily', the Miller's reply is:

> 'By Goddes soule,' quod he, 'that wol nat I,
> For I wol speke or elles go my wey.'

(I.3132–33)

As things unfold, Robyn both speaks and goes his way, and in the end even 'werkes thriftily', in that he wrests an improbable victory from the forces of hegemony on the pilgrimage and in the world. The other pilgrims laughed 'at this nyce cas', and generations of readers, whether they like his kind of humor and revolt or not, called it 'natural', or classed it as fictional 'realism'. In doing so they conceded that the up-for-grabs world of the tale is in some sense a true reflection of the world of experience – just as Robyn hoped they would. But his victory was neither total nor permanent, for his brilliant performance can always become an exemplum of predictable sinfulness by Christian exegetics, part of its case for explaining the whole world. The *Miller's Tale* lives constantly under that threat, since it depends for its effects on Christian discourse and must call into being God's flood, but it is equally true that the Knight and all the fathers whose authority the Knight invokes live under the threat of being exempla of humorless and ineffective *gnofs* like John the Carpenter. Each of these powerful fictions can explain the other by mining under its discursive strategies, and each has ample weapons with which to hold off the incursions of the other.

Notes

1. FREDRIC JAMESON, *The Political Unconscious* (Ithaca, NY: Cornell University Press, 1981), p. 70.

2. M. M. Bakhtin, *The Dialogic Imagination*, trans. M. Holquist and C. Emerson (Austin: University of Texas Press, 1981), p. 342.

3. R. Howard Bloch, *The Scandal of the Fabliaux* (Chicago: University of Chicago Press, 1986), p. 102.

4. Morton Bloomfield, 'The Miller's Tale – An UnBoethian Interpretation', in *Medieval Literature and Folklore Studies*, ed. Jerome Mandel and Bruce A. Rosenberg (New Brunswick: Rutgers University Press, 1970), p. 207.

5. D. W. Robertson, Jr., *A Preface to Chaucer: Studies in Medieval Perspectives* (Princeton, NJ: Princeton University Press, 1962), p. 133.

6. M. Foucault, *Power/Knowledge: Selected Interviews and Other Writings, 1972–1977*, ed. Colin Gordon (New York: Pantheon Books, 1980), p. 82.

7. Bloch, *Fabliaux*, pp. 101–28.

8. Peter G. Beidler, 'Art and Scatology in the *Miller's Tale*', *Chaucer Review*, 12 (1977), 90–102.

9. Natalie Zemon Davis, *Society and Culture in Early Modern France* (Stanford, CA: Stanford University Press, 1975), p. 108.

10. Robert Darnton, *The Great Cat Massacre* (Princeton, NJ: Princeton University Press, 1983), p. 99.

11. C. Muscatine, *Chaucer and the French Tradition* (Berkeley and Los Angeles: University of California Press, 1957), p. 224.

12. Robertson seriously mis-characterizes the setting when he calls it 'vague', except for the lowness of the window and therefore 'only sufficient to make the action understandable', so as to allow only iconic settings to be detailed (*Preface*, p. 258).

13. As Bloch remarks, '. . . comedy is always somewhat gratuitous – undetermined, *de trop*, a surplus added to an already complete universe' (*Fabliaux*, p. 127).

14. Jacques Le Goff, *Time, Work, and Culture in the Middle Ages*, trans. Arthur Goldhammer (Chicago: University of Chicago Press, 1980), p. 49.

15. Keith Thomas, *Religion and the Decline of Magic* (New York: Charles Scribner's Sons, 1971), p. 327.

16. Jacques Derrida, *Of Grammatology*, trans. Gayatri Chakravorty Spivak (Baltimore, MD: Johns Hopkins University Press, 1976), p. 158.

17. See the fine account of the possibilities for borrowing and allusion by Peter Rabinowitz, ' "What's Hecuba to us?" The Audience's Experience of Literary Borrowing', in *The Reader in the Text*, ed. Susan R. Suleiman and Inge Crosman (Princeton, NJ: Princeton University Press, 1980), pp. 241–63.

18. Robert P. Miller makes a quite different assessment of the tale's anti-clerical slant, regarding it as an indictment against Robyn, whom he regards as ignorant and perhaps jealous of the 'real motives' of the 'higher' kinds of life, in 'The *Miller's Tale* as Complaint'; see Robert P. Miller, *Chaucer Review*, 5 (1970), 147–60.

19. Max Horkheimer and Theodor Adorno, *The Dialectic of Enlightenment*, trans. John Cumming (New York: Continuum Books, 1972), pp. 5, 23, and 60.

20. Sigmund Freud, *Jokes and Their Relation to the Unconscious*, trans. and ed. James Strachey (New York: W. W. Norton, 1960).

21. My approach here is in some ways similar to that of EUGENE W. HOLLAND's essay 'Boccaccio and Freud: A Figural Narrative Model for the *Decameron*', *Assays*, 3 (1985), 85–98.

22. Bloch stresses this feature of fabliau, in which the end returns to the beginning, *Fabliaux*, p. 126.

5 The Law of Man and Its 'Abhomynacions'*

CAROLYN DINSHAW

The 'abhomynacions' of Dinshaw's title are the themes of incest which the Man of Law announces in his *Prologue* that he is not going to deal with, but which return at several points in the Tale he tells. In the first section of Dinshaw's chapter (omitted here), the Man of Law is established as a spokesman upholding patriarchy, property and propriety, 'professionally engaged in maintaining society as it is'. Constance's being exported to marry the Sultan is seen as a telling instance of that trade in women – putting women into circulation like goods or currency – that maintains (patriarchal) social order, and the incest prohibition (that disallows keeping women at home, so to speak) is a vital part of such trade, and hence supported by the Man of Law (and indeed, Dinshaw argues, by Lévi-Strauss in his classic analyses of it). Patriarchy's ideal of woman as a 'blank' to be imprinted solely with male desire is, however, ruptured in the Tale by women who have their own desires, including incestuous desires for sons or fathers. At these points of rupture, Dinshaw notes how the Tale strives to efface such threats by, among other things, demonizing these women and excluding them from the realm of 'femynynytee' altogether. Dinshaw in fact sees the *Man of Law's Tale* generally as an exemplary instance (following on the analyses of Pierre Macherey) of the ways in which a dominant ideology works for a resolution of contradictions, presenting itself as a seamlessly coherent, 'natural' and self-evidently legitimate state of things in the face of the opposition that besets it. For further discussion of Dinshaw's work, see my Introduction, pp. 6–9.

. . .

* Reprinted from CAROLYN DINSHAW, *Chaucer's Sexual Poetics* (Madison: University of Wisconsin Press, 1989), pp. 95–112, 235–9.

II

If tales and tale-telling are firmly established as part of patriarchal social organization, it is fitting indeed that Constance when we are first introduced to her in the *Man of Law's Tale* itself, is a tale told by men. The Man of Law opens the narrative with Syrian merchants doing business in Rome. They hear stories about the Emperor's daughter; she is first introduced not in person but in – *as* – narrative: her 'excellent renoun' is declaimed in 'the commune voys of every man' (155). Constance exists as a tale of a virgin. When the merchants return to Syria, they narrate their 'tidynges' to the Sultan, highlighting the story of Constance. And it is with this very story that the Sultan falls in love: he 'hath caught so greet plesance / To han hir figure in his remembrance' (186–87) that he determines he must have her. Middle English 'figure' denotes both 'shape, form' and 'figure of speech', of whom the merchants can be said to be 'maistres' (141). This woman exists not only in but as narrative; she is both 'real' character and linguistic form.

While the merchants are still in Rome, preparing to sail back to Syria, they meet Constance in person. But the parallel narration of loading their ships with merchandise and loading their eyes with Constance underscores her position as a thing – a tale, a commodity – that merchants trade:

> Thise marchantz han doon fraught hir shippes newe,
> And whan they han this blisful mayden sayn,
> Hoom to Surrye been they went ful fayn.
>
> (171–73)

Sent off by her father to marry the Sultan, traveling in a ship from Rome to Syria, she is very obviously not only like the tales but the 'chaffare' of the merchants returning from Rome to Syria. The trade of the woman in marriage is homologous to the trade of goods and the trade of tales, of words. Such an understanding of trade as structuring the use of women and words is well attested in various late-medieval uses of the word 'chaffare'.[1] In Gower's *Confessio amantis*, for example, women are 'that chaffare' that lovers 'take a parte of'. In *Piers Plowman*, it's tidings that are the merchandise: 'Tythes of untrewe thinge [are] ytilied or chaffared.' And marriage itself, in *Hali Meidenhad*, is called 'that chaffere' – that trade, that deal, that (bad) bargain.[2]

The marriage at the outset of the *Man of Law's Tale* is figured forth as the trade of a woman. Such an image turns out to be a precise literary representation of the anthropological analysis of marriage put forward by Lévi-Strauss, who claims that the exchange of women is the very mechanism of marriage and kinship systems. It is the mechanism, he finds, of all social organization. The plot thickens when we recall that his analysis was formulated in the study of *incest* – in an investigation of the universality of the incest prohibition. A look at Lévi-Strauss's *Elementary Structures of Kinship* turns out to be remarkably appropriate to a consideration of the Man of Law's performance: the book is not only an analysis of a power asymmetry between the sexes but an implicit defense of that asymmetry. It is, in other words, a patriarchal text itself, just as is the *Man of Law's Tale*; the workings of its ideology are visible through the same kinds of fissures that we've seen in the Man of Law's performance, lapses having to do with woman's place in a male-dominated structure. Lévi-Strauss belongs in a long ideological tradition of which the Man of Law is an early, card-carrying member; a look at *Elementary Structures of Kinship*, then, will suggest something of great Constancy.[3]

It could be asserted that trade or exchange (I shall use the two words interchangeably) indeed structures every society. As I remarked in Chapter One, Marcel Mauss has suggested that the exchange of gifts constitutes society; he refers to primitive society in particular, but, as Gayle Rubin – to whose article, 'The Traffic in Women', I am again deeply indebted – has acutely discerned, his claims are much more general: he suggests indeed that the gift liberated culture itself.[4] It is evident that society depends on linguistic communication (the trade of words), and on some form of commerce (the trade of goods). But the trade of women? Following and extending Mauss's analysis, Lévi-Strauss suggests that women are the most precious of gifts – 'the supreme gift' (*ES*, p. 65) – and that marriage should be seen as an exchange or trade of these valuables: marriage is 'the archetype of exchange' (*ES*, p. 483). Georges Duby uses this analysis of marriage, we may note, in his study of medieval marriage.[5]

In the regulation of this exchange Lévi-Strauss in fact finds the very basis of social organization: to ensure that these most prized gifts will be circulated widely, distributed evenly, this exchange must be made *between* families and groups. 'It will never be sufficiently emphasized,' urges Lévi-Strauss, 'that if social organization had a beginning, this could only have consisted in the incest prohibition.'[6] The universal prohibition of incest, then, follows from the need for a wide circulation of women if social order is to be maintained. David Herlihy corroborates the applicability of Lévi-Strauss's analysis to the Western Middle Ages: the medieval Church's unusual preoccupation with the prohibition of incest (unprecedented in Roman or Mosaic law), he suggests, forced a 'freer, wider circulation of women through society' and a 'fairer distribution [of women] across social classes'.[7]

So the Man of Law's puzzlingly specific and adamant remarks in his Introduction about tales of incest make immediate sense when considered via Lévi-Strauss's hypothesis of a connection between the exchange of women and the prohibition of incest. When we locate Constance within the clearly delineated structure of commerce in the world of his tale, the remark, in retrospect, gains a particular urgency. For the Man of Law has depicted a society in which women are exchanged, and the prohibition of incest is universal and necessary to that social organization. Further, the power asymmetry that Constance herself bewails as she is being shipped off to Syria ('Wommen are born to thraldom and penance, / And to been under mannes governance' [286–87]) is built into a society based on the exchange of women. Gayle Rubin observes that

> if it is women who are being transacted, then it is the men who give and take them who are linked, the woman being a conduit of a relationship rather than a partner to it.[8]

If, as Lévi-Strauss asserts, the exchange of women is behind the universal taboo, then the power asymmetry, too, between giver and gift, man and woman, is universal.

But it's precisely this issue of power asymmetry between the genders that leads Lévi-Strauss into unresolved contradiction at the end of *Elementary Structures of Kinship*, a contradiction that Rubin also notes. In remarks on method which close the work, Lévi-Strauss compares the work of the sociologist of the family and the linguist. In considering the incest prohibition and language, their respective objects of study, he suggests that both have fundamentally the same function: communication and integration (since 'the relations between the sexes can be conceived as one of the modalities of a great "communication function" which also includes language' [*ES*, p. 494]). Misuses of language and violations of the incest prohibition, therefore, can be grouped together and considered as identical situations. He then draws a conclusion from this conjuncture:

> What does this mean, except that women themselves are treated as signs, which are misused when not put to the use reserved to signs, which is to be communicated?
>
> (*ES*, p. 496)

This conclusion, however logically in keeping with the whole of his analysis of exchange as the basis of kinship relations, creates a contradiction with perceived reality: women are, after all, speakers as well as spoken, active generators of messages as well as passive constituents of them. This contradiction seems to provoke an uneasiness – one Lévi-Strauss exhibits again in 'The Family' – with women readers' potential response to his analysis of their function as empty signs, mere counters in trade.[9] He hastens to add that women are not only spoken, but are speakers as well, and have their own individual 'values'; they are not merely arbitrary significances assigned to empty signs:

> Woman could never become just a sign and nothing more, since even in a man's world she is still a person, and since in so far as she is defined as a sign she must be recognized as a generator of signs. In the matrimonial dialogue of men, woman is never purely what is spoken about; for if women in general represent a certain category of signs, destined to a certain kind of communication, *each woman preserves a particular value arising from her talent, before and after marriage, for taking her part in a duet*. In contrast to words, which have wholly become signs, *woman has remained at once a sign and a value*. This explains why the relations between the sexes have preserved that *affective richness, ardour and mystery* which doubtless originally permeated the entire universe of human communications.
>
> (*ES*, p. 496; my emphasis)

In this penultimate paragraph, Lévi-Strauss lapses into a romantic idiom foreign to the analytical discourse of the foregoing 495 pages. That romantic diction, a break in the academic language, marks the effort of reconciliation: women are, according to his theory, homologous to empty signs; but according to patriarchal myth (or tale), which Lévi-Strauss seems eager to advance here against the exigencies of his own theory, each preserves a mysterious 'particular value'. The contradiction simply remains intact – 'woman has remained at once a sign and a value' – and the diction is heightened to cover it over: 'the relations between the sexes' are romanticized, mystified, and woman is seen as a kind of eternal paradox.

This break in tone at the end of *Elementary Structures* is a crack in the 'monument' (as one reviewer, quoted on the back cover of the Beacon Press paperback, called the book) – a crack in this analysis of masculine prerogative as constituting culture – which reveals its ideological workings.[10] Lévi-Strauss's theory of exchange depends on woman's blankness and intrinsic valuelessness for it to work. The way of all ideology, to adopt Susan Griffin's phrase, is to differentiate the selfsame from the Other, to create a group in power and define all else as lack. Lévi-Strauss's analysis of marriage is fully appropriate to the analysis of the Man of Law's representation in his *Tale* because Lévi-Strauss participates in the same long tradition of thinking – the same patriarchal ideology – as the one that informs the Man of Law's performance. In this ideology it is 'woman' who is indeed an empty 'thing' (*ES*, p. 496), 'a sign and nothing more', whose value is arbitrary and ascribed to her by men. Constance, floating rudderless and will-less in her boat for 'yeres and dayes' (463), is not far behind.

III

A further ideological mystification can be seen in Lévi-Strauss's very focus on the *prohibition* of incest, and it is with this observation that I shall now turn my attention directly to the *Man of Law's Tale* for good. Women may be traded in marriage, but the goods may be spoiled; acts of incest do indeed occur, even if incestuous marriages are prohibited.[11] Incest, in Lévi-Strauss's analysis an act instigated and perpetrated by men, can be seen as in fact another – and more fundamental, because lawless – exertion of control over women. Men make the rules necessary for the establishment of culture and society, but men can break them, too – without, it is a tautology to add, violating masculine prerogative. Incest itself doesn't violate the general principle of masculine dominance, but *narratives* of incest threaten patriarchal social organization because they reveal its violations of its own laws. The Man of Law properly eschews tales of 'swiche unkynde abhomynacions' – in such a move as Lévi-Strauss will later make in his focusing on the prohibition of incest – yet we find throughout his tale the charged presence of incestuous desires and potentially incestuous relationships. Further, what is absolutely disruptive of masculine prerogative, what the Man of Law mentions *first* as a tale not to be told, is the tale of *feminine* incestuous desire; it is *this* tale's uneasily suppressed presence within the *Man of Law's Tale* that I hope, finally, to demonstrate.

In a large number of its folktale sources and analogues, the narrative of Constance's adventures is motivated by incest. Margaret Schlauch has stated persuasively that Chaucer must have known versions of the Constance legend that begin with the exile of the heroine by a father who makes sexual demands. Schlauch argues that the lines in the Man of Law's Introduction regarding tales of incest are Chaucer's announcement of his choice of a version in which this 'most unpleasing feature' has been removed.[12]

> But certeinly no word ne writeth he
> Of thilke wikke ensample of Canacee,
> That loved hir owene brother synfully –
> Of swiche cursed stories I sey fy! –
> Or ellis of Tyro Appollonius,
> How that the cursed kyng Antiochus
> Birafte his doghter of hir maydenhede,
> That is so horrible a tale for to rede,
> Whan he hir threw upon the pavement.
> And therfore he, of ful avysement,
> Nolde nevere write in none of his sermons
> Of swiche unkynde abhomynacions,
> Ne I wol noon reherce, if that I may.
>
> (77–89)

We must attribute choice and revisions of sources, as well as any knowledge of analogues, to Chaucer rather than to the Man of Law himself, since the Man of Law appears to be unaware of his tale's narrative sources and analogues (whereas the narrator of *Troilus and Criseyde*, in contrast, is aware of and resistant to his sources). The Man of Law tells it, we must assume, as he has heard it from the old merchant. But the point is that Chaucer has characterized the Man of Law as reacting to tales of incest; in this way the subsequent *lack* of incest in his tale (even though Chaucer based the tale on a source that doesn't include the motif) serves to delineate the Man of Law's values.

The Man himself seems oblivious to the disparity between what he promises (a tale in which incest has been suppressed) and what he delivers (a narrative structured by incest). I see no indication (no consistent irony, for example) that he is conscious of the pervasive, informing pattern of incest in his tale. But this obliviousness does not serve to demonstrate that the Man of Law is merely dull-witted or perhaps sinful; as spokesman of patriarchal ideology, he does not even register the discord. As Macherey has stated, at the source of ideology we find a desire for reconciliation of opposites, resolution of contradictions.[13] Thus tales of incest are prohibited, and the incestuous potential of relationships in the *Tale* is interpreted by him in some way as legitimate or is not even recognized; actual occurrences found in the well-known analogues have been removed.

In the most popular versions of the Constance legend, the 'accused queen' flees unwanted sexual advances of her father, and her adventures begin as she ends up on foreign shores.[14] But in the *Man of Law's Tale* the motive of the action is converted into the Sultan's desire to marry Constance: reassigned to another man, the desire is made legitimate. The narrative context is thus made fully patriarchal: proper marriage is arranged; dynasties are consolidated; heathens are converted.[15] There may be a trace of the incest motif yet in the *Tale*, Schlauch notes, in Constance's consistent refusal to identify herself throughout her travels: the woman pursued by a spurned lover who is her father and king would have good reason to want to conceal her identity. I shall suggest, later, another reading of Constance's behavior here; suffice it now to accept this as a trace of incest gaping through the patriarchal text.

Incestuous advances of father toward daughter are checked, then, at the outset of the tale, and the daughter's flight becomes a legitimate and celebrated betrothal, spanning East and West and absorbing barbarians into the fold. But this is not the end of intimacy between father and daughter, the Emperor and Constance; their highly charged, emotional reunion at the end of the tale effects the final closure of this narrative of potentially ceaseless wandering. The suggestions of incest at the close of the tale are subtle, but the presence of incest in its suppression at the beginning renders these suggestions compelling at the end. Recalling to the reader's mind the position of daughter *vis-à-vis* father in the Man of Law's description of incest in *Apollonius of Tyre* (Antiochus raped his daughter 'whan he hir threw upon the pavement' [85]),[16] Constance falls onto the street at her father's feet when she sees him at last in Rome:

> And whan she saugh hir fader in the strete,
> She lighte doun, and falleth hym to feete.
> 'Fader,' quod she, 'youre yonge child Custance
> Is now ful clene out of youre remembrance.
>
> 'I am youre doghter Custance,' quod she.

(1103–7)

They embrace and are reconciled; Constance then leaves with Alla for England. After Alla dies, Constance returns to Rome one final time, to her father, and again sinks to the ground: 'And whan that she hir fader hath yfounde, / Doun on hir knees falleth she to grounde' (1152–53). (That Constance's falling actions are voluntary only serves, as will become clear later, to strengthen the implications of incest.) Thus reunited, the two live together 'Til deeth departeth hem' (1158), the phrase echoing late-medieval marriage vows 'to hold and to have, at bed and at burd, for farer for lather, for better for wars, in sekenes and in heil, *to dethe us depart*.'[17]

Constance's relationship to her father, with its undertones of incest, is able to close the tale – narrative closure depending on the *settlement* of disruption – only because the Man of Law does not recognize what it is. He narrates the final reunion as an example of the way the world goes, makes it an exemplification of a platitude: there is, in the sublunar world, joy after woe, just as there will follow woe after gladness. Having spoken of the passing of joy at Alla's death, the Man of Law narrates the final bliss of Constance and her father, then hopes for similar 'joye after wo' (1161) for the Canterbury pilgrims. The conversion of this incestuous relation into a truism about the way of the world – joy after woe, woe after gladness – shows us ideology in action, naturalizing all events according to its values. Reconciliation of father and daughter and suppression of incest in the service of patriarchal propriety stop the wandering progress of the romance, and no discord is perceived or revealed.

The potential of father–daughter incest, announced *a contrario* in the Introduction, thus lurks at both ends of the tale but is absorbed into the proper scheme the Man of Law delineates at the outset. If Constance's father in folktale analogues threatens to violate the rule of reciprocity in trade of women by retaining possession of her, the *Man of Law's Tale* corrects the threat by emphasizing the exchange: it trades Constance with great pomp to the Syrians. The father's incestuous desire is replaced by the Sultan's desire for Constance. But the threat of father–daughter incest does not violate the mechanism of the rule of exchange of women: father–daughter incest creates a trade imbalance, but it does not violate the power and prerogative of males to determine the destination of the female and, consequently, of feminine desire. This is a crucial point: in the economy of female exchange among men, women's desire must 'respon[d] to the desire of others'; woman, if the exchange is to be made expediently, will desire the man to whom another man has traded her.[18] But there is another kind of incest *in potentia* in the *Tale* that I want to uncover, one that does not operate within this structure of mimetic desire and that, therefore, poses a radical threat to masculine prerogative: it is the jealousy of the mothers-in-law, which I read as the potentially incestuous desires of mothers for their sons. These relations are not so easily ignored or absorbed into supports of the patriarchal structure. Schlauch in fact associates the hostility of mothers-in-law toward their sons' wives with matrilineage: the mother-in-law perceives that the wife threatens her dominance in domestic authority as well as in lines of inheritance.[19]

Clearly, the mothers-in-law in the *Tale* are fundamentally threatening to the Man of Law, voice of patriarchy: he expends great energy in excluding these women from society – from Christianity, from 'femynynytee', from all of humankind. These mothers-in-law overtly desire power and control and have the capacity to seize and exercise them. Their abilities to manipulate language in cunning plots

– the Sultaness demands a verbal act of fealty from her followers (344); Donegild exchanges written letters via messenger – appropriate power that is deemed properly patriarchal. Further, these women are responsible for mass butchery and heartless exile, and must, therefore, themselves be extinguished. Nothing less than the murder of the mothers will do: Alla, of course, is later penitent for the murder he commits, but no action other than Donegild's swift dispatch seems adequate at the time. The threat to patriarchy posed by the mother-in-law, I maintain, is radical: it involves not just the rule of the realm, or structures of descent and rules of succession (as Schlauch implies), or even the authority of language. There is the lingering sense, in Alla's penitential journey, that he must be cleansed of the taint of contact with this unnatural creature, this woman with an independent will.

It is in the context of such overtly threatening gestures that the indications of incest function – function perhaps even more powerfully for being so nervously suppressed. The motives of the murderous mothers-in-law are either *too* well accounted for or left entirely vague in the Man of Law's narrative. The Sultaness resents her son's decision to convert to Christianity and refuses to join him in the new religion: 'The lyf shal rather out of my body sterte / Or Makometes lawe out of myn herte!' (335–36). Her violent refusal to accept a change of 'creance' should be adequate to explain the desire to eliminate the Syrians who do renege their faith; granted, mass murder is an extreme reaction, but it is explicable nonetheless in these terms. But an additional explanation is later offered by the Man of Law after 'this cursed dede': 'She hirself wolde al the contree lede' (434). This, too, is a plausible motive, conjuring up the figure of the usurping female, the overweening mother; but the combination of the two explanations seems excessive, and casts her determining motive into doubt. Chaucer here seems to combine Trivet's account of the Sultaness's behavior with Gower's: Trivet explains that the Sultaness resists her son's change of religion, while Gower attributes her actions to envy: 'Than have I lost my joies hiere, / For myn astat schal so be lassed.'[20] Chaucer's splicing of these two versions creates a superfluity that requires explication.

Donegild's motivation is even less clear. Full of 'tirannye', like the would-be usurper the Sultaness, Donegild agonizes over Alla's marriage:

Hir thoughte hir cursed herte brast atwo.
She wolde noght hir sone had do so;
Hir thoughte a *despit* that he sholde take
So strange a creature unto his make.

(697–700; my emphasis)

Alla's mother is undoubtedly not pleased at his conversion to Christianity; like the Sultaness, Donegild too might be understood to be motivated by religious fervor. But such spiritual ardor is not specified, as it is in the case of the Syrian; 'strange creature' is the only suggestion. (Note that Gower gives no motive, either; Trivet gives 'strangeness' of Constance's ancestry and religion, and envy for her popularity among the people).[21] Donegild's 'despit' (699) is more convincingly identified with the angry 'despit' (591) of the young knight in Northumbria whose sexual desire – 'foul affeccioun' – for Constance is rejected. 'Fy, mannysh, fy!' cries the Man of Law at Donegild; 'o nay, by God, I lye – / Fy, feendlych spirit' (782–83). The thrice-uttered 'Fy!' recalls his earlier imprecation apropos of the incestuous love of a woman for a man, Canacee for her brother: 'Of swiche cursed stories I sey fy!' (80). It may be true that, as Drogon of Bergues remarked in his eleventh-century *vita* of Saint Godelive, 'Omnes socrus oderunt nurus' ('All mothers-in-law hate their daughters-in-law'). Drogon identifies this as a piece of popular wisdom, a commonplace saying; such animosity is certainly a widespread folk motif which Schlauch explains in terms of the transition from one phase of family organization to another, a shift from filial allegiance to marital allegiance.[22] I suggest that, whether or not the tale charts a historical shift from matrilineage to patrilineage, as Schlauch argues, the context suggests a quite specific emotional motive for this resentment of mother-in-law for daughter-in-law: incestuous desire of mother for son.

IV

But how can these women be impelled by incestuous desires? Incest would seem to be, in Lévi-Strauss's view at least, an affair of male choice. Behind the taboo, as we have seen, is an economy of exchange which regards women as blank 'things' to be traded. In accord with such patriarchal ideas, in the *Man of Law's Tale* these women with 'unkynde' desires are represented as *not women at all*.[23] The Man of Law becomes rhetorically 'hyperactive', to use Rodney Delasanta's term,[24] when faced with the difficult project of determining how it can be that a woman, the Sultaness, can be so evil; of women we have had so far only the example of the virtuous Constance. In two agitated stanzas he bursts out:

O Sowdanesse, roote of iniquitee!
Virago, thou Semyrame the secounde!
O serpent under femynynytee,

Lik to the serpent depe in helle ybounde!
O feyned womman, al that may confounde
Vertu and innocence, thurgh thy malice,
Is bred in thee, as nest of every vice!

O Sathan, envious syn thilke day
That thou were chaced from oure heritage,
Wel knowestow to wommen the olde way!
Thou madest Eva brynge us in servage;
Thou wolt fordoon this Cristen mariage.
Thyn instrument so–weylawey the while!–
Makestow of wommen, whan thou wolt bigile.

(358–71)

In this Sultaness the Man of Law fixes the origin of all evil: she
is 'roote', 'nest', 'welle' of sin. We might hear this as a typical
antifeminist diatribe, associating all women with Eve as The One
Who Started It All. But as it turns out here, the Sultaness is a *'feyned*
womman' (my emphasis), a 'serpent under femynynytee', like the
Serpent who snakes his way into real women ('Wel knowestow to
wommen the olde way!'). Eve, the first of many, was made Satan's
'instrument'; she was not herself vicious. The Sultaness, not a woman
but a 'serpent', later 'this scorpioun' (404), and finally 'this wikked
goost' (404; removed from even the realm of the living), is truly
malicious. 'Femynynytee' itself is thus kept free of evil, free, in fact,
of independent desire or action.

Similarly, Donegild is explicitly not feminine, not even human:

O Donegild, I ne have noon Englissh digne
Unto thy malice and thy tirannye!
And therfore to the feend I thee resigne;
Lat hym enditen of thy traitorie!
Fy, mannysh, fy! – o nay, by God, I lye –
Fy, feendlych spirit, for I dar wel telle,
Thogh thou heere walke, thy spirit is in helle!

(778–84)

Monstrosity, 'venym' (891), devilishness, and death are associated
with these creatures, and the urgent necessity of their absolute
exclusion from 'femynynytee' is audible in the Man of Law's
overexcited syntax.

The Sultaness and Donegild are excluded from human society not,
primarily, because they are heathens; other heathens (the constable,
Hermengyld, Alla) are treated with respect in this narrative.[25] And

neither are they excluded from 'femynynytee' just because
their desires are 'unkynde'; they are excluded because they have
independent desires at all. They are active women: they want to
retain power over their sons; they want to rule the social order; and
they have sexual desires independent of, and contrary to, the social
order. These desires do not originate in the desires of others, as they
must in society which is founded on the exchange of women.[26] Emily
in the *Knight's Tale* provides perhaps the clearest example in Chaucer
of the feminine desire that conveniently adapts itself to the desires of
those who trade her. We recall that, Arcite having won her in battle,

> she agayn hym caste a freendlich ye
> (For wommen, as to speken in comune,
> Thei folwen alle the favour of Fortune)
> And was al his chiere, as in his herte.

(I.2680–83)

Emily makes herself into what Arcite desires (2683), and turns an
amiable eye toward him. (Note here that when the Knight tries to
explain this phenomenon of the ever-plastic feminine libido, his tone
breaks in the process: 'as to speken in comune . . .'. The break in
tone indicates the Knight's difficulty in explaining this patriarchal
phenomenon; he senses something remarkable in this idea of
feminine adaptability, and has to try to get outside his high-style
aristocratic ideology – to speak commonly – to explain it. The notion
of courtliness as a cover for the patriarchal exchange economy, as
we've seen earlier in *Troilus and Criseyde*, is suggested here as well.)
Later, Arcite dead, Emily uncomplainingly, even blissfully, marries
Palamon. For the smooth operation of the system, women's desires
must conform to the desires of men.

The Man of Law, we might note, seems to be aware of this
condition and the effects it might have on women. Early on in the
narrative he recognizes Constance's unhappy plight as a token of
exchange between men, but is unable, in the terms available to him
under patriarchy, to explain why it must be this way:

> Allas, what wonder is it thogh she wepte,
> That shal be sent to strange nacioun
> Fro freendes that so tendrely hire kepte,
> And to be bounden under subjeccioun
> Of oon, she knoweth nat his condicioun?
> Housbondes been alle goode, and han ben yoore;
> That knowen wyves; I dar sey yow na moore.

(267–73)

In a complete reversal of emotional logic in the last two lines that alerts us to ideology reconciling itself to contradiction – ideology constructing itself – the Man of Law unironically gives the only possible answer under patriarchy: husbands *must be* all good, because women *must be* traded in marriage. He may be able to sense that something is wrong in this gender asymmetry, but he has no way to think of it outside of patriarchal categories. Thus his hasty retreat: 'I dar sey yow na moore.'

The principle of mimetic desire enables the successful exchange of women; women who independently desire, let alone mothers who desire their sons, violate it. The seriousness of this disruption – the anxiety it generates among men – can be discerned by the extreme pressure the Man of Law exerts in his exclusion of these creatures from human society: he uses images of scorpions, snakes, fiends in hell, death. But his trouble with feminine desire is not confined to the two mothers-in-law; it becomes explicit in reference to Constance herself. Female sexual behavior provokes a prurient remark and leads him into paradox when he undertakes to describe what happens on the wedding night of Constance and Alla. Even the mimetic desire of women – their imitative, passive responses – is problematic. He has just mentioned the lavishness of the nuptial feast and entertainments, having deployed *occupatio* to excuse himself from the task of describing them in detail. He could, of course, in the next stanza, use another *occupatio* to extricate himself from the difficulty of describing the saintly, virginal Constance's entrance into sexuality. But he instead brazens it out:

> They goon to bedde, as it was skile and right;
> For thogh that wyves be ful hooly thynges,
> They moste take in pacience at nyght
> Swiche manere necessaries as been plesynges
> To folk that han ywedded hem with rynges,
> And leye a lite hir hoolynesse aside,
> As for the tyme – it may no bet bitide.

(708–14)

The Man of Law suggests that just when Constance has become a wife, on her wedding night, she can't act like one, or can't be one: wives are holy things, but to be wedded means that wives must 'as for the tyme' lay their holiness aside. Wives must stop being wives, as it were, if they want to be wives. The paradox of this wedding night is left intact and reveals a crucial patriarchal formation of woman. 'Hoolynesse' cannot encompass female sexual behavior; what is revealed when wives lay their defining holiness aside is

an effect of masculine desire. The Man of Law depicts a wife as
something that, at least 'for the tyme' (we recall time and maidenhead
as blanknesses to be filled in by men), becomes an 'embodimen[t]
of men's projected needs' (husbands 'take . . . / Swiche manere
necessaries').[27]

It comes as no surprise, then, that any potential of incestuous
relation of Constance to her son Mauricius is entirely absorbed into
and made to further the patriarchal order. Active and independent
drives are what characterize the mothers-in-law, but not this mother.
The relationship between Constance and Mauricius is parallel, rather,
to the relationship between the Virgin Mary and her Son. Mary's
presence is constant throughout the narrative: Constance prays to
her, calls on her for aid; and the Virgin, indeed, finally puts an end
to Constance's perils. The parallels between the two women are clear:
Constance's heart is a 'chambre of hoolynesse' (167), resembling
Mary herself, a closed chamber;[28] she acts as mediator in the
salvation of the Northumbrians (684), just as Mary's role is mediatory
(850); and Constance eventually attains the position of 'queene' (693).
The parallel relationships between the mothers and their sons are
equally clear. Not only does Constance make the connection explicit,
praying to the Virgin to pity Mauricius's plight because she has
suffered the death of her own Son (848–54), but even the iconography
matches: Constance lays her 'coverchief' on Mauricius as she carries
him to the boat of their exile from Northumbria (837), just as Mary
covers Christ at his birth (and later at his death) with her kerchief.
Constance at this point is 'knelyng' on the shore, just as the Virgin is
pictured kneeling at the Nativity. This position of mother kneeling
before son Simone de Beauvoir calls 'the supreme masculine victory',
and, indeed, both maternal roles here subordinate mother to son.[29]
The Virgin is hardly viewed as independent or self-determining
before her Son; Mauricius, we note, eventually becomes emperor.

Thus, instead of being disrupted by an incestuous relationship
between mother and son, the bond between father and son is
powerfully established at the end of the *Tale*. During the feast at the
Roman senator's house, Alla stares into the face of the unknown
young boy as 'The child stood, lookynge in the kynges face' (1015);
Alla recognizes Constance's countenance in him, much to his
amazement, and recognizes him as his son *because* he sees Constance's
countenance therein. Speaking to Constance, Alla later refers to
'Maurice my sone, so lyk youre face' (1063). The woman's image
binds father and son, and, later, grandfather and son (1095–96) in
what must be called the patriarchal gaze. It is the same gaze that
with 'sobre cheere' (97) sees incest between father and daughter but
re-vises it as legitimate, the exemplification of a bland truism. And

it is the same gaze that removes 'tyrannical' women from its line of sight.

V

It seems finally that the operant distinction in the *Man of Law's Tale* is not between good women and bad women. The line between the good female figures and the bad ones in the tale, at first glance so sharp, becomes blurry on closer look.[30] The similarity of the names 'Hermengyld' and 'Donegild' and the fact that Chaucer's treatment of his source enhances this nominal similarity suggest that there is in the narrative some essential resemblance between these figures. Donegild accuses Constance of being an 'elf' who has given birth to a 'feendly creature' (754, 751); she's lying, of course, but the association of Constance with otherworldly and hellish creatures – and, in turn, with the mothers – once made, comes to seem less and less inappropriate: note how many dead bodies Constance herself leaves behind her as she travels from country to country (the Christianized Syrians, the would-be lover in Northumbria, Hermengyld, two mothers-in-law, the would-be rapist on the unidentified shore, more Syrians in revenge).

The vital distinction is rather between all women and all men, or, more precisely, all not-men and all men. 'Woman' in the ideology of the *Man of Law's Tale* is an essential blankness that will be inscribed by men and thus turned into a tale; she is a blank onto which men's desire will be projected; she is a no-thing in herself. The Man of Law's outburst at the Sultaness leaves 'femynynytee' in itself free from sin; 'wommen', he states, are vulnerable to becoming Satan's 'instruments'. This pure instrumentality of woman is, in fact, definitive of her. If 'Eva' demonstrates that bad women are Satan's instruments, Constance demonstrates that saintly women are God's instruments: 'God liste to shewe his wonderful myracle / In hire, for we sholde seen his myghty werkis' (477–78). Constance's defining characteristic, her virtuous suffering, is, indeed, not her own; it results from her father's 'governance', his sending her off – despite her tears – to marry the Sultan in the first place.[31] And her most aggressive gesture, 'hir struglying wel and myghtily' against the thief who would rape her (921), is made possible only by the intervention of Mary (920) and Christ (924). The Man of Law's most memorable images of Constance serve to emphasize her no-thingness: she spends years floating at sea, without a rudder. Hers is the *pale* face in the crowd as she faces her accuser in Northumbria: 'Have ye nat seyn somtyme a pale face . . . ?' (645). And 'deedly pale' again, she walks toward her exile from Northumbria, followed by a crowd (822). In this context, Constance's association with death – all those corpses, mentioned earlier – takes on another valence: as Gilbert and Gubar tautly put it in *The Madwoman in the Attic*, 'To be selfless is not only to be noble, it is to be dead'.[32]

To point out only Constance's blankness and pure instrumentality is, however, to overlook aspects of the narrative that suggest she does have some sense of self-consciousness, indeed, some sense of the kind of 'tale' she herself constitutes. The Man of Law works overtime in imposing biblical and hagiographic identities on Constance, but he is not the only one who is aware of her participation in a larger pattern; Constance is aware of herself in the community of saintly Christians, daughters of the Church (566–74). This fact makes her quite unlike the 'good women' of the *Legend of Good Women*, cut off from the perception of themselves in any kind of community. Not only does the Man of Law use language that associates her with the Virgin Mary (she is a 'queen', 'unwemmed'); Constance herself prays to the Virgin, making her own recognition of saintly analogy clear:

> Thow sawe thy child yslayn bifore thyne yen,
> And yet now lyveth my litel child, parfay!
> Now, lady bright, to whom alle woful cryen,
> . . .
> Rewe on my child.
>
> (848–52)

She makes her own Marian role explicit, just as, earlier, she understands that she and others work as daughters of the Church (566–74). She does have a sense of herself as a saint, as participant in a community whose exemplar is Christ: she senses that her own position under attack in Northumbria is like Susanna's; she may even, as Weissman suggests, enact a sacred parody of the Crucifixion scene as she leaves Northumbria.

Constance has, too, a definite ability to shape her life as a perfect romance, to write, in a sense, her own story. Early on, when she leaves her home for Syria, 'She peyneth hire to make good contenance' (320), demonstrating that she has some awareness of shaping appearances. When she is found by the constable on the Northumbrian shore she tells a little tale about herself, concealing her true identity:

> She kneleth doun and thanketh Goddes sonde;
> But what she was she wolde no man seye,
> For foul ne fair, thogh that she sholde deye.

She seyde she was so mazed in the see
That she forgat hir mynde, by hir trouthe.

(523–27)

She again withholds her identity when she is found on the open sea
by the Roman senator. And she persuades Alla not to reveal it to her
father in Rome when he invites the old man to dine with them. She
thus contrives a denouement full of drama, reversal, and recognition,
in which she utters her own name in the moment of reconciliation
with her father: ' "I am youre doghter Custance," quod she' (1107).
Constance may be a tale told by men, but she seems to be given,
by the Man of Law, a certain power of determining her own
narrative kinesis.

But Constance's limited self-consciousness in fact serves patriarchy
well (as do the romance hagiographies that provide the most
immediate context for Constance's self-portrayal here).[33] The tale she
tells in order to conceal her identity, after all, is that she 'forgat hir
mynde' (524). Dominant ideology (and its expressed system of laws)
controls and manipulates the principle of similarity and difference,
analogy and repetition; if Constance has access to these principles – is
conscious that she is like others (saints, romance heroines, women)
– that consciousness enables her only to suffer and to be constrained.
Her self-perceived identity as saint enables her to do no more than
endure injuries, as does her consciousness of her own womanhood
('I, wrecche womman, no fors though I spille! / Wommen are born
to thraldom and penance, / And to been under mannes governance'
[285–87]). And at the moment of her greatest self-consciousness, the
moment in which she pronounces her own name, Constance plays a
part in a larger system of patriarchal constraint that ends this romance
narrative. Her happiness in reunion with her father – the 'pitous
joye' (1114), the 'wepynge for tendrenesse in herte blithe' (1154) – is
assimilated by the Man of Law into the pattern of joy after woe, woe
after gladness that he identifies as the natural rhythm of earthly life.

It's an ending that appeals to the Host, who commends the tale at
its conclusion as 'a *thrifty* tale for the nones!' (1165; my emphasis).
His enthusiastic response reinforces the smoothly running patriarchal
system that trades women and tales, women as tales. Constance's
minimal self-awareness allows her no more than passivity. But
there's one woman on this pilgrimage who knows that she's
merchandise and uses that knowledge of woman's commodification
to her own advantage: 'With daunger', she assures us, 'oute we al
oure chaffare' (III.521). She knows that 'woman' has been written by
clerks in their oratories. And she takes that 'book of wikked wyves'
and tosses it into the fire.

Notes

1. Hugh of Saint Victor, in his *Didascalicon*, demonstrates an understanding of trade or commerce as a kind of discourse:

> Commerce contains every sort of dealing in the purchase, sale, and exchange of domestic or foreign goods. This art is beyond all doubt a peculiar sort of rhetoric – strictly of its own kind – for eloquence is in the highest degree necessary to it. Thus the man who excels others in fluency of speech is called a *Mercurius*, or Mercury, as being a *mercatorum kirrius* (=*kyrios*) – a very lord among merchants.
> (Trans. Jerome Taylor [New York: Columbia University Press, 1961], bk. 2, ch. 23)

   Cited in EUGENE VANCE, 'Chrétien's *Yvain* and the Ideologies of Change and Exchange', in *Mervelous Signals: Poetics and Sign Theory in the Middle Ages* (Lincoln and London: University of Nebraska Press, 1986), p. 118.

2. JOHN GOWER, *Confessio amantis* 5.6114 (in *English Works of John Gower*, ed. G. C. Macaulay, EETS, e.s. 82 [1900; rpt. Oxford: Oxford University Press, 1957], 2:113); WILLIAM LANGLAND, *Piers Plowman: The B-Text*, ed. George Kane and E. Talbot Donaldson (London: Athlone Press, 1975), 15.105; *Hali Meidenhad*, MS. Bodley 34 and Cotton MS. Titus D. 18 (ed. F. J. Furnivall [1922; rpt. New York: Greenwood, 1969], pp. 12–13, 36–7).

3. CLAUDE LÉVI-STRAUSS, *The Elementary Structures of Kinship*, trans. James Harle Bell, John Richard von Sturmer, and Rodney Needham, rev. edn (Boston, MA: Beacon Press, 1969); hereafter cited, as *ES*, in the text. *Les Structures élémentaires de la parenté*, first published in France in 1949, appeared in a revised edition in France in 1967.

4. See MARCEL MAUSS, *Essai sur le don, forme archaïque de l'échange* (1925); translated by Ian Cunnison, under the title *The Gift: Forms and Functions of Exchange in Archaic Societies* (New York: Norton, 1967); and GAYLE RUBIN, 'The Traffic in Women: Notes on the "Political Economy" of Sex', in *Toward an Anthropology of Women*, ed. R. R. Reiter (New York: Monthly Review Press, 1975), pp. 157–210.

5. Georges Duby notes that 'marriage is at the core of all social institutions', and marriage is a 'treaty . . . concluded between two houses': 'Under such a pact, one of the houses would give up, the other receive or acquire, a woman. The exchange, then, involved a woman'. See GEORGES DUBY, *Medieval Marriage: Two Models from Twelfth-Century France*, trans. Elborg Forster (Baltimore, MD: Johns Hopkins University Press, 1978), p. 4. David Herlihy suggests a Lévi-Straussian analysis of constitutive social exchange (of signs, money, and women) when he links women and money: analysing high- and late-medieval rules of inheritance, he notes that in the common medieval view such rules were tied to exogamy. Referring to the eleventh-century Peter Damian, Herlihy comments: 'The woman must marry out, and she inevitably takes some property with her. The circulation of women thus also produced a circulation of capital'. See DAVID HERLIHY, *Medieval Households* (Cambridge, MA: Harvard University Press, 1985), p. 136.

6. CLAUDE LÉVI-STRAUSS, 'The Family', in *Man, Culture, and Society*, ed. H. Shapiro (London: Oxford University Press, 1971), p. 278.

7. HERLIHY, *Medieval Households*, p. 61.

8. RUBIN, 'The Traffic in Women', p. 174.

9. In 'The Family', Lévi-Strauss – again at the end of the work – acknowledges this uneasiness and tries to provide reassurance:

The female reader, who may be shocked to see womankind treated as a commodity submitted to transactions between male operators, can easily find comfort in the assurance that the rules of the game would remain unchanged should it be decided to consider the men as being exchanged by women's groups. As a matter of fact, some *very few* societies, of a highly developed matrilineal type, have *to a limited extent attempted* to express things that way.

(p. 284, my emphasis)

The heavy qualification here works, in my view as female reader, against such 'assurance'.

10. Robert F. Murphy, from the *Saturday Review*, is the reviewer quoted on the back cover whom I cite here. Gayle Rubin writes of these last paragraphs of Lévi-Strauss, as well as of similar paradoxical passages in Freud:

> It is precisely at such points that the implications of the theory are ignored, and are replaced with formulations whose purpose is to keep those implications firmly lodged in the theoretical unconscious. It is at these points that all sorts of mysterious chemical substances, joys in pain, and biological aims are substituted for a critical assessment of the costs of femininity.

('The Traffic in Women', pp. 202–3)

11. See JUDITH HERMAN and LISA HIRSCHMAN, 'Father–Daughter Incest', *Signs*, 2 (1977), 735–56, for an analysis of 'the asymmetrical nature of the incest taboo under patriarchy': 'Because the taboo is created and enforced by men, we argue that it may also be more easily and frequently violated by men.' But 'a patriarchal society . . . most abhors the idea of incest between mother and son, because this is an affront to the father's prerogatives' (pp. 740–1). Herman and Hirschman present a clinical report of fifteen victims of father–daughter incest.

12. MARGARET SCHLAUCH, *Chaucer's Constance and Accused Queens* (1927; rpt. New York: Gordian Press, 1969), pp. 132–3.

13. PIERRE MACHEREY, *A Theory of Literary Production*, trans. Geoffrey Wall (London: Routledge and Kegan Paul, 1978), p. 194.

14. Schlauch notes that father–daughter incest in the folktales may be the vestige of an earlier matrilineal social organization in Western Europe: the king wants to marry the daughter, after the mother's decease, in order to retain his regal status. The daughter's refusal of her father's advances would, then, suggest a new kind of social organization – patrilineage – and the tale would itself document a transition from female determination of social organization to male determination (*Chaucer's Constance and Accused Queens*, pp. 43–5).

15. Christianity – an ideology that subsumes patriarchy – maintains its sovereignty by denying heathens identity with the rest of humankind, converting them, or killing them. Patriarchy employs parallel methods of suppression, marginalization, appropriation, obliteration. Indeed, in the *Man of Law's Tale* both 'lawes' – 'mannes governance' and the 'newe lawe' of Christianity – create an Other, on whom each is said to impose 'thraldom and penance' (286, 338).

16. Note that this scene does not occur in Gower; and, although the word 'pavement' seems to have been derived from the Latin version, Antiochus there does not throw his daughter to the ground (see *Historia Apollonii regis Tyri*, ed. A. Riese, 2d edn [Leipzig: Teubner, 1893], pp. 2–3). See the note on line 81 in F. N. ROBINSON, *The Works of Geoffrey Chaucer*, 2d edn (Boston, MA:

Houghton Mifflin, 1957), p. 691. This gesture, with its symmetry to Constance's later gestures, seems to be Chaucer's innovation.

17. A vow made at Easingwold in 1484, typical of late-medieval marriage vows, recorded in *Acts of the Chapter of the Collegiate Church of Saints Peter and Wilfred, Ripon, 1452–1506* (Durham: Surtees Society, 1875), 64:162; my emphasis.

18. Rubin makes this point well:

> If a girl is promised in infancy, her refusal as an adult would disrupt the flow of debts and promises. It would be in the interests of the smooth and continuous operation of such a system if the woman in question did not have too many ideas of her own about whom she might want to sleep with. From the standpoint of the system, the preferred female sexuality would be one which responded to the desire of others, rather than one which actively desired and sought a response.
>
> ('The Traffic in Women', p. 182)

See also Margaret Gist:

> It is a commonplace that throughout the Middle Ages marriage was an arrangement of convenience, an enforced legal contract. . . . With such ends in view, it was inevitable that the desire of the woman should be the least significant element in the bargain.
>
> (*Love and War in the Middle English Romances* [Philadelphia: University of Pennsylvania Press, 1947], p. 17)

19. SCHLAUCH, *Chaucer's Constance and Accused Queens*, esp. pp. 33–4.

20. NICHOLAS TRIVET, *Les Chroniques écrites pour Marie d'Angleterre, fille d'Edward I*, in *Sources and Analogues of Chaucer's 'Canterbury Tales'*, ed. W. F. Bryan and G. Dempster (New York: Humanities Press, 1958), p. 167; JOHN GOWER, *Confessio amantis* 2.648–49 (in *English Works of John Gower*, 1:148). On Chaucer's use of these two sources in this scene, see Schlauch, p. 134.

21. TRIVET, *Les Chroniques écrites pour Marie d'Angleterre*, p. 172.

22. 'Verum enimvero hac in parte verum habetur cuiusdam saecularis prudentia dictum quod omnes socrus oderunt nurus' (*La Vie ancienne de sainte Godelive de Ghistelles par Drogon de Bergues, Analecta bollandiana* 44 [1926]: 128); SCHLAUCH, *Chaucer's Constance and Accused Queens*, p. 34. Drogon honors Godelive for her patience in the teeth of marital abuse (she was tormented by both husband and mother-in-law). HERLIHY, *Medieval Households*, p. 114, mentions this saint's life; we remember another Godelive who forms a neat contrast: Harry Bailly's brawny, aggressive wife Goodelief who, reversing the power relations between husband and wife, strikes fear into her husband (ruefully reported by the Host in the headlink to the *Monk's Tale*, after *Melibee*). Harry remarks that she acts nothing like Melibee's Prudence – and we might suspect that she has never read the *vita* of her namesake, either.

23. My analysis in this section is indebted to SHEILA DELANY's chapter, 'Womanliness in *The Man of Law's Tale*', in her *Writing Woman: Women Writers and Women in Literature, Medieval to Modern* (New York: Schocken, 1983), pp. 36–46. Delany problematizes the Man of Law's breaks in style and tone, identifies a reductive conception of femininity, and observes the lack of femaleness of Constance's mothers-in-law.

24. RODNEY DELASANTA, 'And of Great Reverence: Chaucer's Man of Law', *ChauR*, 5 (1971), 288–310.

25. Infidels were not necessarily viewed in the Middle Ages as entirely outside the realm of humankind: as Stephen G. Nichols, Jr., pointed out to me, John Scottus Eriugena, e.g., thought them to represent that half of humanity which rejected God and became the race of Cain. See bk. 5, sec. 38 of his *Periphyseon* or *De divisione naturae* (*PL* 122: 1011).

26. Note that the Sowdanesse herself instigates a trade, thus usurping the masculine role of exchanger: she vows to 'quite' the Sultan in his change of religion (354).

27. 'Embodiments of men's projected needs' is a phrase from CATHERINE A. MacKINNON's pithy article, 'Feminism, Marxism, Method, and the State', in *Feminist Theory: A Critique of Ideology*, ed. Nannerl O. Keohane, Michelle Z. Rosaldo and Barbara C. Gelpi (Chicago: University of Chicago Press, 1982), p. 20.

28. For a discussion of the architectural iconography of the Virgin as closed chamber, see GAIL McMURRAY GIBSON, ' "Porta haec clausa erit": Comedy, Conception, and Ezekiel's Closed Door in the *Ludus Coventriae* Play of "Joseph's Return" ', *JMRS*, 8 (1978), 137–56.

29. SIMONE DE BEAUVOIR, *The Second Sex*, trans. H. M. Parshley (New York: Knopf, 1957), p. 160. MARINA WARNER cites this phrase from *The Second Sex* in her lively and useful discussion of the Virgin's motherhood in *Alone of All Her Sex: The Myth and the Cult of the Virgin Mary* (New York: Random House, 1976), p. 183.

30. Cf. Luce Irigaray's comments on the traffic in women: the exchange of women establishes the operations of patriarchal society, and thus presupposes, among other conditions, 'the equality of women among themselves, but in terms of laws of equivalence that remain external to them' (LUCE IRIGARAY, 'Women on the Market', in *This Sex Which Is Not One*, trans. Catherine Porter [Ithaca, NY: Cornell University Press, 1985], pp. 184–5).

31. See LEE PATTERSON's comments on the *Man of Law's Tale* in his article, ' "For the Wyves love of Bathe": Feminine Rhetoric and Poetic Resolution in the *Roman de la Rose* and the *Canterbury Tales*' (*Speculum*, 58 [1983]): Constance's 'redemptive mission is an effect of her father's tyranny' (p. 692).

32. SANDRA M. GILBERT and SUSAN GUBAR, *The Madwoman in the Attic: The Woman Writer and the Nineteenth-Century Literary Imagination* (New Haven, CT: Yale University Press, 1979), p. 25.

33. I would maintain, in an argument that is beyond the scope of the present chapter, that those very romance hagiographies forming the horizon of expectation for Constance's self-presentation here (and for the Man of Law's performance in general) have the same effect as the one I have analysed for the *Man of Law's Tale*: they uncritically generate, reconfirm, and perpetuate patriarchal ideology. For an example picked more or less at random from an enormous body of literature, consider the popular legend of Saint Mary Magdalene (fourteenth-century text found in the *South English Legendary*, ed. Charlotte d'Evelyn and Anna J. Mill, EETS, 235 [London: Oxford University Press, 1956], 1:302–15; fifteenth-century representation in the Digby play of *Mary Magdalene*, in *Medieval Drama*, ed. David Bevington [Boston, MA: Houghton Mifflin, 1975], pp. 687–753), with its emphasis on conversion, proper lineage, and typological reenactment of Christ's life – properly patriarchal preoccupations, as I have suggested.

6 'Vanysshed Was This Daunce, He Nyste Where': Alisoun's Absence in the *Wife of Bath's Prologue and Tale**

Arthur Lindley

Lindley's article begins with a survey of the vast amount of recent criticism directed at the *Wife of Bath's Prologue and Tale*, criticism flawed in Lindley's eyes by the desire to provide a unified, coherent interpretation of what is a markedly ambiguous and contradictory text. Lindley sees the text as Chaucer's 'intricately ironized' exercise in an anti-feminist discourse that can never be about women *per se* but solely about the male sexual obsessions and anxieties that inhabit such a discourse, and thus as a kind of demonstration of 'the ultimate unknowability of female experience to a male author'. The attempt to make the Wife into any kind of feminist mouthpiece is at odds with the Chaucerian insistence that women are not and cannot be speaking in this text; at most we have a 'drag act' where men play a gross distortion of women. Although Lindley sees the work as Chaucer's 'protest' at the way women cannot be allowed to play themselves in a patriarchal, clerical culture, he is more concerned to see the absence of woman in the text as the sign of a more general 'emptiness' of values within the commercial and materialist culture represented by Chaucer's pilgrimage-party. For further discussion of some of the contradictions arising from Lindley's piece, see my Introduction, pp. 17–19.

I. There is no Single Key

Anyone who has studied the criticism on the *Wife of Bath's Prologue and Tale* will know the sinking sensation that attends the appearance of yet another version of the one, true Alisoun followed, at the requisite two paces, by the one, true Chaucer. Thus, Alisoun the heretical exegete is shadowed by Chaucer the Pauline moralist (for D. W. Robertson), just as Alisoun the battered wife is attended by

---

* Reprinted from *ELH*, 59 (1992), 1–21.

Chaucer the sympathetic humanist (for Robert Burlin). For Kenneth Oberembt, Alisoun the 'temperate' social critic is followed by a Chaucer who is likewise, while for Sheila Delany an antifeminist Alisoun is followed by a rapist Chaucer. In recent criticism, Alisoun-as-feminist-spokeswoman has tended to appear with a Chaucer who is the precursor either of John Stuart Mill (Walter Long) or Luce Irigaray (Barrie Strauss), not to mention Lacan (Louise Fradenburg, of course). John Alford is being only marginally less modest than the norm by announcing that when the Wife is seen as Rhetoric and the Clerk as Logic, 'the two characters immediately become coherent *in every detail*'.[1] The details this reading fails to explain include, by the way, the name Alisoun and the place Bath.

You can group these readings in any number of ways: pro- versus antifeminist (Marjorie Malvern versus Bernard Huppé), for example; or psychological (Burlin) versus archetypal (Robertson). You can divide the Wife's critics usefully into those who wish to remove her from history into the realm of permanent types, as Alford does, and those who wish to put her back again: Mary Carruthers, Dorothy Colmer, David Aers. Even feminist critics can be separated into those who think Chaucer is on their side (such as Peggy Knapp) and those who think he isn't (Delany).[2]

All of these approaches, valuable as they are, share a tendency to reduce one of the most ambiguous, 'dialogic' texts in our literature to a monologic 'right' reading. She's good or she's bad, she's smart or she's dumb, Chaucer's for her or against her. The text is constructed as either/or, not both/and. Thus Robertson, for example, announces that 'Alisoun is not a "character" at all . . . but an elaborate iconographic figure'.[3] This is what I call the fallacy of the single key, which says that Alisoun must hail either from Scripture or from Bath when, manifestly, she hails from both.[4] Rhetorically at least, she's the Wife of Both. Given the enormous critical controversy surrounding this text, it's remarkable how few critics acknowledge its full complexity. With the honorable exceptions of Lee Patterson, Peggy Knapp, and Barrie Strauss, critics tend to approach it in the hope of finding a single, simplifying answer.[5] The uncertainties of the text need to be confronted, however, not eliminated. Reductive answers are precisely what it rules out of play. One of the dangers of a single key, of course, is locking yourself in (or out). Once we've recognized, for example, that the hag is obviously a projection of the Wife, we then have to notice that as someone who denounces property, covetousness, and social privilege, she's also *not* the Wife's representative. What appears to be identity is also opposition. Alisoun's advocate is also her accuser.

In order to make some comprehensive sense of this text, we have to recognize that Chaucer has provided an extraordinary number

of keys for an extraordinary number of wicket gates: Jerome and
Walter Map, the wool trade, the Samaritan woman, birthmarks and
horoscopes, an analogue in Gower, Pauline doctrines of marriage
and the very different marital customs of the land-holding classes of
fourteenth-century England, not to mention enough hints of a murder
mystery to entertain Beryl Rowland and D. J. Wurtele.[6] If Chaucer
meant to create a single key for all these references (and many more),
he has been remarkably unsuccessful. We should remember that
when the knight of Alisoun's *Tale* asks his simple question he gets
any number of more or less right answers before the hag gives him
one general enough to encompass all the rest. We might also
remember Susan Crane's warning that 'when we make the Wife
of Bath coherent, she becomes too easy to dismiss'.[7]

The other thing we have to recognize is that as a character the Wife
is remarkably incomplete. Virtually no part of her story is whole or
trustworthy. Is Jankyn alive? How many Jankyns were/are there?
Was there ever a second Alisoun? Who was the first one's 'dame'?
The list is too long and familiar to need repeating. Far more of
Alisoun is absent than is present. I think we have to take seriously
Marshall Leicester's proposition that 'there is no Wife of Bath',
without using that as a modish way of saying that she is a fictional
character, so that we can get back to the business of discovering her
motives and rhetorical purposes (as even Leicester himself does).[8]
Alisoun is a text whose salient feature is incompleteness. If that text
can be said to be 'about' any single thing, that would be absence: the
absence of other characters (husbands, children, parents); the absence
of the class of people for whom Alisoun seems to speak, other
women; the absence of Alisoun herself. As Patterson reminds us – in
the best single essay on the *Wife of Bath's Prologue and Tale* – Midas's
wife (951–82) was once, in Alisoun's Ovidian source, his barber. We
have to look for the man who isn't there in order to understand the
ambiguity of an apparently simple reference.[9] The barber is not the
only one who disappears. Alisoun's knight, at the point where his life
is about to be settled, has a ludicrously perfunctory and apparently
pointless vision: 'He saugh upon a daunce go / Of ladyes foure and
twenty, and yet mo' (991–92), who disappear, leaving the hag, who
is herself an after-image of a vanished Lady Ragnell and who in turn
will vanish, leaving the beauty who is the solution to (or figment of)
the knight's desires. This text is about who and what isn't there at
least as much as it is about what is. 'Vanysshed was this daunce, he
nyste where' (996). We would do well to inquire why disappearance
– whether of dancing ladies, hags, or Jankyns – is so central a feature
of Alisoun's performance. The absence of a real woman in or behind
this text, I will argue, is the single most significant fact about it.

II. There is no Alisoun

Alisoun's peculiar status as a metafictional puzzle has been widely, if only recently recognized. Carolyn Dinshaw, in a recent issue of *ELH*, puts the basic problem as simply as I could wish: 'The Wife . . . presents in herself a perfect image of a text'; her 'fantasy of the perfect marriage [being] analogous, in her *Prologue* and *Tale*, to the perfect glossing of a text.' Susan Crane calls her 'a fiction who tells a fiction'. Dinshaw's observation, especially when it comes near the head of an essay titled 'Eunuch Hermeneutics', may sound slightly more original and impressive than it is. The burden of Jill Mann's argument in *Chaucer and Medieval Estates Satire* is that the Canterbury pilgrims have their sources less in literal reality than in satiric types, not in Millers but in texts about Millers. More specifically, P. M. Kean has traced the originals of both the Pardoner and the Wife of Bath to the allegorical figures of Faux Semblant and La Vieille in Jean de Meun's sections of the *Roman de la Rose*. Fourteen years ago, Robert Burlin located Alisoun's exact textual source: 'When [she] describes in detail the contents of Jankyn's treasured volume, we have reconstructed the genesis of her *Prologue*. . . . When she attacks its three pages, it is as if she were trying to extinguish the reality of which she is made.'[10] In my own metaphor, the Wife is a kind of Moebius strip: a fictional character originating in an imaginary book (made nevertheless from real authors: Jerome, Theophrastus, Walter Map, Matheolus) that is also an object within her own narrative, against which she can launch an attack that amounts to the attempt to refute her own existence: what we might call a post-emptive strike.[11]

What Burlin fails to address, however, is why, of all the pilgrims, this one should so pointedly and Pirandellianly signal her textuality, her status as one character in search of six authors. What has the puzzle of the Wife's reality to do with the politics of her *Prologue*, her notoriously ambiguous relationship to the priestly antifeminism that she seems at once to parody, attack, and embody? The solution to this puzzle lies, I think, in the solution to a relatively simple paradox: Alisoun is a *lusus naturae* of a common literary kind: a woman born of man, conspicuously without a mother or daughters, but with many fathers, nearly all of them – from St Jerome to Jean de Meun – priests. She is the summation of a tradition of men writing through, at, about, and especially over women, condensed and dramatized by another man (Chaucer) who must, literally or figuratively, have performed her. She is a drag act, a female impersonation, a 'creature of the male imagination'.[12] That is one reason why so much about her – the spurs, the hat like a 'targe' (I.471), the Martian/Venerian horoscope – suggests androgyny. She's what men produce when they think about women. As a woman, however, she does not exist. It is therefore beside the point to treat her as a 'real' woman, no matter whether you try to make a case for her being a feminist heroine (Strauss, Malvern, or the 1989 argument of Peggy Knapp), a battered wife (Burlin), or a 'scourge and a blight' (William Blake.)[13]

It is, in fact, a mistake to try to treat Alisoun as either a consistent emblem or a consistent character, since 'she' is an unstable projection of male fear and desire. To alter Crane's formulation, she is a fantasy who tells a fantasy, the characteristic mode of which is dreamlike exaggeration linked to dreamlike transitions (maiden turning into hag turning into maiden). The *Wife of Bath's Prologue and Tale* is one of the last and greatest of Chaucer's dream-vision poems. The subject of that dream is not woman, but male sexual obsession and the anxieties, guilts, and fears that attend on it. Consistently throughout the text, appeal gives way without transition to threat, seduction to repulsion, advertisement to consumer warning. That process continues to the very end of the *Tale*, where the assertion of mutual submission and harmony is followed immediately by the *Playgirl* fantasy of 'housbondes meeke, yonge, and fresshe abedde' (1259), and the murderous curse against 'nygardes' (1263–64). The *vagina dentata*, of which Alisoun is literature's most famous example, is not a fact of nature but of male fantasy. The Pauline version of that fantasy is the subject and source of Chaucer's text. The women, as Conrad's Marlow says in a related case, are out of it.

As a character, Alisoun presents us not so much with a psychology as a table of contents. A glance through the notes in Robinson will explain what I mean: an opening imitated from the *Roman de la Rose* (12804–5), followed by an argument with male authority and Pauline Christianity imitated from Jerome *Adversus Jovinianum* but incorporating extensive quotation from John 2:1 (11) and 4:6 (14), and from I Corinthians 7:9 (46), 7:39 (47), and 7:2 (51). As most readers will already know, Alisoun's description of life with her three old husbands is a pastiche of Eustace Deschamps's *Miroir de Mariage* (for example, lines 198–202, 233, 235–47, etc.) and/or his source, the *Lamentations of Matheolus* (the source of 129–30), plus Theophrastus's *Liber Aureolus de Nuptiis* (for example, lines 235–47 again, 248–75, 282–92, 293–302, etc.) topped with lashings of the *Roman* (lines 227–28, 229, etc.). The Wife's sexual history draws heavily on that of La Vieille in the *Roman* (for example, 503–14), but, according to Robinson, may also derive from the history of 'la mere' in the *Miroir*.[14] By the time we reach Jankyn's 'book of wikked wyves' at 685, Chaucer is ready to name his sources because Alisoun is about to burn them. The character, having found her authors and found them not to her liking, tries to destroy them, an attempt whose futility is measured by her continuing dialogue with them through Jankyn or with Jankyn through them.

At least one part of her complaint is, of course, famously cogent:

> if wommen hadde writen stories,
> As clerekes han withinne hire oratories,
> They wold han writen of men moore wikkednesse
> Than al the mark of Adam may redresse.
>
> (693–96)

That women have not written – and, even in this case, are not writing – the stories is precisely the point of Chaucer's own version of the book of wicked wives. Like Jovinian, Alisoun represents a conquered and silenced enemy: in her case, women, who are the subject of a debate from which they are excluded, present not as text but pretext.[15] Alisoun, in turn, imitates the authoritarianism of male authority in its ability to exclude other voices. Her husbands are dead, thus silenced and incorporated into her discourse, as Jovinian has been incorporated into Jerome's. She not only speaks for them, with the ambiguous power of mimicry to annihilate the subject even while insisting on its prior existence, she re-enacts the annihilation. She hasn't killed them so much as displaced them, since that is what mimicry does. She eats their words. As the antifeminist clerics have appropriated the voices of women (and Chaucer singles out those, like Jean and Theophrastus, who mimic women), so Alisoun appropriates theirs. Her elaborately repeated 'seistow' (270, 273, 292, etc.) conflates a whole world of male discourse, neatly blending her 'olde dotard shrewe[s]' (291) of husbands with the old dotard clerks who are the source of their purported opinions. At the same time, of course, what 'thou' sayest is literally nothing, since Alisoun says it for you. The old husbands become bystanders at their own marriages. Of all her husbands only Jankyn, briefly, gets to speak in his own voice.

III. This Text is not about Women

In the process of what Knapp calls reappropriation, however, Alisoun necessarily speaks for her clerical enemies as well as for herself.[16] Both the accuser and defender of women, she creates a closed circuit of discourse that effectively excludes other voices, including those of the women for whom she claims to speak. She silences the Prioress and the Second Nun even more thoroughly than she does the Friar and the Pardoner. She is large, she contains multitudes, but only at the cost of turning them all into versions of herself. There is no woman in her *Prologue* who is not named Alisoun; no woman in her *Tale* has a name at all. The 'dame' who taught her to invent dreams (576) might be her otherwise unmentioned mother, but could equally well be La Vieille, Alisoun's literary mother.[17] Throughout her monologue, in fact, there is a remarkable tendency for characters to flow together: the three old husbands with one another; Jankyn with the other clerks from whom he derives his opinions; the fourth husband, who makes Alisoun jealous, with Alisoun, who makes him jealous; Alisoun with her 'gossib' Alisoun. The two women, if there are two, talk exclusively about (the first) Alisoun: the other exists only as a mirror of self. The Wife's purchasing of love when old mirrors the husbands of her youth; the behavior of her last two husbands mirrors her own youthful behavior. She sells her 'bele chose' when young, she buys Jankyn's 'sely instrument' when old. The two sexes are economically and psychologically interchangeable, however much the Alisoun-version of reality may seem to insist on their essential opposition. Trust the tale, not the teller.[18]

Other people exist as mirrors or instruments for the entertainment of the self. Most usefully, perhaps, they exist as audience. The pilgrims, like the old husbands, sit quietly, serving as the pretext for Alisoun to talk to Alisoun about Alisoun. Those who attempt to become participants, like the Friar and the Pardoner, are ruthlessly put down. The other Alisoun knew the Wife's 'privetee / Bet than oure parisshe preest' (531–32). Only your mirror-image knows your secrets; the male authority is out of the loop.

Alisoun's argument with *auctoritee* thus becomes remarkably self-cancelling: two mirroring examples of Keats's egotistical sublime. She talks to herself about the truth of her own discourse, and denies the existence of other truths. Twenty-four ladies vanish, leaving one hag. The one swallows the many. The multitude of answers women give to the question of what they want is displaced by the one answer given by the hag, who may not be human herself. Alisoun, a digest of male authority, silences women by the simple tactic of claiming to speak for them. In the process, she confirms what men say about women because she *is* what men say about women. Since she is herself a text, there is no experience in her history with which she could refute authority that is not itself derived from authority. Manifestly, her experience can neither affirm nor deny what the books say because, being the product of those books, she can have only the 'experience' in them. The loop is closed. Authority, at least when it is male authority pretending to define female experience, is an autoclarificatory system (as Anne Elliot points out to Captain Benwick). Texts confirm other texts, whose authors in turn have become authorities by generalizing from their own (asserted, unverifiable, lost) experience, a process Alisoun and the Merchant will both enact. Both assume that their marriages are all marriages. But her marriages are, also of course, fictions; they exist only in her assertions, which are, as she makes clear, the confessions of a liar.

Sympathetic as the attempts of Knapp, Long, Malvern, Oberembt and others to turn Alisoun into a feminist heroine may be, they miss the point. To try to save the text for humanism by defending Alisoun involves at least three fallacies: (1) confusing her point with Chaucer's (2) confusing her with womankind; and (3) confusing her with a real person. She is none of the above. It is no good theorizing, for example, about the psychological history of someone who exists only as a discourse, even if that discourse were not both internally contradictory and explicitly derived from other texts. Alisoun is absent. The very fact of her performance creates a complex kind of absence: the performer separating herself from the group in order to present herself to it through a confession that is also a screen. This text is not her, this is her act. Aside from that act, there are no available 'facts' except those of her physical appearance. The history given in her *General Prologue* portrait turns out to be proleptic paraphrase of the version given in her own *Prologue*. Unlike the Guildsmen or the Merchant and Franklin, she travels alone; unlike the Miller, Reeve, and Summoner, she is known to no other pilgrim; unlike Roger Ware or Harry Bailley, she has no known sources in actual people.

For all its apparent confessionality, Alisoun's *Prologue* insists on its own secretiveness. She parades her hiddenness, speaking 'after [her] fantasye' (190). Her professed 'entente nys but for to pleye' (192). Alisoun's 'play' is, however, at once a deadly serious defensive tactic and a demonstration of how solipsism can be used as a weapon. Her way of controlling her old husbands, for example, is to use the power of her secrecy against them: she invents plausible charges against herself – 'Thou seydest this, that I was lyk a cat' (348) – puts them into the husband's mouth, then refuses to affirm or deny them, while denouncing his right to think what she has coached him to think. The torment is not betrayal but uncertainty. Killing the fourth husband by creating what she insists was only the illusion of adultery is just a refinement of the tactic. To keep your secret is to hold your power. To withhold your self is to resist being possessed. Alisoun the entrepreneur, of course, offers her sexuality as a substitute for herself: 'Ye shul have queynte right ynogh at eve . . . I shrewe yow, but ye love it [not "me"] wel' (332, 446). Alisoun, meanwhile, makes herself 'a feyned appetit' (417).[19] Her husbands 'know' Alisoun in just the way that we and the pilgrims do: as an impenetrable performance which also signals its unreliability at every turn. At what point(s) in her climactic confrontation with Jankyn is she acting? 'I lay as I were deed', she says (796), but not so dead that she can't watch him reacting to her.

We have to resist the temptation to complete the text precisely because the temptation is so blatant. It is, after all, the one Alisoun uses so successfully on her husbands: I am/am not/am planning on/ never intend having an affair with Jankyn our clerk (check one). It is deceptively easy to invent a story to account for the demise of the fourth husband that the text will not necessarily deny. He could have died of jealousy, natural causes or murder. He could even have died of natural causes at the time he was about to be murdered![20] The multiplicity of possible stories allows us to read in the one we want, but it also prevents us from designating one of those as the 'true' story.

On a more sophisticated level, the Wife's rapid shifts of pose should prevent us from trying to decide which pose is the face and which the mask. It should, in other words, prevent us from doing what Oberembt does when he announces that 'behind all that persiflage in her monologue is a temperate woman espousing a cogent marital theology'.[21] Behind all that persiflage is more persiflage. God knows, it would solve a lot of problems if we could treat the 'wys womman' pose – as Malvern and Long also try to do – as only a parodic mask meant to seduce the male-chauvinist auditor. If that were the tactic, however, you would expect the mask to be dropped in time for sweet, non-sexist reason to triumph (as Oberembt thinks it has [300]). In fact, in both the *Prologue* and the *Tale*, the combative, virulent Wife gets the last – for now – word. The Alisoun who blesses Jankyn's soul (and probably his memory) at the end of the *Prologue* gives way immediately to the router of the Friar and the propounder of the *Tale*, which is announced as another demonstration of the necessity of female sovereignty. At the end of the *Tale* itself, the blessing of marital harmony gives way to the cursing of husbands. Both blessing and curse are part of a performance directed, literally at least, to an automatically estranged audience of twenty-eight men and two nuns. The case hardly allows for the possibility of full, let alone objective, disclosure.

This text does not allow a reader to choose whether the blessing or the curse is 'real' or which one has priority over the other. The *Tale*, after all, doesn't prove any simple case. The hag isn't necessarily the Wife's mouthpiece. The parting curse *can* be seen as a joke already discounted by the happy ending. Rather than trying to find the real Alisoun in this haystack of contradictions, we should see that the contradictions are the point. It solves many problems to pretend that the Wife is really heretical carnality or 'an equalitarian moral revolutionary'.[22] It solves many more, however, to assume that her secrets are indeed secret. On one level of the fiction, then, she is unknowable because her discourse is a screen; her life, like her birthmark, is referred to but never shown. As with the Great Soviet Encyclopedia, one assumes that the contradictory assertions must refer to some facts but those are almost certainly not the ones being stated. Her life, we might say, is a closed book; part of the point being, of course, that male authority cannot know the *privetee* of female experience.

On another level, however, the facts of her discourse do not refer to any actual events, only to the events of other discourses. What Alisoun has actually 'followed' are not her lusts, but her sources. If her performance is not consistent with the psychology of a single, coherent woman, it is consistent with the fears and obsessions of men writing about women. Her words are about other words, those of clerical antifeminism, about which she demonstrates the only truth available in that tautological system: it says what it says. She does, necessarily, what the *Roman* says she does. The text 'proves' what it is programmed to prove. It invents its object – however startlingly life-like that object may seem to be – just as Alisoun invents herself and her world. If she is what clerks say women are, then her husbands, the beasts, are what women say men are. Not surprisingly, the 'beasts' of both fantasies are very much alike, governed by the same desire to possess without being possessed. Alisoun is most like her clerkly inventors in wishing to define the other while exempting herself from counter-definition.

The clerkly author possesses his subject by 'glosyng' it, as Jankyn does, both verbally and sexually, to that animated text, Alisoun (509). Alisoun is Jankyn's book in the double sense of having been made out of it and being contained (defined, interpreted) in it. Like it, she is also his property, the thing he acquired along with 'al the lond and fee' (630) when Jankyn the would-be cleric became Jankyn the merchant and marital adventurer. He uses the book as an instrument of control through definition. Their marital conversation consists of his reading her identity to her, very much as she has earlier lectured her first three husbands. Sexual glossing gets Jankyn his property, by the same means that Alisoun got it before giving it to him. Textual glossing gives him the illusion of authority over it. The common thread linking clerks, wives, and merchants is, of course, acquisitiveness.[23]

It is important to see just how much Jankyn and Alisoun are the same person, aside from a minor difference in their *sely* instruments. One problem with Robertson's antifeminist reading of Alisoun, which privileges the authority of clerks over women and blames Alisoun for a constitutional unwillingness to heed that authority, is that it is a blow from a clerk – defrocked but still claiming scholarly authority and striking in defense of authority – that has made Alisoun deaf.[24] Her inability to hear is not inherent but induced, by clerks as much as by her own sinfulness. 'I was beten for a book, pardee!' (712). You cannot talk about that book, as Robertson tends to, as if its authority were abstract and beyond scrutiny; you have to talk about the use to which it is put. Jankyn, that conjunction of clerkly, commercial, and male sexual acquisitiveness, does three things to Alisoun: he beats her 'on every bon' (511), he 'glosses' her (509), and he reads to her (669–87). All three are methods of control. The violence of the blow is simply reading carried on by other means. 'Who wolde suppose / The wo that in my herte was, and pyne', says Alisoun, referring at this point only to the reading (786–87).

Like Alisoun, however, Jankyn is also constructed by his book. He speaks through it, it speaks for him. We never hear him use his own words until after she takes the book away from him. It gives his personal complaints the appearance of universality and objectivity; it makes him (*inter alia*, a fortune-hunter and a wife-beater) into the victim of his wife; and it allows him to go on claiming the authority of the orders he has renounced. Jankyn and his book form a closed circle of mutual reinforcement: his experience confirms its authority, its authority confirms his interpretation of that experience. *The Wife of Bath's Prologue and Tale* is notoriously a monologue full of other monologues, each of which requires the presence of a silenced other. Alisoun's harangue, the hag's sermon on *gentilesse*, Jankyn's reading are all monologues pretending to be dialogue. In each case, the speaker pronounces on the nature of the other while the other listens and groans. In each case, the voiced one tells the unvoiced that it is so because we, the authorities, say so. In this text, habitually, people do not talk to each other but to themselves.

As Jankyn reads, the book stands literally between himself and Alisoun, a physical as well as mental intermission. Naturally enough, Alisoun's rebellion consists of attacking the book and her final possession of Jankyn necessarily involves burning it: the would-be 'code user' literally breaking the code.[25] As Alisoun tells it, of course, getting the book out of the way produces – after a spasm of inarticulate rage – the magical transformation of both parties. Like the marriage of Dame Ragnell in the analogue, it breaks a spell, here releasing a loving husband and a devoted, solicitous wife. Neither of these creatures is ever seen, however, because they are absent from the clerical text out of which Alisoun has been made. There is no counterbook to 'Valerie and Theophraste', save perhaps for the one the Wife tries to make out of the story of Gawain and Ragnell in her *Tale*. And now, of course, Jankyn is gone and the Wife has returned to being what clerical authority says she must be. Through the gap Chaucer has induced in the discourse of antifeminism we are allowed to glimpse the possibility of a sexual relationship outside the logic of control and subjugation. Not surprisingly, perhaps, the tale Alisoun tells turns on the ability of women to evade control by evading definition.

IV. Alisoun's Text

The most striking thing about the women in *The Wife of Bath's Tale* is their combination of power and insubstantiality. The King abdicates the power of life and death to the Queen who passes it along to the hag. Both women are nameless, however – no longer Guenevere and Ragnell – like all the other women in the *Tale*. The nameless women show a remarkable tendency to flow into one another: the maiden who is the victim of the knight is displaced by the Queen who is his judge; she in turn is displaced by the hag on whom the Queen's power devolves; the hag becomes the knight's bride and, when assured of his submission, becomes a ravishable maiden.[26] As we have seen, twenty-four dancing ladies – women plural – are liable to turn into one hag – woman singular – who in turn speaks for all women. The court ladies mirror the Queen's responses both to the crime and the answer. The many individual replies to the knight's question merge into the one general reply. We cannot avoid seeing the women as aspects of one personality, avatars of one goddess, nor seeing that all the aspects are 'defined' by their relation to the knight. They are his victim, his judge, his salvation, his desire.

'Defined', in this case, does not mean controlled, since the women remain impenetrably mysterious even while playing their roles to (with? upon?) the knight. The knight rapes the maiden 'maugree hir heed' (887), but what her 'heed' is remains undefined, except perhaps through the actions of the hag who displaces her. But why does this hag want this knight, especially since he has been stripped of the name he bears in the analogues – he is not Gawain – as well as all the qualities that made his original desirable? The answer is available neither to him nor to us. Along with her name, the loathly lady has lost all external signs of identity: she no longer has relations (a brother who is a giant) nor location (in Gower's version, she is the Princess of Sicily), and her choice no longer has an explicit logic. She wants him because she wants him. We do not even know whether she is enchanter or enchanted. She is mysterious precisely because she is entirely self-contained. In the analogue what happens in the bed is self-revelation: the lady tells her name and her story, then she turns back into her real self. In the Wife's version, she turns into somebody else. It is seldom noticed that the chief function of the hag's curtain lecture is to deflect personal questions into general statements about nobility and old age, even as the hag avoids exactly identifying herself with the categories. She will be noble 'whan that I bigynne / To lyven vertuously' (1175–76): not quite yet, not quite certainly. As the knight is about to find out, she is not necessarily old. Her speech is not self-revelation; it displaces self-revelation, just as the general question of what women want displaces the particular question of what the maiden wants. Everyone recognizes that the knight's quest is for a non-answer to a non-question.[27] It is not often seen, however, that the non-question displaces real questions: it is a way that women avoid talking to men while pretending to explain themselves. What is the hag doing for all that long sermon? She is protecting her privacy, preserving her absence.

The knight's question is not, of course, his. A woman asks a question about women (in response to a crime against a woman) and another woman answers it, using the knight as a kind of ventriloquist's dummy. Simply because he is a man, he cannot know the answer. (This is, in every sense, a fool's errand.) He can only know what women tell him. As many critics have noted, the answer he receives is a public one, what the Queen and her ladies will accept, not necessarily what they believe.[28] None 'dar seye nay' (1019), which is not the same as saying yes, even if public affirmation (in the presence of men) could be trusted. The knight is left with little choice except to take it on faith: it is so because they seem to say so. And, of course, the 'right' answer is partly belied by the plethora of other answers, all partially endorsed by Alisoun, that the knight has previously received. It is most obviously belied by the hag's own submission – 'she obeyed hym in every thyng' (1255) – when she has obtained his.[29] The answer functions as a declaration of solidarity and exclusion. Women close ranks behind it, safe from having to reveal their individual answers. It is a means of securing absence.

Alisoun's *Tale*, I think, suggests that a woman's real connection is with other women. The hag knows what the Queen will accept. After all, they are aspects of the same personality. Women in the Wife's tale operate in the same way she conceives of clerics doing: they form a closed circle of discourse from within which they pronounce on themselves and on the other.[30] The knight, standing outside the circle, is compelled to accept their auctoritee: 'he / Constreyned was' (1070–71). The women who accept the answer compel him to marry the woman who gives the answer. They are a conspiracy – oddly enough, considering their source – of silence. As we should have learned from Alisoun's *Prologue*, the more she speaks the less she reveals.

The knight learns nothing from his experience except blind submission, though even a critic as astute as Susan Crane can talk of his being guided 'to change for the better'.[31] He learns to parrot the hag's answer without even seeing that it has any application to himself. He surrenders to her curtain lecture as silently as Pertelote submits to Chauntecleer's. He gives up the sovereignty because he is unable to choose: 'I do no fors the wheither of the two' (1234). His earlier reference to 'youre wise governance' (1231) is no more than the customary language of surrender. It doesn't even directly acknowledge that she has promised to 'fulfille youre worldly appetit' (1218). To the end of the story, he has no idea whom or even what he has married. He knows what he wants, beauty and submission, but not who has given them to him. He fails to learn partly because he is manifestly stupid, but also because he is male, and this text invites the most serious doubts about whether either sex can understand the other, except as a reflection of itself. In both the *Prologue* and *Tale*, the sexes can be reconciled by magic, not by education.

Women in this text are absent because, after all, a man wrote it, using texts by other men, which are necessarily about men's experience of women. The reality is elsewhere. With a nice doubleness, Chaucer shows us the two sexes as at once mirroring and mutually mysterious: ultimately not knowing one another and probably incapable of doing so, but longing to know, since being imprisoned in one's sexual identity is only a more generalized form of being imprisoned in one's self. Even Alisoun dreams of mutuality.

V. Alisoun's Non-entity

Let us not whitewash, however. Even Stalin, we must suppose, dreamed of being loved, like Milton's God. The most important fact about Jankyn is that he too is not there. Whatever the quality of the love Alisoun gave him, he did not survive it. Like virtually every other external thing in her life, he's absent. 'Vanysshed was this daunce, she nyste where.' However much Alisoun may be imprisoned by the discourse of male authority, she is still more imprisoned by her own isolation and cupidity. Her motto might well be that of Marlowe's Barabas: *'Ego mihimet sum semper proximus'*: roughly, 'I am always closest to myself'.[32]

The parallel with Barabas, not so great an associative leap as it might seem, reminds us of something more theologically serious than the sexual paranoia of celibate clerks: that the Wife's unreality – the dissolution of her past into fictions and her present into poses – also identifies her with privative evil. We do, in fact, arrive back where Robertson assures us we always do: at the doctrine of *caritas*. By a typical indirection, Chaucer leads us through the false problem of the 'evil' of women to the true problem of the evil of *cupiditas*. Like all the great Satans, including the Pardoner as well as Barabas or Iago, Alisoun is not so much an actor as an act, a mask without a face. In the great paradox that descends from Augustine and Origen into the orthodoxy of medieval Christianity, *malum est non ens*: evil is not-being; that is, it exists phenomenally without existing essentially, since it represents a turning away from not only the source of good but the source of reality, God as absolute Being. Evil is thus a deprivation, an absence. Satan's first satanic act, as in Milton's version (*Paradise Lost*, 5.853–66) is to deny his own birth, just as the first authority Alisoun rejects is Christ (9–23).[33] Satan's act of autonomy is the first step toward becoming the father of lies, the self-made creature of unreality. Having negated your essential being you can exist in the world only through appearances, as a protean shadow, taking on the form and voice of others. From the Pardoner down to Richardson's Lovelace, evil is linked with acting and mimicry.[34] You must keep talking, as Alisoun does, or you will vanish, as the Pardoner (symbolically at least) does.

In terms of this doctrine, Alisoun is a figure of evil precisely because she represents personality detached from any essential core, language detached from substantial referents. She's a balloon filled without air. All her waxing amounts to the multiplying of zero. *Amor* converted to the uses of *cupiditas* is, of course, necessarily barren, productive neither of love nor of life. When we define Alisoun in the present, we must speak almost entirely in terms of absence: no love, no friends, no children, no future. 'I have had my world as in my tyme' (473): the tense is past. As is widely recognized, the mode of the *Prologue* is elegy. Alisoun's world is defined by what is missing, dead, or unborn.

Unreality longs for reality and builds itself fantastic substitutes, a Pandemonium substitutes for Heaven. (The creation of substitutes for unsatisfactory reality is the underlying activity of both halves of the text.) An undercurrent of self-rejection pervades Alisoun's discourse. The woman of wealth, via the hag (1177–1206), praises virtuous poverty. 'Whan that I bigynne to lyven vertuously', then I will be noble, then I will be something. The more Alisoun denies love the more, in the cell of herself, she dreams of it. The implicit fairy tale of her life with Jankyn transforms itself into the explicit fairy tale of the hag and the knight (a fiction that will in turn breed other fictions in

the *Tales*: January and May, Chauntecleer and Pertelote). Her tale is a
parable not only of man's inability to know woman except carnally,
but also of the most aggressive forms of *cupiditas* – the knight's rape
of the maiden, the hag's purchase of the knight – converting magically
to love, just as the hag's flesh acquires the self-renewing power
of spirit.

The hag's transformation only compounds the sense of unreality
that goes with her being the *alter ego*, the distorted rewriting, of
Alisoun.[35] In this text, the logic of devotion to the flesh and the
material world ends in the attempt to deny their reality. *The Wife of
Bath's Tale* is a sustained figuration of the unreality of the material
world. What has the knight married: a beautiful young woman who
appeared to be a crone or a crone who appears to be a beautiful
woman? Whatever, it is a blessing without substance. When the
knight grants the hag the right to choose what she will be, she
chooses unreality. What is presented as self-determination is actually
a choice determined by the 'worldly appetit' (1218) of the other. To
control him by his desire she must be controlled, literally shaped, by
that desire.[36]

D. W. Robertson reminds us that Alisoun and the hag, faced with
the problems of aging and death, choose ' "renewal" through the
desires of the flesh [which] must necessarily prove to be illusory'.[37]
That, I would say, is almost exactly half the point. The *Prologue* and
Tale taken together force us to think in terms of two apparently
opposed forms of non-being: the imposed unreality of woman
glossed and defined by the desires, words, and authority of men
(what we can call Alisoun's political absence); but also the more
fundamental unreality of privative evil, which chooses the world of
illusion and thus generates its own unbeing (Alisoun's existential
absence). The hag is presented by Alisoun, deceptively, as a woman
speaking for other women, but she is also an elf-queen, a succubus,
offering in place of woman a ghostly substitute: the shadow of men's
desire and women's desire to be desired.[38] The *Tale*, like the *Prologue*,
is at once sinister and wistful, embodying both the action of *cupiditas*
and the dream that it will, somehow, transform itself into *caritas*,
from foul and loathsome to fair and loving. In the *Tale*, certainly,
the acquisition of beauty is inseparable from the renunciation of
sovereignty. If the hag chooses the renewal of the flesh, she chooses
it in a form – renewal through the gaining of love – that can easily
figure the desired renewal of the spirit. As always, the text is
multiple, not single.

It is not, I repeat, necessary to defend Alisoun in order to defend
women. The true case against her is not sexually linked. She is not
'right' because her husbands are wrong, any more than she is fertile

because her enemies are celibate. As her five husbands together demonstrate, lust and cupidity are human sins, not female ones. The Jankyn who marries an old wife for her money is, obviously, the moral equivalent of the young Alisoun. Like Becky Sharp, she is a sucker for the bargains of this world. Like Barabas, she is an embodiment of the curiously innocent wickedness of privative evil at play in its toyshop of the flesh. The absence of her *ens*, her essence, the evanescence of her goods, the loss up to which her life adds are qualities which apply to nearly all the pilgrims regardless of sex. The emptiness of economic man and woman, for whom all relationships are those of ownership, debt, and thralldom, is a property of the unstable world of material transaction. Her solitude and absence convey a fundamental comment on the values of the class of pilgrims to which she belongs, not least her chief accuser, that man of insubstantial substance, the Merchant.

The Wife of Bath's Prologue and Tale are about woman, but also about more than woman. They remind us of the illusory evil of women as imagined by clerical authority in order to remind us of what evil (in the Augustinian sense) really is. They parody an official interpretation of woman in order to remind us that interpretation creates the thing it pretends to describe. In doing so, they remind us of that fundamental problem of the *Canterbury Tales*: that of knowing the other who lies behind the other's performance. Alisoun's absence reminds us that Alisoun is in the eye of the beholder, and that her sins – especially the desire to control and define others – are also the sins of those who imagined her. When we think of Alisoun as a text, we are reminded that no woman has taken part in the creation of this 'woman'. I take that to be Chaucer's intricately ironized protest at the silencing of women in the official culture of which he was a part. But it is something more. Far from being what Wayne Shumaker once called him, 'a docile scholar', Chaucer is magisterially subversive.[39] This text is an authoritative warning about the dangers of authority. It is a sustained demonstration of the incompleteness of all texts and of the dangers of that necessary imaginative act we perform to complete them. We create the Alisoun we see, Chaucer's Alisoun is an absence.

Notes

1. D. W. ROBERTSON's famous discussion of the Wife as heretical 'exegete' and figure of carnality is in the *Preface to Chaucer* (Princeton, NJ: Princeton University Press, 1962), 317–31. ROBERT BURLIN's section on Alisoun is in *Chaucerian Fiction* (Princeton, NJ: Princeton University Press, 1977), 217–27 (the description of her as 'battered' is on p. 218). For a description of Alisoun

as a moderate social critic, see KENNETH OBEREMBT, 'Chaucer's Anti-Misogynist Wife of Bath', *Chaucer Review*, 10 (1976), 287–302. SHEILA DELANY's chapter, 'Strategies of Silence in the Wife of Bath's Recital', in *Medieval Literary Politics: Shapes of Ideology* (Manchester: Manchester University Press, 1990), 112–29, concludes with the insistence that the case of Cecily Chaumpaigne should be understood as literal rape (128–9). LOUISE FRADENBURG, 'The Wife of Bath's Passing Fancy', *Studies in the Age of Chaucer*, 8 (1986), 31–58, discusses the Wife as 'an image of the absent, the regressive, the heart's desire' (32) with primary reference to J. LACAN's 'God and the *Jouissance* of the Woman' in *Feminine Sexuality: Jacques Lacan and the École Freudienne*, ed. Juliet Mitchell and Jacqueline Rose (New York: Norton, 1982). WALTER LONG, 'The Wife of Bath as Moral Revolutionary', *Chaucer Review*, 20 (1986), 273–84, compares the Wife's objections to labelling of women with Mill (278–79) and quotes Mill on '"the sultan-like . . . sense of superiority" men have traditionally felt over women' (280). BARRIE STRAUSS, 'The Subversive Discourse of the Wife of Bath: Phallocentric Discourse and the Imprisonment of Criticism', *ELH*, 55 (1988), 527–54, draws heavily on LUCE IRIGARAY's *This Sex Which Is Not One*, trans. Catherine Porter with Carolyn Burke (Ithaca, NY: Cornell University Press, 1985), and on Julia Kristeva. See Strauss's note 11 (55). JOHN ALFORD, 'The Wife of Bath versus the Clerk of Oxford: What Their Rivalry Means', *Chaucer Review*, 21 (1986), 110 (my emphasis).

2. MARJORIE MALVERN, ' "Who Peynted the Leon, Tel Me Who?" Rhetorical and Didactic Roles Played by an Aesopic Fable in the *Wife of Bath's Prologue'*, *Studies in Philology*, 80 (1983), 238–52; BERNARD HUPPÉ, *A Reading of the 'Canterbury Tales'* (Albany, NY: State University of New York, 1964), 107–35; MARY CARRUTHERS, 'The Wife of Bath and the Painting of Lions', *PMLA*, 94 (1979), 209–22; DOROTHY COLMER, 'Character and Class in the *Wife of Bath's Tale'*, *JEGP*, 72 (1973), 329–39; DAVID AERS, *Chaucer, Langland and the Creative Imagination* (London: Routledge and Kegan Paul, 1980), 83–9, 146–52. PEGGY KNAPP, 'Alisoun Weaves a Text', *Philological Quarterly*, 65 (1986), 387–401; reprinted as 'Alisoun Looms' in Knapp's *Chaucer and the Social Contest* (London: Routledge, 1990), 114–28.

3. ROBERTSON (note 1), 330.

4. As HOPE WEISSMAN writes, 'With a characteristically late medieval richness of determination, Chaucer summons the materials of both experience and authority to supply the concrete details of the portrait' ('Antifeminism and Chaucer's Characterization of Women', in *Geoffrey Chaucer: A Collection of Original Articles*, ed. George Economou [New York: McGraw-Hill, 1975], 105).

5. LEE PATTERSON, ' "For the Wyves Love of Bath": Feminine Rhetoric and Poetic Resolution in the *Roman de la Rose* and the *Canterbury Tales'*, *Speculum*, 58 (1983), 656–95.

6. BERYL ROWLAND, 'On the Timely Death of the Wife of Bath's Fourth Husband', *Archiv*, 209 (1972–73), 273–82; D. J. WURTELE, 'Chaucer's Wife of Bath and the Problem of the Fifth Husband', *Chaucer Review*, 23 (1988), 117–28. On the marital customs of the land-holders, see MARY CARRUTHERS (note 2).

7. SUSAN CRANE, 'Alison's Incapacity and Poetic Instability in the Wife of Bath's Tale', *PMLA*, 102 (1987), 26.

8. MARSHALL LEICESTER, 'Of a Fire in the Dark: Public and Private Feminism in the *Wife of Bath's Tale'*, *Women's Studies*, 11 (1984), 157–78. The quotation is 175.

9. Line references are to *The Riverside Chaucer*, gen. ed. Larry Benson (Oxford: Oxford University Press, 1987). Unless otherwise indicated, parenthetical line numbers in the text refer to Ellesmere Fragment III. All other references are

by fragment and line number. I have also consulted the notes in *The Works of Geoffrey Chaucer*, ed. F. N. Robinson (Cambridge: Riverside, 1957), 697–704. PATTERSON (note 5), 657.

10. CAROLYN DINSHAW, 'Eunuch Hermeneutics', *ELH*, 55 (1988), 27. Dinshaw elaborates her version of the Wife as text in *Chaucer's Sexual Poetics* (Madison: University of Wisconsin Press, 1989), 113–31; CRANE (note 7), 20; JILL MANN, *Chaucer and Medieval Estates Satire* (Cambridge: Cambridge University Press, 1973); P. M. KEAN, *Chaucer and the Making of English Poetry* (London: Routledge and Kegan Paul, 1972), 217–18 (Pardoner), 275–76 (Wife); BURLIN (note 1), 226.

11. SUSAN SCHIBANOFF, 'The New Reader and Female Textuality in Two Early Commentaries on Chaucer', *Studies in the Age of Chaucer*, 10 (1988), 71–108, extends this body of observation by considering Chaucer as the possible originator of the glosses on *WBP&T* in the Ellesmere manuscript and Alisoun herself as a figure for the new, private reader. DELANY (note 1) discusses the problem of trying to construct the Wife as a 'resisting reader' of clerical antifeminism (112–29).

12. PATTERSON (note 5), 687.

13. PEGGY KNAPP, 'Alisoun and the Reappropriation of Tradition', *Chaucer Review*, 24 (1989), 45–52; WILLIAM BLAKE, 'Description Catalogue' (1809), in *Chaucer: The Critical Heritage, Volume I: 1385–1837*, ed. Derek Brewer (London: Routledge and Kegan Paul, 1978), 256.

14. The major sources mentioned here (Jerome, *Adversus Jovinianum*, Walter Map, the relevant passages of the *Roman de la Rose*, Gower's 'Tale of Florent', 'The Marriage of Sir Gawaine', 'The Weddynge of Sir Gawain and Dame Ragnell') are given in *Sources and Analogues of Chaucer's 'Canterbury Tales'*, ed. W. F. Bryan and Germaine Dempster (Chicago: University of Chicago Press, 1941). The section concerning the *Wife of Bath's Prologue and Tale*, 207–68, is edited by B. J. Whiting. The Wife's scriptural references are noticed by ROBINSON (note 1), 697–704. The notes to this text in the *Riverside Chaucer*, 864–74, record much the same body of information. SCHIBANOFF's discussion (note 11) of the glosses in the Egerton and Ellesmere MSS, indicates that Chaucer's earliest editors recognized that the *Prologue* and *Tale* are a tissue of intertextual references (see especially 71–92). The argument for Matheolus as the source of the passages usually ascribed to Deschamps is made by ZACHARIAS P. THUNDY, 'Matheolus, Chaucer, and the Wife of Bath', in *Chaucerian Problems and Perspectives: Essays Presented to Paul E. Beichner*, ed. Edward Vasta and Zacharias Thundy (Notre Dame: University of Notre Dame Press, 1979), 24–58. ROBINSON (note 1) offers 'la mere' as source for the wife in his notes to lines 576, 583 (701).

15. Chaucer's only female source, Marie de France, whose fable of the lion is referred to at III.692, is not, in the original, concerned with women or marriage, see her *Fables*, ed. A. Ewant and R. C. Johnston (Oxford: Oxford University Press, 1966), 30–1.

16. PEGGY KNAPP, 'Alisoun of Bath and the Reappropriation of Tradition', *Chaucer Review*, 24 (1989), 45–52.

17. See the Riverside edition's note on this line (870).

18. In the case of this text at least, I disagree strongly with ELAINE TUTTLE HANSEN's assertion that 'the Chaucerian poet . . . finally invokes the myth of female difference, through his representation of women and Woman' ('Fearing for Chaucer's Good Name', *Exemplaria*, 2 [1990], 33). The Wife, as

(mis-)interpreter of her own text, mystifies the difference. The text minimizes practical differences, even while insisting on the ultimate unknowability of female experience to a male author. You can, of course, insist, as Hansen does, that this is a case of Chaucer suppressing 'the very real threats to the male poet' (33) posed by a recognition of his similarities to women. Here, however, it is more obviously a case of the author revealing and the character concealing.

19. Alisoun's substitution of her commodified body for her self is noted by STRAUSS (note 1), 535–6, and by AERS (note 2), 149–50.

20. See WURTELE (note 6), 117–28.

21. OBEREMBT (note 1), 295.

22. LONG (note 1), 282.

23. I think Dinshaw confuses the issue when she argues that 'the appropriative nature of glossing has a particularly masculine valence'. As Dinshaw concedes in the next paragraph, the Wife is 'a glossator herself' (*Chaucer's Sexual Poetics* [note 10], 123). Appropriation, whether of Alisoun by Jankyn or of the knight by the hag, is what Alisoun's text is all about.

24. Jankyn's name ('Johnny') is the diminutive of John, as in 'Sir John', the cant name for a priest, applied to both the Monk (VII.1929) and the Nun's Priest (VII.2810) by Harry. See the Riverside gloss on 'John' (1319). Alisoun refers to Jankyn's reading from the book of wicked wives as 'prech[yng]' (641).

25. I have borrowed the description of Alisoun as a frustrated code user from PHILIP WEST, 'The Perils of Pauline Theology: The Wife of Bath's Prologue and Tale', *Essays in Arts and Sciences*, 8 (1979), 8.

26. BRITTON J. HARWOOD notices a somewhat simpler version of this pattern: 'Having been dishonored, the maiden becomes a hag. When honor is vested in her once more, she becomes a maiden again': 'The Wife of Bath and the Dream of Innocence', *Modern Language Quarterly*, 33 (1972), 272.

27. See, for example, DELANY (note 1): 'It is what logicians term a non-question, a pseudo-problem' (125).

28. See CRANE (note 7), 23; also ROBERT KASKE, 'Chaucer's Marriage Group', in *Chaucer the Love Poet*, ed. Jerome Mitchell and William Provost (Athens: University of Georgia Press, 1973), 52.

29. The most famous explication of the contradiction between the hag's answer and her later behavior is by CHARLES A. OWEN, 'The Crucial Passages in Five of the *Canterbury Tales*: A Study in Irony and Symbol', in *Chaucer: Modern Essays in Criticism*, ed. Edward Wagenknecht (Oxford: Galaxy, 1959), 259–64.

30. ROBERT STURGIS, 'The *Canterbury Tales'* Women Narrators: Three Traditions of Female Authority', *Modern Language Studies*, 13 (Spring 1983), 41–51, thinks benignly that Alisoun draws other women into 'an ever-expanding community of women bound by female solidarity against male domination' (45). There are, however, no women present who could be drawn into an alliance of wives. In that sense, Alisoun addresses a phantom audience. Their function, like that of Jankyn's authorities, is to allow the speaker to declare herself a majority. Given the make-up of the pilgrim audience, exclusion is surely more the point than inclusion. Alisoun's claims of universality are a projection of solipsistic isolation: the mirror-image of 'clerkes . . . in hire oratories'.

31. Crane (note 7), 23; see also Knapp, *Chaucer and the Social Contest* (note 2): 'Embedded deep in this story is the untraditional idea that men must learn from women' (127).

32. Christopher Marlowe, *The Jew of Malta* (1.1.192), in *The Complete Plays*, ed. J. B. Steane (Harmondsworth: Penguin, 1969), 354.

33. For Satan's speech declaring himself 'self-begot, self-raised' (5.860), see *The Poems of John Milton*, ed. James Holly Hanford (New York: Ronald, 1953), 332.

34. I summarize this tradition and some of its literary effects in 'The Unbeing of the Overreacher: Proteanism and the Marlovian Hero', *Modern Language Review*, 84 (1989), 1–17.

35. Strauss (note 1), discusses the hag's transformation as a 'complex doubling of [the knight's] desire' (545); he does not see her reality, 'he sees his desire' (546).

36. Warren Ginsburg, 'The Lineaments of Desire: Wish-Fulfillment in Chaucer's Marriage Group', *Criticism*, 25 (1983), 203, citing Augustine's belief that 'language has its origin in desire', argues that 'ultimately the Wife's desires make her a metaphor for language itself'.

37. Robertson (note 1), 381.

38. On the incubus and succubus as medieval figures, see the Riverside editor's note to III.880 on page 873.

39. Wayne Shumaker, 'Alisoun in Wanderland: A Study in Chaucer's Mind and Literary Method', *ELH*, 18 (1951), 88.

7 The Powers of Silence: The Case of the Clerk's Griselda*

ELAINE TUTTLE HANSEN

Hansen reads the subordination of Griselda to Walter in the *Clerk's Tale* as at once an instance of the 'powerlessness of real women in history' and, more significantly, as the undoing of male control over behaviour that takes patriarchal idealizations of 'wommanhede' to the limits of comprehensibility and beyond. The Clerk-narrator's shifting loyalties to both the male and female protagonists in his Tale bespeak, Hansen argues, the uncertainties of Chaucer's own attitudes 'toward the problematic issues of gender and marital conflict', and what Hansen sees as the string of jocular or unconvincing interpretations of his Tale that the Clerk appends at its conclusion only serves to trivialize and distance these issues. Beyond the Clerk's desire to escape the contamination of a womanhood that he is forced to identify with on several levels, Hansen posits the evasiveness of Chaucer himself, wishing to step out of the problems of 'sexual politics and gendered poetics' into a realm of transcendent aesthetic 'play'. Unlike the majority of critics in this volume therefore, Hansen argues for Chaucer's identification with the patriarchal attitudes of many of his tellers, rather than for a Chaucer who stands back from and criticizes such tellers. For further discussion of Hansen's work, see my Introduction, pp. 7–8.

> To take a stand would be to upset the beautiful balance of the game.
> (Richard A. Lanham, 'Chaucer's *Clerk's Tale*:
> The Poem Not the Myth')

To most Chaucerians, it is by now either commonplace or irrelevant to point out that the *Clerk's Tale*, like so many of Chaucer's poems, situates a strong female character in what one modern editor describes as 'a context of masculine authoritarianism'.[1] Recognizing this situation does not seem to resolve the interpreters' fundamental

---

* Reprinted from ELAINE TUTTLE HANSEN, *Chaucer and the Fictions of Gender* (Berkeley: University of California Press, 1992), pp. 188–207.

confusion about the Tale's meaning. This confusion, in fact, is one of the few things that a number of critics can agree upon: whatever its specific significance, this poem appears to many to be bound up with its ambiguities and contradictions, the insolubility of its many problems.[2] The force of gender conflict in the Tale is thus at once recognized and neutralized; if Chaucer takes no definitive position on the victimization of women that he so clearly depicts, then we need not raise charged and difficult questions about misogyny and great Western art, and we can instead contemplate 'the beautiful balance of the game', a playful, aesthetic foreclosure of the problems of sexual politics and gendered poetics.

Here I want to recharge the question of the impenetrability of the *Clerk's Tale* with further consideration of the nature of 'masculine authoritarianism' in the poem. The text offers readers a fundamentally equivocal – and hence rich and compelling – confrontation with patriarchal power, a confrontation necessitated and implicated by the literary project foregrounded in all the Chaucerian fiction I have examined thus far: the representation of a male author telling, with great verbal skill and studied, multivalent ambiguities, the story of a female character. In the first part of my discussion, focusing on the female character and her multiple, slippery significations, I argue that the tale of patient Griselda addresses central questions about women and power and articulates a clear paradox. Woman's insubordination is, as our lexicon suggests, a derivative of her subordination. In the second half of the chapter, focusing on the representation of the male author, I ask again what kind of men, in Chaucerian fiction, choose to tell such stories about women, and why and how such men might well prefer to play games and make jokes rather than take a stand.

'This is ynogh, Grisilde myn.'

(IV.365, 1051)

From one point of view, the plot of Griselda's story demonstrates how a woman may rise to the highest position of hegemonic power, becoming the honored wife of a wealthy lord and a co-ruler of his kingdom, through her archetypally acceptable behavior: utter submissiveness and essential silence. Griselda is a complicated figure of both class mobility and the classless (or cross-class), feminized ideals of Christian thinking. She succeeds in rising from poorest peasant to ruling aristocrat – and at another level even serves, the Clerk reminds us, as an allegorical figure for the patient Christian soul – by living up to her culture's image of perfect femininity, by willfully accepting and even reveling in the powerlessness of her position.³ To some modern readers, of course, Griselda may not in this way represent a positive model of female power, but rather the kind of prescriptive antifeminist propaganda for which the medieval period is well known.⁴ Even from the naturalistic point of view that the Clerk sometimes at least insists on, the happy ending brings the heroine the dubious reward of permanent union with a man whom the Clerk, embellishing his sources, has characterized as a sadistic tyrant, worst of men and cruelest of husbands (although not, he suggests, unrealistic or atypical in this regard). The Clerk's peculiar handling of the Griselda story both supports and complicates such responses by exploring the implications of Griselda's paradoxical position as a woman: the fact that she attains certain kinds of power by embracing powerlessness; the fact that she is strong, in other words, because she is so perfectly weak. The Tale suggests on one hand that Griselda is not really empowered by her acceptable behavior, because the feminine virtue she embodies in welcoming her subordination is by definition both punitive and self-destructive. On the other hand, the Tale reveals that the perfectly good woman *is* powerful, or at least potentially so, insofar as her suffering and submission are fundamentally insubordinate and deeply threatening to men and to the concepts of power and gender identity upon which patriarchal culture is premised.

The *Clerk's Tale* specifies early in the plot that even legitimate exercises of direct power only endanger a woman's well-being. Immediately after his description of Walter and Griselda's marriage, the Clerk, following his sources, points out how swiftly and remarkably the good peasant girl is transformed into the perfect noblewoman. In the space of a few stanzas (393–441), we learn that after her marriage Griselda is beloved by Walter's people and famed in many regions; people travel to Saluzzo, we are told, just to see her. Not merely a paragon of 'wyfly hoomlinesse', she also serves the public interest (the 'commune profit', 431) by acting in her husband's absence as a peerless adjudicator who settles all disputes with her 'wise and rype wordes' (438). The passage seems in its own right to document Griselda's innate 'virtue' – but the root of the word 'virtue' itself, from the Latin for 'male person', signals what the *Clerk's Tale* subsequently affirms: a *virtuous woman*, the stuff of folk tales and saints' legends, is a contradiction, a semantic anomaly, a threat to the social order and to the stability of gender difference and hierarchy.

Walter, it appears, recognizes part of this threat right away. Griselda's public virtue, her ability to exert a power at once masculine in kind and superhuman in degree, would seem to vindicate the sovereign's willful choice of an unsuitable bride beyond his wildest dreams; people soon say, according to the Clerk, that Griselda is literally a godsend. But Walter's decision to torture and humiliate her as a wife and mother comes, according to the narrative, after she has been acclaimed as a saintly ruler, and so the narrative sequence implies on the contrary that such virtue in a woman only provokes male aggression. A woman's public powers, even if they are conferred upon her through her husband and divinely sanctioned, cannot be integrated with her proper identity as a female and a wife. Griselda's supposedly unusual and seemingly innate ability to rule wisely and well, to pass good judgments and speak in ways that men admire and respect, to assume, that is, the power and position normally assigned to the best of men, fails to empower her or enable her to escape her subordinate gendered status. Her situation may in this way remind us of a point made by modern feminist analyses of history: the occasional existence of a strong, wise, and successful female in a position of power is the exception that proves the rule; the token Virgin Mother or queen or bourgeois female entrepreneur does not alter the material position of most women or the conventional definition of the feminine. To prove her 'wommanhede', Griselda must suffer and submit; the more obviously unsuitable part of her virtue – her allegedly inherent but nevertheless unnatural manliness and power – must be punished and contained.

One reason why Griselda's public virtues must be controlled, why the good woman of any social class must be defined as silent and submissive, seems patent. If a peasant woman can so easily rule as well as a noble man – or even better – then Walter's birthright and the whole feudal system on which it depends are seriously threatened. This realization is surely part of the Clerk's meaning when he remarks, near the end of the tale, that it would be 'inportable', or intolerable, unbearable, if real wives behaved like Griselda. His comment seems intended to heighten the pathos and abstraction of his portrait of Griselda and to express yet again his alleged sympathy with her situation as a woman; it also suggests, however, his sympathy with Walter and his understanding that it is precisely Griselda's saintliness, her superhuman – or inhuman – goodness, her feminine ability to be just what he asks her to be, that (rightly, or at least understandably) enrages her husband. For as the tale goes on to disclose, if Walter is at first shown up, defeated, and made powerless by the position and authority he hands his wife, which she so effortlessly and successfully wields, he is again all but undone by the self-abasement that he then demands and that she, ever obedient and adaptable to her situation, so easily and successfully performs. Galled by the unbearable way in which this woman eludes his tyranny by refusing to resist and define it, he can only torture her again and again, seeking to determine her elusive identity as well as his own, to find the Other in Griselda, someone he can master in order to find himself.

The series of seemingly unmotivated trials proving Griselda's worth also emphasizes that the better Griselda is, the more she must suffer, or that the more she suffers the better she must be. While this principle is consistent with medieval Christian thought, we shall see at the close of the tale that one logical conclusion of this potentially fatal prescription for female virtue proves troubling. The end of the heroine's suffering must in a sense spell the end of her virtue, and what voice Griselda has is silenced, her story finished, when Walter finally stops torturing her. And what makes Walter stop, after the third trial, may be his eventual understanding of the paradoxical sense in which this woman continues to win, in venerable Christian fashion, by losing so fully and graciously to a tyrannical man.

The last scene of the tale becomes crucial to our understanding of the complex interaction of the subordination and insubordination of the female; Griselda almost beats Walter to the draw. She has been called back to the palace to clean it up for Walter's second wedding, and, as the nobles sit down to dinner, Walter calls the old wife over to ask how she likes his beautiful new one. But in the preceding stanza we have learned that Griselda is already busy praising the girl and her brother 'So wel that no man koude hir prise amende' (1026). When Walter, who hasn't apparently noticed what she's up to, foolishly invites her to come center stage for a moment, in her rags, Griselda seizes the opportunity to protest and celebrate, at the same time, her own treatment at Walter's hands. First she wishes him well of his lovely young bride; at the same time that she once again accepts and cooperates in her own abasement here, she subtly praises herself, born again into better circumstances, and engages in the competition between women, even between mother and daughter, that her culture enforces. She goes on to warn Walter not to torment the maiden as he has tormented 'mo' ('others'), as she tactfully puts it; Griselda predicts that the well-born creature could not endure what the poor one could. Her strategy recalls her earlier move when she responded to banishment with the longest, most pathetic speech in the poem (814–89), but this time Walter knows better than to let his patient wife have the floor for more than one stanza. He is at this point said to 'rewen upon hire wyfly stedfastnesse' (1050), and while the chief sense of 'rewen upon' is 'to feel pity or compassion for', we may also think of the more familiar sense of the verb, one which was also current in Middle English: 'to regard or think of . . . with sorrow or regret, to wish that (something) had never taken place or existed'.[5]

Walter must indeed regret Griselda's surpassing wifely steadfastness, because whichever way he turns, it all but defeats his lordly urge to dominate. When in the next stanza he tells Griselda, '"This is ynogh, Grisilde myn"', we are reminded that he said this once before, when she gave her initial promise (365), and in retrospect the repetition may underline for Walter the dangers inherent in the way Griselda from the beginning sought to exceed his demands for wifely subordination. In setting the conditions for their marriage, he asked only that she would do what he wished, and never contradict his will. She promised far more: a perilous merging of wills ('But as ye wole youreself, right so wol I' [361]), which would in fact imply her full knowledge of his will and thus destabilize the power differential and difference between them; and a surrender of her own life ('In werk ne thoght, I nyl yow disobeye, /For to be deed, though me were looth to deye' [363–64]), which again would defeat his intention to keep her, alive, under his thumb. When, at the end of the story, he sets the limit to her excessive self-abasement, which is beginning to be coupled with the self-assertion it always entails, we cannot be sure whether he intends to call a halt to her suffering or to her emergent powers of subversive speech – powers paradoxically dependent on his continued oppression of her. When he goes on to seal Griselda's lips with kisses, her reaction is telling. She is so stunned, the Clerk says, that for a moment she cannot hear Walter's astonishing concession that she has finally proved herself in his eyes: 'She herde nat what thyng he to hire seyde; / She ferde as she had stert out of a sleep' (1059–60). Griselda's temporary deafness and stupor represent, I suggest, her unwillingness to hear that the nightmare is over. She knows that any power she has lies only in continuing to excel at suffering, that she can speak only to assent to being silenced, and that the promise of a happy ending precludes her potential for martyred apotheosis, and forces her to awaken into the reality of her material, gendered powerlessness.

In the second half of this chapter I shall explore what happens after this climactic moment, in the multiple endings of the *Clerk's Tale*, as the Clerk himself confirms Griselda's powerlessness at many levels, but let me conclude this section by underscoring some implications of the reading I have just offered. Griselda has threatened to escape Walter's tyranny by willfully refusing to resist it, and it is possible to argue that he keeps testing her because given his view of selfhood and power, her behavior can only seem to him unmotivated, implausible, irritating, and even inhuman. As the Clerk says after the second trial, Walter 'wondred' at his wife's patience; if he hadn't known better, he would have thought that she took some perverse or treacherous delight in seeing her children murdered (687–95), and modern readers have frequently complained that Griselda was not a good enough mother. In one way Griselda's behavior is certainly both perverse and treacherous, not because she fails to protect her children against paternal infanticide and thus to live up to ideals (and realities) of motherhood, but because she lives up all too well to certain ideals of womanhood and thus makes manifest their latent powers. Walter cannot and does not solve the mystery or negate the threat that her perfect womanly behavior poses; he merely stops trying to do so and stops giving his wife the chance to act in ways that he cannot understand or control.

Just as she remains a mystery and a threat to Walter, so too Griselda remains an unresolved problem for the Clerk and for his audiences. The *Clerk's Tale* suggests, and generations of modern interpreters confirm, that Griselda is a 'humanly unintelligible' entity, as one critic puts it, comprehensible and coherent only at the allegorical level that the Clerk at once entertains and undermines.[6] In an unusual way, the inhumanity and perhaps inhumaneness of Griselda's perfect femininity confirms that the human is often posited as equivalent to the masculine in the symbolic order that reaches from the Western European Middle Ages into more recent centuries. At the same time, the problem she presents – the unintelligibility of the perfectly good woman, or perhaps of any woman – is the most threatening thing about her. Griselda's embodiment of the archetypally feminine position thus not only insists on the absence and silence and powerlessness of real women in history but also marks again the limits of power for masculine authority (Walter), for the male author (the Clerk), and for the audience attempting to fix the meaning of the female character in the tale.

Grisilde is deed, and eek hire pacience.

(IV.1177)

Viewed as a poem about either a woman's subversive silence or her silenced subversion, the *Clerk's Tale* thus affirms two conclusions about the history of masculine and feminine power in Western culture. It suggests that 'maleness', as Catharine MacKinnon has put it, has often been perceived as 'a form of power that is both omnipotent and non-existent, an unreal thing with very real consequences'.[7] It also explains why Woman, identified as absence, is a fearsome ideal for both real women and masculine presence. Turning the focus of my reading to the Clerk now, I want to suggest that the oft-noted and characteristic ambiguity of the tale is most fruitfully read as a reflex of his position as a male story-teller, which turns out to be much the same here, where the narrator is an unbeneficed cleric writing in a specifically religious mode and explicitly translating from Latin, as when he is a secular court poet translating from the vernacular. To support and flesh out this claim, it is possible to compare the subtle Clerk of the *Canterbury Tales* with one narrator who exemplifies the coyness, insecurity, and playful evasiveness that we see in the narrators of all the earlier dream-visions and *Troilus and Criseyde*: the poet of the *Legend of Good Women*.

   The *Clerk's Tale* and the *Legend of Good Women* are not, as far as I know, frequently compared, but the comparison is in fact indirectly suggested within the *Canterbury Tales*, where the Legends are invoked in the preface to the *Man of Law's Tale*, a poem that, in the most common ordering of the Tales, comes right before the *Wife of Bath's Tale*, to which the Clerk in turn is responding. The link between the *Man of Law's Tale* and the *Clerk's Tale* is reinforced by the fact that both are female saints' lives, potentially or actually bracketing the Wife's monstrous tale of feminine misrule. The Clerk may emphasize this point with his two allusions to the Man of Law's heroine, Constance: one when Walter finally admits that Griselda is 'constant as a wal' (1047), and one when the Clerk says that we should all be, like Griselda, 'constant in adversitee' (1146). And even if we read the tales in another order, or discount the dramatic interaction between tellers altogether, the analogies between Griselda in the *Canterbury Tales* and the female saints of the *Legend of Good Women* are obvious. All these women are represented as archetypally passive. They put the love of a man above all other responsibilities, even above life itself. As a direct consequence of this love they endure great suffering. (The heroines of the earlier poem almost all die; Griselda's survival, at least until the *Lenvoy de Chaucer* proclaims her demise, may thus indicate either a flaw in her goodness, or the story's need, like Walter's, to keep her alive in order to punish and contain her perfection.) The unremarked similarities between the men who tell this kind of story, the narrator of the *Legend* and the Clerk of Oxenford, are equally obvious and perhaps more subtly interesting, and three prominent features of their performances warrant comparison: the ostensive circumstances under which they tell their stories, the changes they make in their sources, and their closural strategies.

   In both the *Legend of Good Women* and in the *Canterbury Tales*, the audience is made privy to specific circumstances or preconditions, outside and prior to the narratives of good women, that occasion each act of story-telling and hence oblige us to speculate about the dramatized motives and attitudes of both the poet/dreamer of the earlier poem and the Clerk of Oxenford, and to see each narrator's voiced personality as part of the meaning of his fiction. In the

Canterbury Tales, not in a dream but in the framing matter of his tale, the Clerk, like the narrator of the *Legend*, is commanded to tell a story – 'Telle us som murie thyng of aventures' (15) – by the Host, a figure who like Cupid in the dream assumes godlike powers of judgment and behaves like a tyrant. The Host first makes fun of the Clerk's unaggressive, even effeminate behavior: 'Ye ryde as coy and stille as dooth a mayde / Were newe spoused, sittynge at the bord' (2–3). He reminds the Clerk that he agreed to submit to the Host's authority when he entered into the 'pley' (10). The Clerk's professional status is also underscored by the Host's prohibitions against an overly didactic or boring tale in the 'heigh style' associated with learned clerks (18). In the *Wife of Bath's Prologue* (separated from the *Clerk's Tale* only by the *Friar's* and *Summoner's Tales*), clerks in general, again like the poet/dreamer of the *Legend of Good Women*, have already been associated with and castigated for their literary antifeminism. The Clerk appears to accede more meekly to the tyrant's commands than the dreamer does, just as we would expect from the quiet, virtuous, willing learner introduced in the *General Prologue*. But even before the tale proper begins, the coy Clerk also quietly defies the Host's orders by translating, within an ostensibly disparaging framework ('Me thynketh it a thyng impertinent' [54]) almost all of Petrarch's 'prohemye' to the story. This is presumably just the kind of elevated, clerkly fare that the Host hoped to forestall, and its inclusion clearly suggests that this Clerk has his own share of the impertinence he displaces onto Petrarch, that crafty impudence associated with others of his profession throughout the *Canterbury Tales*.

If we are obliged to recognize even before we begin to listen to their stories that both the Clerk and the poet/dreamer of the *Legend of Good Women* have somewhat comparable axes to grind with specific reference to a male figure of alleged sexual and literary authority, then their subsequent representations of good women confirm the wary reader's suspicions that, as in all literature, bias and resentment and special pleading color the stories. The Clerk, as we shall see, disguises himself and his motives more cleverly than the poet/dreamer of the *Legend* (or other story-tellers, like the Wife of Bath and the Pardoner); he is so discreet, in fact, that at least one modern critic sees his performance as 'a rarefied act of literary-critical wit', executed not in the 'voiced style' of the other Canterbury pilgrims but in the manner of Petrarch himself, as 'man *of letters*, a posited ideal character, created, displayed, and caught only in the act of writing'.[8] This argument may disclose the Clerk's intentions quite accurately, but the alleged neutrality of the man of letters does not stand up under close inspection of the minor additions and revisions the Clerk makes to his two apparent sources, Petrarch's Latin version of Boccaccio's Griselda story and an anonymous French translation of Petrarch. In one early addition, for instance, the Clerk aims a direct blow at the Wife of Bath by supplementing the original description of Griselda with these lines: 'No likerous lust was thurgh hire herte yronne. / Wel ofter of the welle than of the tonne / She drank . . .' (214–16). No such comment is found in either the Latin or French version of the story; it recalls to attentive listeners or readers the Wife's self-proclaimed drinking and sexual habits and her memorable observation that 'A likerous mouth moste han a likerous tayl' (III.466). In light of the insults that the Wife hurled at clerks as a profession and at her Janekyn in particular, the Clerk's allusion cannot be accidental or innocent; and so too the subject of his tale – a patient, submissive married woman who is faithful to one husband despite his insufferable exercise of *maistrie* – must be interpreted by the audiences of the *Tales* as a central part of the interpersonal, voiced drama of the poem as a whole.

In another set of additions and revisions, the Clerk's strategy may again be profitably compared to the narrator's in the *Legend of Good Women*. As I have argued elsewhere, alterations in all of the legends consistently reshape the heroines into figures like the narrator's Cleopatra, less active, aggressive, and passionate, or like his Thisbe, less noble, more flawed, and more feminine.[9] So too, as J. Burke Severs has documented, Walter in the Chaucerian version is 'more obstinately wilful, more heartlessly cruel', while Griselda's 'gentleness, her meekness, her submissiveness' are more pronounced.[10] Together, these changes, like many of the alternations in the Legends, call attention to the heroine's feminine powerlessness with respect to a ruthless, self-centered, all but omnipotent man with whom she herself purports to be in love, and hence to her victimization; Griselda's suffering, no matter how we view its signification, arises specifically from the actions of a cruel, deliberate, and decidedly male oppressor, and the war between the sexes is on again. At the same time, the Clerk's version of the Griselda story, like the poet/dreamer's treatments of his good women (and his bad ones), stresses the heroine's archetypal femaleness, as Petrarch certainly does not. Note, for instance, this minor change in Walter's motivation: according to the Clerk, what he is seeking and testing in his wife is not her patience or obedience or ability to live up to her vows but her 'wommanhede'. Whereas in Petrarch (as in the anonymous French version) Walter is said to admire her *virtutem eximiam supra sexum supraque etatem* (a virtue beyond her sex and age),[11] the Clerk gives us Walter (here like Troilus) 'Commendynge in his herte hir wommanhede, / And eek hir vertu, passynge any wight / Of so yong age' (239–41). The translation effectively alters the entire thrust of the passage; Griselda still transcends her youth, but notably she does not transcend the expected limitations of gender. Instead, she exemplifies, first and foremost, what has become an almost holy (or mock-holy) ideal in the *Clerk's Tale* as in the *Legend of Good Women*: the abstraction of certain gender-specific characteristics into the ideal state of 'wommanhede'. After Griselda passes her last test, Walter reiterates his motivation: ' "I have doon this deede / For no malice, ne for no crueltee, / But for t'assaye in thee thy wommanheede" ' (1073–75). Again his self-justifying claim, original to the Clerk's version (and in defiance of the Clerk's subsequent injunctions), brings Griselda into line with the heroines of the Legends as type and embodiment, if not caricature, of the idealized medieval good woman.

In another set of even more obvious additions to his source materials, his own intrusive comments on the characters' behavior, the Clerk also underscores the issues of gender difference and marital conflict so central to the *Legend of Good Women* and so common in the *Canterbury Tales*. Just as Walter celebrates Griselda for her 'wommanhede', the Clerk repeatedly notes that Walter's behavior is typical of a certain type of 'housbonde' or 'wedded' man (698, 622) who needlessly tries his 'wyf' (452, 461) and her 'wyfhod' (699; note that in this line 'wyfhod' is mentioned before 'stedefastnesse', just as in lines 239–40 'wommanhede' comes before 'vertu'). In another original comment, after drawing the standard analogy between Griselda and Job in line 932, the Clerk observes:

> . . . but as in soothfastnesse,
> Though clerkes preise wommen but a lite,
> Ther kan no man in humblesse hym acquite
> As womman kan, ne kan been half so trewe
> As wommen been, but it be falle of newe.
>
> (934–38)

This particular moral to the story, just one of many we will be offered, is found nowhere in Chaucer's sources, but the superiority of women to men, especially in terms of humility and fidelity, is the same highly unoriginal point that the narrator of the *Legend of Good Women* has been commanded to make. The qualifying, tonally odd turn at the end of the Clerk's comment – no man can be as humble or half as true as woman can, unless it has just happened recently – is also reminiscent of the odd jokes that the poet/dreamer often throws off at the end of his legends. Here and there such jests may indicate, like a knowing wink of the eye, the speaker's amused

131

distance from the *querelle des femmes* and/or his actual loyalties. Moreover, the Clerk's implicit separation of himself from those other clerks who 'preise wommen but a lite' is, I suggest, part of his attempt to show himself sympathetic to the cause of women, even at the expense of professional solidarity. So too in an earlier intrusion he poses a rhetorical question to the female members of his audience: 'But now of wommen wolde I axen fayn / If thise assayes myghte nat suffise?' (696–97; compare the narrator of the *Legend*'s 'And trusteth, as in love, no man but me', 2561). The Clerk's strategy in this kind of commentary is remarkably similar to the poet/dreamer's attempts in the *Legend of Good Women* to ingratiate himself with supposed women listeners and demonstrate his unique sympathy with their gender. But despite his efforts to deny that he is the epitome of 'clerkhede', to condemn needless male cruelty and to sympathize with Griselda as archvictim of patriarchal tyranny, the Clerk is finally not able or willing to distance himself from a specifically masculine attitude toward feminine virtue.

The fact that the Clerk's perspective is not morally universal, as many modern critics have assumed, not actually sympathetic to women, and not artistically neutral is dramatically confirmed at the conclusion of the tale, where what we might call the excess of endings has the same effect as the apparent incompletion of the *Legend of Good Women*.[12] Although they appear to close in such radically different ways, both endings are definitely and strategically equivocal, designed to compound readers' uncertainties about the meaning of the narratives, about the narrators' respective attitudes toward the purposes of stories and story-telling, and especially about Chaucer's attitudes toward the problematic issues of gender and marital conflict. In the case of the *Clerk's Tale*, the story-teller addresses the problem for men that he has discerned in the story of the good woman by shifting his ground, dismantling the fiction of feminine virtue by at once denying in various ways that Griselda is a woman and reaffirming that he is a man.

There are several endings to the *Clerk's Tale*. The narrative itself first concludes with a completely closed and happy ending: Walter and Griselda live 'Ful many a yeer in heigh prosperitee'; their daughter is married to one of the worthiest lords in Italy; Walter brings Griselda's old father to court and takes care of him for the rest of his days; and Walter's son succeeds to the lordship of the land and makes a fortunate marriage (1128–37). At this point, the Clerk departs briefly from Petrarch to add that Walter's son, however, did not test his noble wife, and that 'This world is nat so strong . . . As it hath been in olde tymes yoore' (1139–40). This comparison between the hardiness of wives then and now, between the fabular or literary and the real, implies that Griselda is not like real women, and this point will be picked up three stanzas later, where it leads directly to the Clerk's reference to the Wife of Bath and then to the envoy.

First, however, another possible ending to the story, a religious moral, is offered, prefaced by a closing call to attention, 'And herkneth what this auctour seith therfoore' (1141). The subsequent moral is found in both Petrarch and the French versions; the point is not that wives should adopt Griselda's humility but that all human beings should be as 'constant in adversitee' as she is: again, then, Griselda is not really a woman. Following this, a third conclusion to the tale is initiated with a second closing formula, 'But o word, lordynges, herkneth er I go' (1163), and in the next two stanzas the Clerk playfully does precisely what he has just told his audience not to do. Returning to the notion that it would be hard 'now-a-dayes' to find two or three live Griseldas in a town, he de-allegorizes the notion of 'assay' from the religious interpretation of Griselda's trials to offer this comment on material women, who fall so short of the ideal female malleability that his tale prescribes:

> For if that they were put to swiche assays,
> The gold of hem hath now so badde alayes
> With bras, that thogh the coyne be fair at ye,
> It wolde rather breste a-two than plye.
>
> (1166–69)

He then goes on to dedicate a blessing (in contrast to the Wife's parting curse) to the Wife of Bath and 'al hire secte', who are implicitly presented as the real, living examples of that superficially fair coin that will not bend.

With a third parting call to attention – 'Herkneth my song that seith in this manere' (1176) – as if he realized that our minds may well be wandering or at least confused by this plethora of contradictory conclusions and applications of his tale, the Clerk offers what now stands as the last ending to the text, titled in many manuscripts *Lenvoy de Chaucer*. Here, as in the preceding two stanzas, the speaker interacts directly with the other pilgrims and links the story we have just heard to the question of marital sovereignty. Now reading the heroine not as a paradigm for all humanity but as an historically real character, dissociable from her ideal virtue, the speaker replicates Walter's move, saying, in effect, 'This is enough': 'Grisilde is deed, and eek hire pacience, / And bothe atones buryed in Ytaille' (1177–78). He warns husbands that they will fail if they try to test their wives. Turning to 'noble wyves', he advises them not to let any clerks tell a story about them like the story of Griselda; and in the remaining stanzas he presents advice couched as the most extreme version possible of the Wife's already extreme philosophy of female dominance.

The Clerk's disclaimer two lines before the beginning of the Envoy – 'And lat us stynte of ernestful matere' (1175) – has encouraged modern readers to see the ending as comic play that protects the seriousness of the tale. In a frequently cited appraisal of this 'concessionary comedy', for example, Charles Muscatine argues: 'The Clerk admits the opposition purposely, so willingly and extravagantly as to make safe from vulgar questioning the finer matter that has gone before.'[13] Such a reading is consistent with Freud's view of humor as a healthy, even precious, defense mechanism wherein the humorist takes on the psychic part of both father and child; the superego speaks like a parent to the frightened ego, saying ' "Look here! This is all that this seemingly dangerous world amounts to. Child's play – the very thing to jest about." '[14] But what, exactly, is the young male ego of the Clerk so frightened of? And how is it the 'finer matter' of Griselda's story that the envoy makes safe?[15] As Freud further suggests, the humorist always repudiates suffering and affirms the ego's invulnerability; humor, then, would seem far more likely to trivialize, even undercut, a heroine whose power is equivalent to her capacity to embrace suffering and who can subordinate her own ego so completely to the cultural superego (the Law of the Father, the domination of Walter).

Given the similarity of the Clerk and the narrator of the *Legend of Good Women*, I conclude from the nature of the jest attempted in the envoy that the Clerk is simultaneously afraid of women and afraid of being (like) a woman. What frightens the Clerk so much that he has to joke about it is, first, the power of Griselda, the silenced woman, and her inhuman, celebrated capacity to suffer. This power, within the tale, has also frightened her husband Walter, in ways I have suggested; the envoy reveals that it is, moreover, paradoxically reminiscent of the power attributed by the Clerk to women like the Wife of Bath. What Griselda and the Wife seem to have in common is their capacity, manifested in opposite ways, to escape or at least lay bare the operation of male tyranny by exceeding, in different directions, its enunciated limits. Second, I submit, the Clerk may be frightened by his own likeness to Griselda, a parallel often drawn by readers.[16] As a youth whose manhood is openly questioned by the Host, as an unbeneficed young cleric, and as a story-teller translating a renowned author, the Clerk occupies a marginal and insecure position in the culture that wants to rule the day, the hearty manly world organized and policed both by the menacing Host of the *Canterbury Tales* and by the literary tradition embodied in the authority vested in Petrarch and the Latin source text. If Griselda exceeds the demands of her husband, so too the Clerk exceeds the demands of translation, and nowhere more than in the excess of endings to his tale. While the Clerk's sympathy with women may be suspect, then, his identification with the feminine position and hence his insight into the nature of a certain kind of psychic oppression is plausible, and it is as frightening to him as it is to a woman like the Wife.

The Clerk's strategy at the end of his tale suggests both his fears and his defense against them. By playing in the envoy at taking the shrew's part, he continues to dissociate himself – now, however, with tongue quite obviously in cheek – from the crude antifeminism of men like Walter, who seriously and mistakenly expect women to submit to masculine dominance and who underestimate the powers of their victims. At the same time, he implies that after all he has managed to transcend the merely literal response to the tale's pathos that his ostensive sympathy with Griselda might indicate and that he is in fact distanced by his superior learning and wit from the whole field of sexual warfare. Like the narrator of the *Legend of Good Women*, the Clerk finally signals that he is neither for real women nor against them; he is just playing a game, not the courtly cult of the marguerite but something not very different, a game played for and about men, and one that entails the transmission of the patriarchy's values, courtly or religious, through stories about idealized female figures. Griselda, then, is not finally unintelligible and threatening, she is just implausible; her suffering and its finer meanings can be forgotten. This is all there really is, the comic ending says, to the seemingly dangerous world of women and the war between lordly husbands and long-suffering wives – the very thing to jest about.

Freud, again like many modern Chaucerians, values humor for its 'liberating' element and sees something 'fine and elevating' in what he calls 'the triumph of the ego': 'It refuses to be hurt by the arrows of reality or to be compelled to suffer.'[17] But as humor liberates the humorist, does it liberate everyone? What about people who cannot laugh off the arrows of reality, who cannot refuse to be compelled to suffer – what about people like Griselda, whose only power lies in suffering? What about those who are the targets of real arrows, the butts of jokes, like the Wife of Bath? The Clerk's humorous ending deflates rather than protects Griselda's virtue, surely, and deflects us from both the real experience and the figurative value of her suffering and endurance; in liberating and elevating himself, then, he devalues and dismisses the feminine power of silence without liberating women from the complementary myths of absence or excess. The envoy in particular not only trivializes but also preempts the voice of a woman like the Wife of Bath, exaggerating just the sort of 'vulgar' response – something short of throwing his books into the fire – that she might indeed offer to a story like the Clerk's. Griselda, I have suggested, is made temporarily deaf, like the Wife, when Walter suddenly undergoes a dramatic reversal and agrees that she has proved her worth and can stop being tested; her story ends and her voice is silenced when the misogyny and fear that brings her into being finally comprehends how dangerous it is to let her suffer so visibly and well. In the same way, the Wife's position is silenced and disarmed by the Clerk's reversal when he impersonates her voice and takes up in jest precisely the kind of argument she might make.

The tale's reception, moreover, suggests that the vocal men on the pilgrimage have not been fooled into thinking that the Clerk is really on women's side in all this, or that the telling of this tale could possibly serve to liberate any wives from the domination of husbands that they are compelled to suffer outside the worlds of story and jest. In the link between the *Clerk's Tale* and the *Merchant's Tale*, we hear the Host's enthusiastic response to the story of Griselda, which he wishes his wife could hear. The Merchant, another manly man, begins the next tale in the series by comparing his own shrewish wife to Griselda. Disguised, but not completely so, as sympathetic to women, the Clerk nevertheless affirms to other men his proper maleness by offering them a comforting example of how both virtuous and vicious women alike may be silenced, and Griselda's meaning is reduced to its most minimal and least threatening level. The Host and Merchant have been accused of distorting the tale, and indeed they simply ignore the Clerk's half-hearted, clearly ambivalent and finally subverted warning that we should view Griselda not as a woman, but as a figure for the human soul.[18] But their response, biased as it may be, is invited by the Clerk's presentation.

The audience outside the poem may be more alert to the tale's subtleties, but modern critics at least have not been able to agree on its significance in a persuasive way either. And one of the problems that plagues more skillful interpreters outside the pilgrimage is the identity, not to mention the intentions, of the speaker in this poem, and especially in the envoy. Apart from the teller of the tales of *Melibee* and *Sir Thopas*, the Clerk is the character most often associated with Chaucer and his point of view, one of the few pilgrims usually thought to be treated with little irony and left in control of his own story. At the same time, the voicing of the envoy is particularly problematized by the scribal heading, *Lenvoy de Chaucer*, invoking the author's name at just the point where the joke is made. Robinson's explanatory note seems either obvious (aren't all the dramatically appropriate tales finally composed by Chaucer?) or confounding: 'The song . . . is Chaucer's independent composition. But it belongs dramatically to the Clerk, and is entirely appropriate.'[19] It points, however, to the importance of the fact that insofar as Chaucer speaks, it is only through the dramatic composition of other characters and other voices. Here, as in all the earlier dream-visions (and perhaps again with special relation to the *Legend of Good Women*, whose narrator also likes to make obscure little jokes about the ladies), the poet develops and plays on both the proximity and the distance between himself and the narrator of the story. To the extent that both proximity and distance remain in evidence, he creates the possibility of writing about his own limitations and biases with a penetrating self-scrutiny and an ironic self-reflexivity, and hence at the same time implying that he has in some sense escaped these limits and can be caught only in the equivocal act of writing and the liberating gesture of humor. Like Griselda, again, the figure of Chaucer transcends ostensive limits because he admits in play to perceiving and accepting them. In his marked equivocation, so central to the game, he figures himself in and as one who realizes the powers of silence and unintelligibility that he usurps from and finally denies to his female heroines.

Whereas many modern readers have posited a radical break between early and late Chaucerian fictions, one of my aims in discussing selected *Canterbury Tales* is to underscore some lines of thematic and rhetorical continuity that are especially visible to a feminist criticism interested in the problem of masculine identity and authority. The *Clerk's Tale* highlights such continuity, and we see how the evasiveness of the narrator and his position, so characteristic of all the early poems, manifests itself in an even more emphatic way in the *Tales*: through the creation of other fictive speakers altogether, with their own proper, fictive names, at different degrees of distance from the author, in the fiction of the framed collection. Here the functional moves toward the self-disguise, self-division, ambiguity, and resistance that I trace as empowering strategies in all the earlier poems proceed a logical step further toward the position of 'negative capability' and aesthetic transcendence that becomes the hallmark of the humanist artist and earns Chaucer his status as Father of English poetry, even as he plays the child and perhaps identifies with children.[20] Through this further step in self-effacement, brought out so clearly in the Clerk's performance, the figure of the poet avoids precisely the predicament that the remaining male story-tellers I am interested in here – the Miller, Knight, Merchant, and Franklin – to varying degrees reflect: any representation of Woman seems to entail a revelation of the male speaker's anxiety about his manliness, his status and identity. Again, this revelation goes hand in hand with a discourse that is thoroughly misogynistic, but the strategic intersection of the present, impersonated male narrator and the absent author has served to liberate Chaucer from the self-revealing, self-destructive side of the misogyny that powers the literary canon.

Notes

1. JOHN H. FISHER, ed., *The Complete Poetry and Prose of Geoffrey Chaucer* (New York: Holt, Rinehart and Winston, 1977), p. 145. The article from which the epigraph is drawn appears in *Literature and Psychology*, 16 (1966), 157–65.

2. For other readings like Richard Lanham's (see epigraph on p. 121) that locate meaning in the contradictions and tensions that the Clerk brings to his story, see DOLORES WARWICK FRESE, 'Chaucer's *Clerk's Tale*: The Monsters and the Critics Reconsidered', *Chaucer Review*, 8 (1973), 133–46; WARREN GINSBERG, ' "And Speketh so Pleyn": The Clerk's Tale and its Teller', *Criticism*, 20 (1978), 307–23; LLOYD N. JEFFREY, 'Chaucer's Walter: A Study in Emotional Immaturity', *Journal of Humanistic Psychology*, 3 (1963), 112–19; PATRICK MORROW, 'The Ambivalence of Truth', *Bucknell Review*, 16 (1968), 74–90; J. MITCHELL MORSE, 'The Philosophy of the Clerk of Oxenford', *Modern Language Quarterly*, 19 (1958), 3–20; and ROBERT STEPSIS, '*Potentia Absoluta* and the *Clerk's Tale*', *Chaucer Review*, 10 (1975–76), 129–42.

3. See CAROLINE WALKER BYNUM, *Holy Feast and Holy Fast* (Berkeley: University of California Press, 1987), for a discussion of the feminization of medieval Christian practice and theory, and especially Chapter 10, 'Women's Symbols'.

4. For a discussion of Chaucer's relation to the antifeminist tradition as it emerges in 'images . . . which celebrate, with a precision often subtle rather than apparent, the forms a woman's goodness is to take', see HOPE PHYLLIS WEISSMAN, 'Antifeminism and Chaucer's Characterizations of Women', in *Geoffrey Chaucer: A Collection of Original Articles*, ed. George D. Economou (New York: McGraw-Hill, 1975), pp. 93–110.

5. See *Oxford English Dictionary*, rue, v.1, sense 1.

6. MARSHA SIEGEL, 'Placing Griselda's Exemplary Value by way of the *Franklin's Tale*', paper presented at International Congress on Medieval Studies, Kalamazoo, MI, May 1982.

7. CATHARINE A. MACKINNON, 'Feminism, Marxism, Method, and the State: An Agenda for Theory', *Signs*, 7 (1982), 543.

8. ANNE MIDDLETON, 'The Clerk and His Tale: Some Literary Contexts', *Studies in the Age of Chaucer*, 2 (1980), 149.

9. For a more complete discussion of this point and others in the Legends, see my 'Irony and the Antifeminist Narrator in Chaucer's *Legend of Good Women*', *Journal of English and Germanic Philology*, 82 (1983), 11–31, as well as the discussion in Chapter 1 of this study.

10. *The Literary Relationships of Chaucer's Clerk's Tale* (New Haven, CT: Yale University Press, 1942), pp. 231, 233.

11. I take the Latin quotation from the convenient edition of Petrarch's *Epistolae Seniles*, Book XVII, Letter III (with a facing edition of *Le Livre Griseldis*) in

Sources and Analogues of Chaucer's Canterbury Tales, ed. W. F. Bryan and Germaine Dempster (Chicago: University of Chicago Press, 1941), pp. 296–331. The text of Petrarch's version is translated in ROBERT DUDLEY FRENCH, *A Chaucer Handbook* (New York: F. S. Crofts, 1927), pp. 291–311.

12. For a sampling of different approaches and conclusions all based on the fundamental premise that the Clerk's answer to the Wife of Bath presents the obviously sensible, beautiful, 'universal' refutation of her equally obviously monstrous and ridiculous perversion, see S. K. HENINGER, JR., 'The Concept of Order in Chaucer's *Clerk's Tale*', *Journal of English and Germanic Philology*, 56 (1957), 382–95; THOMAS H. JAMESON, 'One Up for Clerks', *Arts and Sciences* (Winter 1964–65), 10–13; LYNN STALEY JOHNSON, 'The Prince and His People: A Study of the Two Covenants in the *Clerk's Tale*', *Chaucer Review*, 10 (1975–76), 17–29; ALFRED KELLOGG, 'The Evolution of the *Clerk's Tale*', in *Chaucer, Langland, Arthur: Essays in Middle English Literature* (New Brunswick, NJ: Rutgers University Press, 1972), pp. 276–329; MORROW, 'The Ambivalence of Truth'; IRVING N. ROTHMAN, 'Humility and Obedience in the *Clerk's Tale*, with the Envoy Considered as an Ironic Affirmation', *Papers in Language and Literature*, 9 (1973), 115–27; JEROME TAYLOR, 'Fraunceys Petrak'. For readings that stress the Clerk's (or Chaucer's) sympathy with women, see for example HARRIET HAWKIN, 'The Victim's Side: Chaucer's *Clerk's Tale* and Webster's *Duchess of Malfi*', *Signs*, 1 (1975), 339–61; VELMA RICHMOND, 'Pacience in Adversitee: Chaucer's Presentation of Marriage', *Viator*, 10 (1979), 323–54; and MORSE, 'The Philosophy of the Clerk'.

13. C. MUSCATINE, *Chaucer and the French Tradition* (Berkeley: University of California Press, 1957), p. 197.

14. 'Humour' (1928), in *Collected Papers*, vol. 5, ed. James Strachey (New York: Basic Books, 1959), p. 220.

15. The term 'purity' is one Muscatine insists on; see MUSCATINE, *Chaucer and the French Tradition*, p. 196.

16. For a good analysis of the similarities between narrator and female character in this case, see CAROLYN DINSHAW, *Chaucer's Sexual Poetics* (Madison: University of Wisconsin Press, 1989), pp. 135–7.

17. 'Humour', p. 217.

18. MIDDLETON, 'The Clerk and His Tale'. The Host's words, lines 1212a–g, are found in only one family of manuscripts, including the Ellesmere manuscript and Hengwrt 154. Robinson identifies them as 'without doubt genuine', perhaps part of a canceled job. See also ELEANOR HAMMOND, *Chaucer: A Bibliographical Manual* (New York: Macmillan, 1908), pp. 302–3, and AAGE BRUSENDORFF, *The Chaucer Tradition* (London: Oxford University Press, 1925), p. 76.

19. *The Works of Geoffrey Chaucer*, note to line 1177, p. 712; John Koch argues, however, that the Envoy is spoken by the author; ('Nochmals zur Frage des Prologs in Chaucers "Legend of Good Women" ', *Anglia*, 50 [1926], 65); for recent comment that supports Robinson's view, see THOMAS J. FARRELL, 'The "Envoy de Chaucer" and the *Clerk's Tale*', *Chaucer Review*, 24 (1990), 329–36.

20. For the argument that Chaucer identifies with children and plays the childish role in the *Canterbury Tales* in particular, see LEE PATTERSON, ' "What Man Artow?" Authorial Self-Definition in *The Tale of Sir Thopas* and *The Tale of Melibee*', *Studies in the Age of Chaucer*, 11 (1989), 117–75.

8 Umberto Eco, Semiotics, and the *Merchant's Tale**

Carolyn P. Collette

Collette's article draws on Eco's writings on semiotics to read the *Merchant's Tale* as a 'labyrinth' of metaphorical relationships that mutually enrich each lexical item. Like much reader-response theory, Eco's work argues for an interpretative partnership between readerly creativity and the constraints laid down by the original text, and Collette sees this as an attractive compromise position, enabling us to acknowledge how we construct the texts we read while simultaneously recognizing the 'otherness' of the Middle Ages.

Semiotics applied to literary criticism is but one of a host of new perspectives from which to examine our responses to Chaucer's art.[1] Most Chaucerians trained in what were popularly understood as Donaldsonian or Robertsonian criticism realize that neither approach by itself can fully open to modern readers the complexities Chaucer has created in his work; we realize, too, that a combination of these two approaches is better than either alone, but still not entirely satisfactory, because their premises ignore questions central to modern criticism in general, and to medieval literature in particular. Every time we try to comprehend a Chaucerian text we must first encounter a series of challenging questions, questions we often avoid answering: What is the text we are reading? What, precisely, is our relation to it? Where does it exist – on the page? in the past? in our minds? Can we ever know the text in a way similar to the way fourteenth-century men and women knew it? Ought we to try?

Adapting semiotics to the literary criticism of medieval texts can help to focus these questions, to delineate their dimensions and implications. In the following pages I would like to explore what happens when one applies some of Umberto Eco's semiotic heuristics about aesthetic texts to the *Merchant's Tale*. First, however, it will be helpful to focus briefly on the distinctions between medieval and

---

* Reprinted from *Chaucer Review*, 24 (1989–90), 132–8.

modern semiotics and to summarize some of the pertinent aspects of Eco's theories about aesthetic texts.

Eco, I think, would be the first to acknowledge that Western thought has, from the Classical era, been interested in the relations among signs, words, and their referents in the world of matter and ideas; yet he would also caution us to remember that a crucial distinction separates medieval sign theory and modern semiotics. For the medieval 'semiotician', working in the Augustinian tradition, for example, all signs derive their meaning from a priori Being and from knowledge latent in the mind of the receptor. Such knowledge, in its turn, is a reflection of Divine Being, antecedent to all expression. All signs ultimately refer, however imperfectly, to the Divinity in whose service, and by whose creative love, they come to be.

Over the course of the last twenty years, Eco has been developing a sign theory of increasingly labyrinthine proportions; an increasingly complex theory of semiotics as an extended network of culturally created referents and interpretants; and a theory of a mazelike world of potential meanings through which the individual mind moves, sorting, correlating, fusing. These stand in contrast to medieval theories. Eco posits an ever-widening *spiral* of possible connections among interpretants and signs, and he increasingly focuses on the individual as a creator of meaning. Augustine, by contrast, posits a *circle* of initial perception, followed by inference, meaning, understanding, and full perception grounded in faith. For Augustine, signs at their best can only indicate reality; for Eco, they shape reality.

Noting this crucial difference, we must stop to consider what we are doing when we read a medieval text semiotically. Even given the obvious fact that medieval semiotics was a continuously developing theory of epistemology and understanding, and even given that, as Eco says, by the late Middle Ages the rationalists, at least, understood the cultural basis of perceptions about the universe,[2] we must recognize that we are dealing with a modern literary critical method that can make no claims to open up a medieval text as medieval semiotics would have done. The semiotic study of literature, like many other modern literary critical theories, is interested in meaning, specifically in how a modern reader understands meaning.

Within the terms of this proviso, however, we can say that Eco's theories about aesthetic texts in general, and about the function of metaphor in particular, are apt to the study of Chaucer, because their nexus with the text lies at the intersection of cultural codes and individual interpretation, an intersection familiar to Chaucerians. In his three major works in English, *A Theory of Semiotics* (Bloomington, 1976), *The Role of the Reader* (Bloomington, 1979), and *Semiotics and the Philosophy of Language* (Bloomington, 1984), Eco has delineated with progressive and increasing clarity a theory of the aesthetic text as a heightened and thus extremely complex form of semiotic communication. Passing beyond Peircean models of semiotic triangulations, as well as beyond any notion of sign theory as a matter of equivalents, he has moved increasingly toward what he terms a theory of 'responsible collaboration' between writer and reader, summarized for our purposes in the following passages from *A Theory of Semiotics*:

> Like a large labyrinthine garden, a work of art permits one to take many different routes, whose number is increased by the criss-cross of its paths.
>
> First of all the comprehension of an aesthetic text is based on a dialectic between acceptance and repudiation of the sender's codes – on the one hand – and introduction and rejection of personal codes on the other. . . . In the interpretive reading a dialectic between *fidelity* and inventive *freedom* is established. On the one hand the addressee seeks to draw excitement from the ambiguity of the message and to fill out an ambiguous text with suitable codes; on the other, he is induced by contextual relationships to see the message exactly as it was intended, in an act of fidelity to the author and to the historical environment in which the message was emitted.
>
> . . . The semiotic definition of the work of art explains why, (i) in the course of aesthetic communication an experience takes place which can neither be reduced to a definite formula nor foreseen in all of its possible outcomes; (ii) yet at the same time this 'open' experience is made possible by something which should have (and indeed has) a structure at all levels. Thus the semiotic definition of an aesthetic text gives the *structured model* for an *unstructured process of communicative interplay*.
>
> (pp. 275–76, italics in original)

We need to make one further point here about historical distance. In the labyrinthine garden of medieval literature the modern reader finds a maze of crisscrossing individual paths and cultural codes – in our case medieval and modern codes. This richness produces a constant theorizing, a constant testing, and, I would argue, a constant self-consciousness about our reading. Even if we could know all the items in a code, could, for instance, have a map of how the semiotic paths crisscross in the imaginary garden of a medieval text, it is not at all certain that we would traverse the same paths in the same order as a medieval reader. And this is the paradox that lies at the heart of reading a medieval text, a paradox that Eco helps us to recognize: while we know instinctively that the more we learn about the world of ideas, people, places, and events that Chaucer's audience knew, the better our criticism, we must constantly deal with doubts about how heavily we can depend on our knowledge, about how certainly we can correlate it with Chaucer's or his audience's. Eco's theories of interdependent creation legitimatize both modern readings and attempts to understand fourteenth-century codes. They suggest that we cannot accept one without the other, but they also urge us to remember that we are modern readers, first and foremost, and that the text comes alive through our sensitive reading.

A semiotic reading of some parts of the *Merchant's Tale* can provide an example of how we can combine medieval and modern understandings.[3] For the purposes of this essay we will consider several instances of figurative language, what Eco, following Aristotle, categorizes as metaphor. This broadly-conceived notion of literary language, the umbrella-term 'metaphor', is the locus where the semiotic process is most intense, most clearly at work, and hardest to define. In essence, metaphor creates a dynamic moment of meaning. Eco describes it as a cognitive instrument, not an ornament, as 'at once a source of clarity and enigma' (*Semiotics and the Philosophy of Language*, 102). The first sort of metaphor I want to consider is the explicit analogy. Phrases like, 'A man may do no synne with his wyf, / Ne hurte hymselven with his owene knyf' (1839–40)[4] depend on the interplay of four elements. In the first case the analogy, simply stated, is man:wyf=man:knyf. In Eco's theory a semiotic reading of such a metaphor depends surely upon the codes each word brings to the metaphor, but also, and more importantly, on what happens to the codes once the four signs are placed in the dynamic relationship of the metaphor. In that relationship each takes on properties of the other,[5] dropping 'noncoincident' traits, reinforcing their common traits. The mind almost automatically sifts signs in this way, helping the author and the phrase to render new meanings. Here 'man' may be understood in the first instance as husband, in the second as a wielder of tools. This relationship then brings to bear a new meaning on the word 'wife'. Is the man in fact the controller of the wife as he is of the tool? Does the wife indeed remain passive until the man 'animates' her for his own purposes? Even as we consider these possibilities, we remember that the word 'knyf' signifies such interpretants as a dangerous and powerful tool, a sharp instrument, a means of exercising power. In the midst of a comparison designed ostensibly to show Januarie's blind confidence that he can control and dominate his wife utterly, we find, following Eco's lead, that Chaucer links the ideas of wife and knife to create the idea of woman as ironically powerful, dangerous, potent. The apparent sense of the

analogy, a woman, like a knife, can be manipulated, is expanded
to include, a woman, like a knife, is very dangerous. As readers we
almost automatically sense the irony of the phrase, as semioticians
we understand the dynamics of how that irony comes to exist.

This is a perfectly straightforward, modern reading of an
apparently significant passage. Something less apparent is found
near the end of the text,[6] where May says to January, who has just
witnessed his own cuckolding, 'But, sire, a man that waketh out of
his sleep, / He may nat sodeynly wel taken keep / Upon a thyng,
ne seen it parfitly, / Til that he be adawed verraily' (2397–2400). The
MED records two principal meanings for *adawen*:[7] 'to dawn, become
day, shine'; and 'to awaken from sleep, recover from a swoon'. If we
follow the theory of coincident traits and move from this passage
back into the text, something unusual happens here. What appears
initially as the primary meaning in this passage, to awaken – for
January has certainly been 'sleepy' throughout the tale – fades in
comparison to a meaning that arises when the word is heard in
conjunction with a strong pattern of recurring signs associated with
May. At various points in the story we have seen May described as
like the day: 'As fressh as is the brighte someres day' (1895); 'lyk the
brighte morwe of May' (1748). These two systems of signs work
together in the reader's mind when we remember that January has
sought to control May, and that Chaucer has continually linked
Januarie's fantasies with other bright things that evoke ideas of light,
of sun, and day – with mirrors and gardens, the world of signs that
comprise his own misconception of himself as potent, young, and
lusty. January tries to appropriate to himself the world of light
and fruitfulness signified in the tale by May, by the mirror of his
imagining, and by the blossoming garden. Yet at the end he is
revealed as not *verailly adawed*, not truly part of that world, just as
he is not truly a part of his own, real world of age and folly. Eco's
theories help us to see the blindness theme of the tale in a new way;
it is not just that January is blind to the truth, but that he is not part
of the world of light and youth, no matter how hard he tries to be.
In more than one sense things don't dawn on (or in) January.

Finally, meaning in the tale can derive from an even more
encompassing kind of metaphor, that derived from linking three
major signs in the tale: first, the mental mirror through which
Januarie envisions his ideal wife; second, the wax which represents
Januarie's initial expectation of how he can mold May to his wishes,
a sign which later figures in making the key to the garden as well
as in a series of verbal references to impression and impressability;
and third, the garden whose fertility yet sterility marks it as a place
of illusion, projection, self-indulgence. If we follow our theory of

metaphor, these three signs work together both because they
are heavily encoded with referents and interpretants intelligible to
Chaucer's audience, and because their particular conjunction in this
tale produces an effect that transforms each in the presence of the
others, an effect that reinforces coincident traits and thereby produces
a dynamic moment – a metaphor.

In reading this broad metaphor we need to develop a degree
of self-consciousness, a structure through which we can grasp the
unstructured play of semiotic elements. Certainly we begin by trying
to track down the full range of their referents and interpretants in
late fourteenth-century English. On the other hand, we will never
realize their full meaning if we stop there. Along with knowledge
must go an understanding of what happens in the 'moment' of
metaphor, when codes are joined and fused, employed and
transcended, present yet fundamentally altered by their being joined
in this pattern by the collaboration of author and reader. This latter
sort of understanding is available to us even if we cannot know all
the interpretants these signs would have evoked during the fourteenth
century, even if we cannot replicate a fourteenth-century experience
of metaphor. We acknowledge the world of codes and signs in which
these signs existed even as we realize that the dynamic moment of
their union in this one pattern of Chaucer's and ours takes them out
of that world and places them in ours.

What happens if we consider this broad metaphor with a
heightened self-consciousness? The mirror's interpretants of clarity
and truthfulness fall away in the presence of the wax's passivity, its
impressionability, so that the mirror reveals itself to us in terms of its
passivity. It is a sign of vanity, an instrument that will give back to
one what one brings to it, it exists not to give truth but to confirm
impressions. Coupled to this interpretation, the garden, the *locus
amoenus*, the *hortus conclusus*, at first interpretation a clear, standard
literary and religious sign, appears to us as a sign of how individuals
seek to impress their wills on nature. It is, after all, Januarie's
construction, a projection of his mind – like the mirror – an attempt
through imagination to impress on reality a pattern he very much
desires to see. The garden, on this level, exerts a reciprocal effect on
the mirror and on the wax, suggesting the fertility, the creativity
inherent in both the imaginative process of conjuring up images of
the kind of wife one wants and in the process of molding the world
to one's wishes. Both the wax used to make the key and the tender
heart reposing in May are 'impressed' with images which also give
rise to 'creations' – the key in one instance, and a willing adulteress
in the other. It goes without saying but it is probably most interesting
of all that a heavy irony must govern our understanding of the terms

'creativity' and 'imagination', especially in regard to the idea of impressionability. Irony arises from one of those 'moments' of metaphor when signs fall away, but in the instant before doing so, provide a norm against which and through which we can apprehend the flash of wit that turns codes inside out and in so doing produces irony and humor.

We can use a theory of semiotics, combining historical cultural knowledge, even while realizing that codes so learned cannot provide the whole basis for literary analysis, even while realizing that each of us will retain different references as central, while dropping others. The point is that such a reading, admittedly self-conscious as it must be, helps us to answer those initial questions of what the text is, where we stand in relation to it. It helps us understand how we combine knowledge of fourteenth-century culture with our own intuitions, and it reminds us how much the text is a creation of imagination, both the author's and the reader's.

Notes

1. For an introduction to contemporary thinking on this subject see *New Perspectives in Chaucer Criticism*, Donald Rose, ed. (Norman, 1981), particularly Florence Ridley's article, 'A Response to Contemporary Literary Theory and Chaucer', in which she summarizes the driving force behind the current examination of modern critical theory in relation to Chaucer as a desire for a theory or theories that will 'enhance our comprehension of or our pleasure' in Chaucer's texts (p. 42).

2. *Semiotics and the Philosophy of Language* (Bloomington, 1984), p. 103.

3. In many respects the *Merchant's Tale* is an ideally semiotic tale. Signs from both medieval and modern 'codes' permeate that tale. January visualizes his fantasies and lives his life of folly dependent on external signs he often misreads; broad references to a variety of texts, to the Bible, as well as to mythological figures, also work to create a network of intertextual allusions, echoes, and parodies.

4. All citations of the *Merchant's Tale* are from *The Works of Geoffrey Chaucer*, ed. F. N. Robinson, 2nd edn (Boston, 1959).

5. For a fuller discussion of this point, see *Semiotics and the Philosophy of Language*, p. 76.

6. On the importance of the ending of an aesthetic text in understanding the whole, see *The Role of the Reader*, p. 26.

7. On the restrictive potential of dictionaries see *Semiotics and the Philosophy of Language*, p. 58f., where Eco discusses classification and offers a critique of the Porphyrian tree.

9 Metafictional Strategies and the Theme of Sexual Power in the *Wife of Bath's* and *Franklin's Tales**

JOHN STEPHENS AND MARCELLA RYAN

The authors here contest a traditional male reading of the *Franklin's Tale* in which a patronizing attitude towards the 'inept' femininity of Dorigen goes hand in hand with an acceptance of the ideal of marital happiness the Tale supposedly lays before the reader. On the contrary, Dorigen should be seen as the victim of a patriarchal authority that dissembles itself in the 'illusion' of caring and concern for the female, just as the illusion of the rocks' disappearance represents in the Tale the cloaking of an aggressive male sexuality underneath the rhetoric of *fin amour*. However, the *Franklin's Tale*'s constant attention to metafictional elements alerts the reader to the process of fiction-making itself as an 'illusion', and offers a kind of 'self-dismantling' of textual authority (the text/reader relationship being analogous to that between male/female) which encourages the reader to 'penetrate the conventions of discourse' and unmask the (male) illusions therein. Even so, Stephens and Ryan see little that is positive in the roles of the women characters themselves in Chaucer's *Tales*: Dorigen's fate is one of submission and silence and, in the equation made between verbal and sexual power, a 'clitoridectomized' role dependent on men for its activation; by comparison, where a woman does briefly achieve sexual and verbal power, as with the old hag towards the end of the *Wife of Bath's Tale*, this is quickly effaced by the transformation scene leading to another male illusion of 'the ideal object of desire'. For the authors, Chaucer held 'a bleak view of male–female relations': though sympathetic to the women who are constrained by the superficial and simplified versions of themselves that constitute male objects of desire, and though allowing his women speakers some access to the deeper levels of discourse that challenge such versions, he sees 'little prospect for change' in the relations between gender and power in his own day. This is no reason, however, why modern readers

* Reprinted from *Nottingham Medieval Studies*, 33 (1989), 56–75.

should not offer a more substantial challenge to the superficial and simplified interpretations of a male interpretative tradition.

'The picture allows any number of readings, including the correct one.'
(E. H. Gombrich, *Art and Illusion*, p. 278)

I

New directions in literary theory and critical practice over the past twenty years have brought with them a potential for generating fresh approaches to Chaucer, often by bringing neglected aspects of his works into the foreground of attention.[1] By the late 1970s structuralist and post-structuralist concern with theories of the sign had provoked re-readings of Chaucer and a concomitant re-writing of literary history, particularly with respect to the influence of medieval sign theory on literature.[2] Another approach was initiated at about the same time by Arlyn Diamond's pioneering feminist essay on 'Chaucer's Women'.[3] Perhaps because here, as in other areas, feminist criticism has to function in the context of an established and often hostile critical discourse, studies following on from Diamond have been slow to appear. The aim of this essay is to explore how some post-structuralist contributions to the theory of narrative enable a feminist re-reading of two of the *Canterbury Tales*.

One covert barrier to a shift of emphasis within criticism of the *Canterbury Tales* is the way critical tradition privileges certain groupings of tales and readings of them. Our present concern is with the tales framing the so-called 'marriage group'; that is, the sequence of tales assumed to stage a dramatic debate over male/female relations. Despite substantial shifts in critical emphasis, the notion of the group has remained as a critical reflex throughout the sixty-odd years since Kittredge's formulation of it in 'Chaucer's Discussion of Marriage'.[4] So whether it is argued, for example, that the tale-teller relationship discloses a theme other than the individual narrator's overt purpose,[5] or that the narrator himself is more concerned with a theme other than 'marital relations',[6] it still seems generally held that in some sense the *Franklin's Tale* is to be seen as the final word on the subject of marriage, and that 'Chaucer himself is speaking in the tale',[7] thereby furnishing his own answer to the argument begun in the *Wife of Bath's Tale*. Readers of Chaucer have had to wait a long time for David Aers's argument that a reading which accepts the tale's romance 'happy ending' at face value is, while valid, nevertheless naive, because the absence from the narrative of any process of regeneration 'means that we have no ground for any faith whatsoever in the [tale's] final assertions'.[8] The reason that authorial point of view has been identified so readily here rather than in other tales is because the apparent attitude of the tale can be made to conform so well to a ruling attitude of twentieth-century Anglo-American society, and it is thus assumed that Chaucer, in his wisdom, thinks the same way. So what happens if the tales are considered from an entirely different perspective – if, in short, the reader reads 'as a woman'?[9] It might be objected that this is a modern concept, and thus an anachronism if applied to the *Canterbury Tales*, but Diamond has properly pointed out the pervasive 'attention to the "problem" of women' in Chaucer's works (p. 64), and to this can be added the argument that the discussion of *Troilus and Criseyde* in the *Prologue* to *The Legend of Good Women* reflects a contemporary fourteenth-century woman's reading of the great romance. It is also pertinent to observe that the argument over the 'marriage group' has been largely carried on by male critics with male attitudes. For example, Alfred David (in *The Strumpet Muse*) gives a sensitive and sympathetic account of the Wife of Bath, seeing her as a character trying to find a way to live in a society which 'does not allow an intelligent woman any self-respect unless she is a saint or martyr' (p. 156), but nevertheless still finds it humorous that 'she at the age of forty responds to the call of Nature like a girl of sixteen' (p. 150). Such a comment seems to originate in the moral and sexual assumptions which are brought to the text, rather than in the text itself, and suggests some important questions: is middle-aged female desire inherently comic? does Chaucer's *text* suggest that it is? how might another kind of reader respond, especially one who might well be female and possibly forty?[10]

The very title 'marriage group', and what this conveys about the theme isolated for comment, limits discussion to a particular category of experience, and privileges this over other experiences. Likewise the optimistic resolution seen in the *Franklin's Tale* links this particular view of male/female relations to 'some of the moral values most worth cherishing',[11] thus assuming that the tale underpins the modern concept of marriage. If it is to be accepted that the relations between the sexes are explored through the tales, and through their interaction, and that the Franklin represents some kind of deliberated conclusion, it should also be recognized that more is at issue than marriage relations. The parameters for discussion of these tales are effectively set by the language in which the erring knight of the *Wife of Bath's Tale* couches the answer to the question 'What thyng is it that wommen moost desiren':[12]

> Wommen desiren to have sovereynetee
> As wel over hir housbond as hir love,
> And for to been in maistrie hym above.

(1038–40)

All sexual relations are included in the key terms of the knight's answer – *sovereynetee, housbond, love, maistrie* – and all of these terms are collocated within ten lines in the marriage contract at the beginning of the *Franklin's Tale* (lines 742–51). To limit the perspective to marriage thus tends to exclude the other relationships which pivot on sexual power, such as that of Dorigen and Aurelius or Damyan and May in the *Merchant's Tale*. Further, the received view that the *Franklin's Tale*, whatever else it does, presents an exemplar of the compromise necessary for a happy marriage, and within that a picture of the ideal wife, seems increasingly unlikely to find favour among modern female readers. A pertinent resituation of the question at the heart of the *Wife of Bath's Tale* is offered, in another context, by Hélène Cixous in her much more recent paper, 'Castration or Decapitation?':

> Another question that's posed in History, rather a strange question, a typical male question, is: 'What do women want?' . . . To pose the question . . . is to pose it already as answer, as from a man who isn't expecting any answer, because the answer is 'She wants nothing' . . . Nothing because she is passive. The only thing man can do is offer the question 'What could she want, she who wants nothing?' Or in other words: 'Without me, what could she want?'[13]

The question in the *Wife of Bath's Tale* may have been posed by the queen as women's representative, but the antifeminist context is quite similar to that referred to by Cixous, and the path travelled by Woman from here to the end of the *Franklin's Tale* is that from aggressiveness to passivity: Dorigen will 'want' what the male characters of the tale decide she wants. For a female reader to accept that the *Franklin's Tale* defines marital 'sovereyn blisse' is for her to accede to the power relationships which underlie such a reading. That the *Canterbury Tales* themselves avoid authoritative structures of this type is suggested by the conflict between *experience* and *auctoritee* which Chaucer refers to in so many works and which he places at the centre of the Wife of Bath's performance.

The idea of the unauthoritative text is something of a paradox, since the way the world is experienced is always partly determined by some form of authority. The rebellion of the Wife of Bath, for example, is circumscribed from the outset insofar as she attempts, in her theoretical preamble, to oppose biblical and patristic authority on their own ground and is thus condemned to misuse a discourse which has already marginalized women. The antifeminist material she then draws on in describing her married life completes the process rather than presenting the picture of a woman in revolt against specific examples of male authority. In the *Franklin's Tale*, Dorigen's moment of revolt is against the highest authority, the Creator, and she is effectively punished for this. But what really determines her behaviour is her subjection to the authority of social conventions. This is expressed by a sculptural analogy in lines 829–31 of the tale:

> By proces, as ye knowen everichoon,
> Men may so longe graven in a stoon,
> Til som figure therinne emprented be.

The lines begin to describe how Dorigen's grief for her absent husband is somewhat ameliorated. The figure is significantly *not* the 'running water wears away stone' cliché, but a figure which suggests that Dorigen can be reprinted and should be re-formed by external influences. She has, after all, already been transformed in a little more than a year from an independent woman to a classic hysteric whose desire, whose being, has been reduced to a response to her husband's presence or absence:

> For his absence wepeth she and siketh . . .
> Desir of his presence hire so destreyneth
> That al this wyde world she sette at noght.
>
> (817–21)

Her subsequent behaviour is similarly 'imprinted' by authoritative structures – the unintended promise to Aurelius may be motivated by her obsession with her husband's safety, but it is structured by a conventional literary game which decrees that a lady test her would-be love by allotting him tasks. Similarly, her decision to commit suicide is overtly predetermined by the multitude of exemplars already drawn together to illustrate that death is preferable to unchastity (and which limits the possibilities to these alternatives anyway). Her hesitation in the latter event is usually nowadays dismissed as comic, but its more immediate function – to serve as a reminder that the unpalatable options decreed by authority might not be definitive – should question that attitude.

The language of criticism also becomes an issue here. Burlin, for example, describes this scene in typical marginalizing language:

Dorigen's 'high resolve' is 'eroded by garrulity', and 'where
the Franklin had intended to give us the elevated style of a noble
lady faced with a tragic dilemma, a peek over Chaucer's shoulder
confirms that he has produced a much more human and engaging, if
somewhat hysterical and even occasionally silly woman'.[14] Just as the
critic peeps over Chaucer's shoulder, the reader is invited to peep
over the critic's authoritative shoulder to behold a picture of inept,
though somewhat endearing femininity. Must the modern female
reader therefore accept this as one more art-work which exemplifies
an unpalatable, if conventional, attitude to women, or can she
distinguish the work from the critical mediation of that work and
set her own experience against the authority of traditional ways of
reading the text? It is not just a question of what modern readers are
to do with attitudes apparently endorsed in earlier literatures that are
now no longer acceptable, but rather whether such attitudes are so
readily to be found in this grouping from the *Canterbury Tales*. Of
central importance here is the assumption that it is possible to see as
Chaucer saw, whereas his attitudes may not be anywhere available
to us in the *Canterbury Tales*. If we return to the *Franklin's Tale*'s
sculpting analogy, we might well ask whether the figure reflects a
socially inscribed view, or an awareness of what is happening to
Dorigen, or a more covert recognition that a powerful, broadly-based
authority fears, subjugates and confines the Other, the not-male.

A range of interpretative possibilities thus exists, and it may be
illuminated by implications for reading Chaucer which have emerged
from recent accounts of author/narrator/audience relationships and
metafictional strategies. In the fictional world of the *Canterbury Tales*,
the literary author creates his own order of reality, peopled with his
own creations in their own space, subject to his will, but generally
modelled on the forms and social conditions of the real, phenomenal
world previously created by the 'author of Nature', as he is called in
Boethius and John of Salisbury.[15] The analogy applies crucially to the
recreation of Woman. As the *Merchant's Tale* reminds the reader, the
first Creator made woman subordinate to man and for man:

> The hye God, whan he hadde Adam maked,
> And saugh him al allone, bely-naked,
> God of his grete goodnesse seyde than,
> 'Lat us now make an helpe unto this man
> Lyk to hymself'

(1325–29)

Woman is continually re-created in these tales through the
perceptions of her expressed through fictional narrators. The author

himself seems removed, distanced by the complex structure of the *Canterbury Tales* which mediates all attitudes through old stories and their present narrators: the narrators occupy a space and time coextensive with late fourteenth-century England, but their stories often do not.

In this manner, the gap between experience and authority can be widened by exploiting the difference between 'then' and 'now'. The patterns and restrictions of the real world can be loosened, and commented upon, by transporting the audience to other times and/ or places, to when the land was 'fulfild of fayerye' and the religious authority of Holy Church did not yet control 'illusion', to when anything is possible and anything can be said. The stories become the responsibility of their tellers, not of the author, as is early argued in the Prologue to the *Miller's Tale* – albeit a tongue-in-cheek argument, already undermined by its similarity to the Miller's abdication of responsibility due to drunkenness. This is a double movement, the removal of the author and the reminder of his presence, which brings to the foreground the fiction-making process and the responsibility of the reader for both readings and misreadings. It is, after all, a fiction, so the confirmation or subversion of large notions such as morality or authority take place in that secondary world whose recreation is shared by the narrators of the tales and the readers. Of particular interest to us here are elements within the fiction which are embedded, digressive, or disruptive, and which function not only to extend the reader's sense of a narrator's fallibility, but also as effective metafictions. These elements mirror the narrative processes of the tales as a whole and thematize key linguistic and societal concepts – for the 'marriage group' tales, these concepts revolve around the struggle between male and female for sexual power.

The observation that the narrators are themselves narrated is crucial to any reading of these tales, because each deals, in some way, with illusion as story event and as theme, but each also embodies, overtly or covertly, an awareness that narrative itself is the making of illusion. In both tales, we would argue, a self-commentary is discernible in three, related ways: in the self-consciousness of the narrator's narrating (an aspect which has long received detailed critical attention); in a highly-developed linguistic self-awareness (generally covert, but approaching overtness in the *Franklin's Tale*); and in the use of a number and variety of story events – sometimes presented more or less discretely, sometimes tightly woven through the text – which thematize the fiction-making process and imply a commentary on the power relations between narrator and reader. We would further argue that, although this is not necessarily consciously worked out, the text/reader relationship bears strong analogies to the

power relationships between male and female (not to speak of
other power relationships), and through the analogy each of these
mirrors the other. Narrative authority is like sexual authority: the
reader may be dominated, seduced, abused, even violated, or may
in (re-)producing the text exploit its gaps and weaknesses to question
the authority of the text and the attitudes present within it. In the
history of English literature, Chaucer is probably the first great
dismantler of his own texts, employing what we might think of as
broadly metafictional techniques in order to alert the reader to the
processes of narration, and thence to the instability of meaning and
to the plurality of readings.

II

The capacity of language, especially literary language, both to
communicate and to impede understanding deeply concerns Chaucer,
and this concern is reflected in the extent to which the problem of
unstable signification is central to a reading of the *Franklin's Tale*.
In the *Canterbury Tales*, the head-links and prologues (where they
exist) usually provide some indications about both the themes and
emphases of the following tale. Here, though, the foreground theme
of *gentillesse*, conjoined with the Franklin's social aspirations, has
proved to be an indeterminable element in the interpretation of the
narrative, and has given rise to an irreconcilable plurality of opposing
readings. The prologue presents a comparable difficulty in the
attention it draws to the tale's rhetoric: this has received an ample
amount of critical comment, which usually links it to the social
aspiration theme to reveal a narrator 'uneasy . . . with the rhetorical
requirements of his chosen genre'.[16] Although Burlin praises the
Franklin's play on the three meanings of colours as 'witty' (p. 60),
there is more involved than mere polysemy:

> Colours ne knowe I none, withouten drede,
> But swiche colours as growen in the mede
> Or elles swiche as men dye or peynte.
>
> (723–25)

The verbal sign is arbitrary. What it conveys can be contextualized
and recontextualized. It can be manipulated to suggest that by
opposing the artifice of rhetorical language with the direct
experiencing of a flower there might be a more direct access to
unmediated reality, or that the concrete mimetic effects of the plastic
arts or of craft are a more accessible kind of making. The question of

what *gentillesse* denotes has teased commentators for decades, but this is just another straw in the wind here, for the whole tale is characterized by a pervasive sense of denotative fade and drift, a linguistic phenomenon endemic to the Middle English lexicon but rarely so extensively exploited as in this text. For example, it is cultivated in such localized examples as the polyptoton of lines 742–43, where instead of intensifying meaning the rhetorical device marks the emptying of meaning from *lord*:

> To take hym for hir housbond and hir lord,
> Of swich lordshipe as men han over hir wyves.

The nominalist/realist debate is evoked in lines 751–52, when Arveragus abjures the traditional patriarchal role but insists on retaining the appearance of it:

> Save that the name of soveraynetee,
> That wolde he have for shame of his degree.

He keeps the name (*nomen*) but not the thing (*res*). The signifier points nowhere; it has become an unsigning sign which will, nevertheless, reclaim its signifying power by the end of the tale (already foreshadowed here in the emphatic syntax, and especially in the *name/shame* internal rhyme which suggests a signified for *name*). Finally, on the largest scale, meaning is so set adrift that Dorigen's firm and apparently unambiguous rejection of Aurelius can be re-encoded by him to bring about a meaning opposite to her intention.

A major effect of this linguistic openness is to create gaps which no imaginative endeavour on the part of the reader is able to close. By the end of this tale an unbridgeable gap has been exposed between the formal closural features of story – the main characters having all been returned to their proper states and positions – and the very open-ended thematic elements. In a tale in which no meaning has remained stable for very long, any answer to the Franklin's celebrated closing question, 'Which was the mooste fre, as thynketh yow?', will be as true, or as false, as any other. Needless to say, however, Dorigen is rarely considered as a possible contender: *fredom* seems to be a male preserve. She is included, for example, in Mann's paper, where she is ranked below Arveragus and above Aurelius, since she shares (albeit in a 'considerably shaken' form) the virtues of 'trouthe' and 'married love'; her dependence on Arveragus to sustain these virtues is stressed (pp. 21–22).

In contrast to the open ending of the *Franklin's Tale*, the *Wife of Bath's Tale* uses its fairy-tale genre to present what appears to be a

interpreting literature by his own experience. But this remains an externally controlled interaction with the text, since the clerk (author) directs and manipulates:

> And whan this maister that this magyk wroughte
> Saugh it was tyme, he clapte his handes two,
> And farewell al oure revel was ago.

(1203–4)

The episode deliberately exposes the creation of illusion. Within the story as it subsequently unfolds, the clerk goes on to use his skill and knowledge to weave the illusion which almost unravels Dorigen. Simultaneously, the narrator envisages an audience as passive and easily directed as Aurelius in the study. For example, the audience is never *shown* the marital happiness of Arveragus and Dorigen; rather, it is rhetorically asserted by means of the inexpressibility topos ('Who koude telle, but he hath wedded be, / The joy, the ese, and the prosperitee / That is bitwixe an housbonde and his wyf?' – 803–5). More obviously, the narrator intrudes to direct audience attitude towards the dubious use of magic, or towards the dubious morality of a husband making his wife available sexually to another man for the sake of honour (and thus glossing over the moral relativism in arguing that Arveragus's action is justified because of its effect on Aurelius).[20] So, by placing this model of author-reader relationship *en abyme* Chaucer has inscribed within the text an implicit commentary on both the fictional processes of the containing narrative and on the power relationships operative at story level. Now, since within the story it is the clerk who is the master of illusion and the weaver of fictions, the threatening black rocks which his art, as it were, glosses over, take on added symbolic suggestiveness, coming to represent the covert meanings which rise up to subvert the text.[21] The rocks are a threat to Dorigen's well-being whether they are visible or hidden, but she misperceives the nature of this threat. She first sees it as directed against Arveragus, whereas, in reality, it proves to be directed against herself. As a catalyst, the rocks are responsible for the terms in which Dorigen rejects Aurelius, for the illusion which brings about her death-or-dishonour dilemma, and hence for Arveragus's decision to send her to Aurelius. In each situation, the rocks are closely linked with Dorigen's sexuality and mark her progressive loss of freedom and independence. It is noteworthy, too, that Dorigen's most cutting remarks to Aurelius are already couched in a language which assumes male sovereignty: 'What deyntee sholde a man han in his lyf / For to go love another mannes wyf, / That hath hir body whan so that hym liketh?' (1003–5), so it is hardly surprising that Arveragus should later feel that her body is at his disposal. If the *Franklin's Tale* culminates in a discussion of male/female relationships, the rocks might have to be seen as the latent assumption of male sexual power which underlies the whole discussion.

We have suggested that the scene in the clerk's study depicts Aurelius's recreation of a literary fiction, culminating in a picture of

> his lady on a daunce,
> On which hymself he daunced, as hym thoughte.

> (1200–1)

The scene is also, of course, a sexual fantasy (even without insisting on the common use of dance as a sexual euphemism),[22] and mirrors the way that Dorigen, as an object of male desire, is only another illusion created in different ways by the men in her life. This insight applies generally to the 'marriage group' women, presented *en abyme* in the *Franklin's Tale*, and as informing structure in the *Wife of Bath's Tale*.

IV

A crucial strategy for exploring the struggle between male and female for sexual power is found in the *Wife of Bath's Tale*, in the thematic interchange between sexual acts and speech acts, sexual power and verbal power. The knight's initial assertion of sexual dominance is to be expiated by a task whose whole object is primarily verbal but which leads him to the bed of the old woman. There, his sexual failure prompts her extended verbalizing. The length and digressiveness of her discourse, together with the way it presents an inverted mirror-image of the overt didacticism of the tale (that is, the narrator's thesis that power in a relationship should rest with the woman), suggests that it has a *mise en abyme* function, and thus thematizes the tale's general interchange of sexual power and verbal power. Furthermore, by incorporating a substantial segment of received, authoritative moral opinion, the text also thematizes didacticism. Through the interrelation of the two by embedding the intertextual expression of elevated morality within an argument directed towards the acquisition of sexual and emotional power, the text discloses a flaw within the argument which contributes towards an undermining of the narrator's didactic purpose. The wedding-night situation also emphasizes the symbolic function of the old woman: she is Woman as Man fears she might be – unattractive but, or perhaps because, sexually voracious, assertive, demanding and verbally powerful.[23] A comparison with the wedding-night scene from the *Merchant's Tale* (1709–1857) is very informative about the treatment of sexual power and sexual dominance, and about explicit and implicit attitudes towards women. The roles of the two women make a strong contrast, with May's silence and submission being directly opposite to the old woman's sexual and verbal assertiveness. The old woman's initial claims on the young knight – I love you . . . I'm your wife . . . I saved your life . . . I never did anything to offend you – present a range of ultimately untenable arguments for deserving to be loved. The gap between male and female is concisely expressed in the knight's reply when, on first demanding that the young man fulfil his promise, the old woman asks to be 'thy wyf . . . and eek thy love' (1066) and is met with the rejoinder 'My love? . . . nay, my dampnacioun!' (1067): 'woman, for man, is death. This is actually the castration complex at its most effective' (Cixous, 'Castration or Decapitation?', p. 48). The crux of the matter lies in who will have control over the transactional aspect of sexuality. It is a question of dominance, illustrated in the knight's two sexual encounters within the tale, the first a selfish taking from the non-speaking physically powerless maiden, the second a failure with the aggressive loquacious old woman. When confronted with female sexual aggression he is stricken with sexual reluctance, if not dysfunction. The old woman's taunting him with being *dangerous* (1090) is not calculated to help either,[24] since as a term more frequently applied to women it only thinly conceals an accusation of impotent effeminacy and marks the old woman's assumption of sexual and verbal dominance. Throughout history, women have been characterized as garrulous, chatterers, 'jangleresses', and so on, precisely because pejorative terms are needed to dismiss female claims to verbal efficacy.[25] The use of such terminology reduces the importance of the feminine capacity for language; once reduced, control is easier.

The Old Woman's verbal fluency contrasts with the ineffectual talkativeness of the *Franklin's Tale*'s Dorigen, for if verbal power and sexual power are interchangeable, there are some pertinent comments to be made on Dorigen's lack of verbal/orgasmic capacity. By twisting her words and using them to gain power over her, Aurelius effects a direct transfer of sexual power. In more basic terms, woman's resolve to say 'no', to refuse sexual relations, is brushed aside and transformed into an affirmative: women don't know what they really want, after all, and usually say the opposite. It does not matter whether it is with respect to Arveragus or Aurelius, Dorigen is allowed no desire other than that imposed upon her by male wishes. In the same way, the notorious 'black rocks' speech is a pointless questioning of the order of things: that is not woman's role (neither Dorigen's nor the Wife of Bath's) and so the rocks themselves are taken and used against her. Her speech is, as it were, clitoridectomized, just as successfully as the knight in the *Wife of Bath's Tale* is symbolically castrated by the old woman's clear assumption of sexual and verbal dominance. Dorigen goes on extending her long list of virtuous women, a speech which never climaxes but merely dissipates, until the dominant male arrives to take control.

V

The dilemma posed for the young knight at the end of the *Wife of Bath's Tale* adroitly shifts attention from the question 'What do women want?' to the question 'What do men want?'. The answer has been present throughout the tale, and is already inscribed in the opening lines. It seems to us inadequate to read the opening as no more than an ironic rebuke of the pilgrim-friar and as the tale's first example of the Wife's aggressive and digressive story-telling, since it raises very clearly the relationship between sexual power and fiction-making. Like the *Franklin's Tale*, this tale strongly asserts its own fictiveness at the outset by highlighting temporal and societal differences between the experiences in the text and the experiences of the narrator and audience. The readers must, nevertheless, participate actively in the creation of this fictive space *in illo tempore* ('In th' olde dayes of the Kyng Arthour'), and hence must constantly measure their subjective responses to text events against the formation of these events as textual fictions. The difference between past and present, once established, is immediately effaced. The Wife makes ironical use of the argument (elsewhere to be found, presumably seriously, in the *Franklin's Tale*) that Christianity has freed the modern world from the power of lesser supernatural phenomena – ironical, because the conceptual shift from the lexical set 'elf-queene, fayeryes, elf' to 'incubus' is repeated in the shift from the set 'lymytours, holy freres' to, again, 'incubus'. The equation is carefully prepared by the repetitions and deictic tightening of lines 872–73:

> For ther as wont to walken was an elf,
> Ther walketh now the lymytour hymself,

and then pushed home by lines 878–81:

> Wommen may go now saufly up and doun.
> In every bussh or under every tree

Ther is noon oother incubus but he
And he ne wol doon hem but dishonour.

By narrowing the focus of the opening lines to sexuality, and
by presenting 'elf' and 'friar' as signifiers pointing towards the
one signified (here rephrased by 'incubus'), the text asserts that
woman's role as sexually exploited object has remained unchanged
(or even worsened, if sex has lost the element of *fayerye* 'magic').
And, of course, what the rape at the beginning of the story proper
demonstrates is that not even *in illo tempore* could women 'go . . .
saufly up and doun' because of the attitudes and depredations of
human males. What men want is the availability and subservience
of women, an attitude which the tale seeks to overthrow both by the
thematic implications of the questions it poses and by its narrative
strategies which lead the reader through a pattern of ignorance and
disclosure. In comparison to Gower's 'Tale of Florent' or *The Marriage
of Dame Ragnell*, the *Wife of Bath's Tale* makes heavier use of suspense,
so that the reader's understanding of events is usually no more
informed than the young knight's. At the same time, the queen's
question, 'What do women most desire?', is both the central issue
and a deconstructive agent within the tale. The answer will always
be arbitrary, and, in common with *Dame Ragnell*, the *Wife of Bath's
Tale* builds in the recognition that the possibilities are limitless. The
seekers in *Dame Ragnell* fill entire books, and the Wife prefaces her
list of possible answers with the information that the knight 'in this
mateere' could nowhere find 'Two creatures accordynge in feere'
(923–24). This openness is sustained right up until the moment at
which the question must be answered, in contrast to the analogues,
in which the reader is informed of the answer in advance. Nor is it
told that the queen already knows the answer, which is another
contrast to the analogues. In both of those, the asker of the question
complains of being betrayed when given the correct answer, whereas
in the *Wife of Bath's Tale* the proferred answer is laid before a
conference of women representing all states ('wyf . . . mayde . . .
wydwe') and then adjudged to be correct. The main effect of this
difference is on the reader's interpretation, since it remains unclear
whether the test has been completely arbitrary, or whether the
power inhering in knowledge has been entirely shifted to the old
woman who has the answer and uses it in quest of her own sexual
regeneration, the recuperation of *fayerye*. Again in contrast to the
analogues, the *Wife of Bath's Tale* conceals from both the knight and
reader the promise which the old woman intends to exact, not
disclosing this until the moment of exaction (and thus shifting the

moral ground). The delayed timing of these disclosures, in our view, forces a more rigorous examination of the reader's subjective responses to the events themselves and their meanings.

The paradigm for this process of withholding and disclosure is presented *en abyme* in the story of Midas (951–82). The episode stands out for its manifest digressiveness, being an exemplum illustrating the only suggested answer to the queen's question which the narrator dismisses. It has a contrapuntal relation to the tale within which it is placed, mirroring textual concealment and deferral on the one hand, and textual disclosure on the other. Whereas the knight of the tale is in search of something unknown to him or the reader, Midas's wife is in possession of knowledge she should conceal but feels constrained to disclose. As literary texts prefer indirection to outright statement, and so practise concealment, when Midas's wife can no longer remain silent she whispers her secret to the water, thus re-encoding it. The episode is then truncated at the point of disclosure and so forever defers its consequence. For the conclusion, the reader is referred to another text, the putative source, Ovid's *Metamorphoses*, where it will be found that the story concerns not Midas's wife but his barber. As mere story, nevertheless, the *Wife of Bath's Tale* version resolves the conflict between concealment and disclosure by re-encoding. As we have suggested earlier, re-encoding takes place at the end of the tale itself, when the knight's choice not to choose enables a dismantling, still at story level, of the restrictive pairs 'old and ugly, therefore faithful', or 'young and beautiful, therefore unfaithful' and a re-encoding as 'fair and good'. In its immediate context, the Midas story also functions as an antifeminist stereotype, the depiction of the chatterbox untrustworthy woman. Has the ending of the Wife's tale likewise done more than increase the number of stereotypes from two to three, substituting the conventional object of male desire – the beautiful woman who is possessed sexually and exclusively – for objects either undesirable or feared? The first option offers conventional, safe, boring marriage, where the wife is 'trewe, humble' and subservient ('nevere yow displese') but sexually undesirable; the second threatens with female sexuality rampant and out of control. For the price of allowing his wife *maistrie*, the knight wins the ideal object of desire. It is, once again, a matter of transaction, which the tale's final (and most literal) disclosure suggests that the knight has won:

> 'Cast up the curtyn, looke how that it is.'
> And whan the knyght saugh verraily al this,
> That she so fair was, and so yong therto,

For joy he hente hire in his armes two ...
And she obeyed hym in every thyng
That myghte doon hym plesance or likyng.

(1249–56)

The cue is 'obeyed', which suggests that the long-deferred consummation coincides with an actual return to male dominance. In both the analogues, the actual transformation of the woman coincides with the knight's resolve to consummate the marriage despite his partner's sexual unattractiveness, so the subsequent question of sovereignty is of diminished impact, since each young man has already proven his worth. By deferring the transformation as it does, the *Wife of Bath's Tale* makes all pivot on the issue of *maistrie* and loses all.

VI

What emerges from this approach to the *Canterbury Tales* is that Chaucer presents a bleak view of male–female relations, rather than the more usual assumption of a movement towards optimism. The major tool that women are shown to possess with which they can subvert the authority of those over them is their creative capacity, usually taking the form of power with language. Thus the Wife of Bath, in the longest prologue of the *Canterbury Tales*, illustrates the female's power with words in her ability to create an interesting discourse from her personal experience rather than from reliance upon authority and old stories, and so displays a natural ease in story-telling not enjoyed by the male narrator of the *Franklin's Tale*. In the *Wife of Bath's Tale* this capacity overtly offsets woman's sexual vulnerability to the demands and abuses of physically dominant men. It does not eradicate the abuse, but the power is a form of compensation. A comparable verbal power is achieved by May in the *Merchant's Tale*. She is totally inarticulate up to and through the wedding night and, apart from four lines of reported thought (1982–85), does not speak until the moment she is asserting her virtuousness to Januarie even as she signals her would-be lover to climb the tree. This coincidence of contrary sign systems asserts a loss of virtue concomitant with the gaining of voice. The linking of verbal power with sexual unfaithfulness reduces that power to verbal deceit and declares it illicit, with the result that sympathy is withdrawn or withheld from these female characters. The obverse of these women with voices is Dorigen; she sees herself as having a choice between sexual indignity or death, but Arveragus, selecting

the former for her, then formulates her next choice as one between
silence or death:

'I yow forbede, up peyne of deeth,
That nevere, whil thee lasteth lyf ne breeth,
To no wight telle thou of this aventure . . .
Ne make no contenance of hevynesse,
That folk of yow may demen harm or gesse.'

(1481–86)

In place of verbal dissembling which gains a modicum of freedom,
Dorigen is sentenced for her errors to channel her creativity into
silent suffering. For woman to exercise her creative abilities in other
ways, and thus to rebel against her prescribed role, is to re-create Eve
and confirm the received view of woman as the root of sin. Dorigen,
then, follows the way of submission which constitutes goodness
in the male conception of woman. This attitude is succinctly, if
unwittingly, expressed by Donald C. Baker in his study of 'Dorigen's
Complaint': 'Each exemplum brings home solidly its implication,
sometimes tragic, sometimes humorous: all vital matters require
complete confidence and trust in one's mate; it is evident that the
decision is to be left to Arveragus.' Baker then matches this with 'the
decision of the husband that his wife's word is more important than
any consideration touching him', and concludes that the moral is the
'necessity of complete mutual trust, rather than sovereignty as the
essential ingredient of any marriage'.[26] What is described here, though,
is mutual trust based on female submission and male decision-making,
which looks to us suspiciously like male sovereignty. The *Franklin's
Tale*, as a model for marital bliss, can thus be extremely appealing to
males, since it suppresses the creative and verbal capacities of the
female which are put to use in the *Wife of Bath's* and *Merchant's Tales*
to humble the male and in turn give some degree of satisfaction to
the women, even if the pattern of sexual submission is not itself
broken. What does seem clearly illustrated by the case of Dorigen
is the way control over the lives of women is maintained under
the guise of caring and concern. This not only marks Arveragus's
behaviour at the crisis, apart from a short outburst, but also appears
throughout Aurelius's speech to Dorigen in which he courteously
reminds her of her promise and his deep love for her, but all his
words of concern are an obvious lead-up to the blunt conclusion, 'But
wel I woot the rokkes been aweye'. The incidents illustrate how men
create and sustain the illusions which support desire: readers have
had little difficulty in seeing through the illusions of Aurelius, though
those of Arveragus have proved more resistant.

We have suggested that an approach to these tales which locates itself outside the habits of traditional male reading and examines the illusion that is fiction, and especially those aspects of it showing a strong textual self-consciousness, might bring out a different emphasis within the attitudes towards the illusions and realities ascribed to characters in that fiction. It then seems arguable that the relationship between the metafictions embedded in the tales and the recurrent theme of sexual power discloses a similarity between the author's creative power over language and fiction and women's creative verbal power which substitutes, in various senses, for actual sexual power. But if, as this seems to indicate, Chaucer recognized the predicament of women, sympathized with them and saw their capacity for fulness of life, he also saw little prospect for change in a world where elves are succeeded by friars, where the shackles of imagination give way to the authority of flesh-and-blood men, and where the creative and sexual capacities of women were either unacknowledged or feared.

Notes

1. The starting-point for this essay was a paper by Marcella Ryan, and then our overlapping interests prompted its evolution as a collaborative project.

2. As, for example, by EUGENE VANCE in 'Mervelous Signals: Poetics, Sign Theory, and Politics in Chaucer's *Troilus'*, *New Literary History*, [cited as *NLH*], 10 (1970), 293–337.

3. ARLYN DIAMOND, 'Chaucer's Women and Women's Chaucer', *The Authority of Experience: Essays in Feminist Criticism* (Amherst: University of Massachusetts Press, 1977), pp. 60–83.

4. G. L. KITTREDGE, 'Chaucer's Discussion of Marriage', *Modern Philology*, 9 (1912), 435–67. The view did not go unchallenged, of course; see JAMES L. HODGE, 'The Marriage Group: Precarious Equilibrium', *English Studies*, 46 (1965), 289–300.

5. Thus in Alfred David's reading of the *Wife of Bath's Tale* the question of sovereignty is finally subsumed into an account of the power of fiction to transcend the limitations of experience (*The Strumpet Muse* [Bloomington & London: Indiana University Press, 1976], Chap. IX).

6. The *Franklin's Tale* has long been read as an illustration of *gentillesse*, to which the marriage issue is subsidiary; the watershed study here is LINDSAY A. MANN, ' "Gentilesse" and the Franklin's Tale', *Studies in Philology*, 63 (1966), 10–29. The position has been restated, with minor modifications, in MARY J. CARRUTHERS, 'The Gentilesse of Chaucer's Franklin', *Criticism*, 23 (1981), 283–300.

7. MORTON W. BLOOMFIELD, 'The Franklin's Tale: A Story of Unanswered Questions', *Acts of Interpretation: Essays . . . in Honor of E. Talbot Donaldson*, ed. Mary J. Carruthers and Elizabeth D. Kirk (Norman, OK: Pilgrim Press, 1982), p. 196. The whole essay is a good example of the trait we are pointing to: not itself directly concerned with 'the marriage debate', it hedges on the central issue and half-consents in a parenthesis.

8. DAVID AERS, *Chaucer* (Brighton: Harvester, 1986), pp. 98–9.

9. Particularly illuminating discussions of this principle are: MARY JACOBUS, 'Is There a Woman in This Text', *NLH*, 14 (1982), 117–41; JONATHAN CULLER, *On Deconstruction* (London: Routledge and Kegan Paul, 1983), pp. 43–64 ('Reading as a Woman').

10. Gender-based value judgments have become so institutionalized within criticism that they are reproduced by writers of either sex. Thus CARRUTHERS, 'Gentilesse', 294–5 assumes that Dorigen's behaviour is 'unbearable', and that both she and the audience find it to be so, whereas Arveragus's decision to send her to Aurelius is 'an act of moral courage'. The reading pivots on lines 1472–86, but, like most *Franklin's Tale* criticism, ignores the physical threat uttered by Arveragus which concludes the section.

11. TREVOR WHITTOCK, *A Reading of the Canterbury Tales* (Cambridge: Cambridge University Press, 1968), p. 177.

12. All quotations from the *Canterbury Tales* are taken from F. N. Robinson, *The Complete Works of Geoffrey Chaucer*, 2nd edn (Oxford & London: Oxford University Press, 1966).

13. HÉLÈNE CIXOUS, 'Castration or Decapitation?', *Signs*, 7 (1981), 45.

14. ROBERT B. BURLIN, *Chaucerian Fiction* (Princeton, NJ: Princeton University Press, 1977), p. 200.

15. *Boece*, 1 pr.6, 245–50; 3 pr.5, 720–25; 3 m.6, 760–65; JOHN OF SALISBURY, *Polycraticus*, ed. Migne, *Patr. Lat.*, lib.ii, cap.xxix, 475. The idea also appears in *Troilus and Criseyde*, 3.1016 and 1765. See also PETER HAIDU, 'Repetition: Modern Reflections on Medieval Aesthetics', *Modern Language Notes*, 92 (1977), 882–3.

16. ROBERT B. BURLIN, 'The Art of Chaucer's Franklin', *Neophilologus*, 51 (1967), 61.

17. For cogent discussions of this concept, see: TADEWZ KOWZAN, 'Art "En Abyme"', *Diogenes*, 96 (1976), 67–92; KEIR ELAM, *Shakespeare's Universe of Discourse* (Cambridge: Cambridge University Press, 1984); LINDA HUTCHEON, *Narcissistic Narrative* (New York and London: Methuen, 1984).

18. JUDITH FERSTER, 'Interpretation and Imitation in Chaucer's Franklin's Tale', *Medieval Literature: Criticism, Ideology & History*, ed. David Aers (Brighton: Harvester, 1986), p. 160.

19. MARCELLE THIEBAUX, *The Stag of Love: The Chase in Medieval Literature* (Ithaca, NY and London: Cornell University Press, 1974), p. 104.

20. MANN (p. 17) best exemplifies those readings which choose to see Arveragus's decision as a calculated risk, intended to put pressure on Aurelius.

21. The symbolism of the rocks has been much discussed since OWEN's influential 'The Crucial Passages in Five of *The Canterbury Tales*: A Study in Irony and Symbol', *Journal of English and Germanic Philology* [cited as *JEGP*], 52 (1953), 294–/. HODGE, pp. 296–7, reviews earlier interpretations, advances 'a symbol of Dorigen's love for Arveragus', and suggests that the Franklin doesn't understand the implications of his own story or the symbolism of the rocks, and hence the tale is undermined from within.

22. There are various references in *Midde English Dictionary* under *daunce* 4.(a), where dancing is synonymous with sexual activity, The most obvious is *Troilus and Criseyde*, 4.1431.

23. DIAMOND (p. 62) observes that medieval antifeminism expresses not 'contempt for women's inadequacies . . . but fear of their power'. See also NIKKI STILLER, *Eve's Orphans: Mothers and Daughters in Medieval English Literature* (Westport, CT and London: Greenwood Press, 1980), pp. 63–85.

24. *MED, dangerous* 2.(a) 'difficult to deal with or to approach . . . haughty, aloof': in examples in amatory contexts the term is always applied to women. Compare also *daunger* 4.(a) 'Resistance offered to a lover by his lady love'.

25. See also the remarks on the 'battle of the sexes for linguistic primacy' in SANDRA M. GILBERT and SUSAN GUBAR, 'Sexual Linguistics: Gender, Language, Sexuality', *NLH*, 16 (1985), 515–43 (esp. 523 ff.).

26. DONALD C. BAKER, 'A Crux in Chaucer's *Franklin's Tale*: Dorigen's Complaint', *JEGP*, 60 (1961), 63.

10 The Subject of Confession: The Pardoner and the Rhetoric of Penance*

LEE PATTERSON

Patterson reads in the Pardoner's performance a self-representation as a penitent, using the late-medieval discourse of confession, that also incorporates a rejection of such a discourse. Before discussing the Pardoner's own 'motivational complexity', Patterson sets this in the context of other late-medieval texts and ecclesiastical injunctions (this survey has had to be omitted here) that reveal the problematics of confession, in particular the thin dividing line between the fruitful recognition of one's sins and the perils of despair. The Pardoner's penitence, read in Oedipal terms as the desire for atonement with the Father (and the Pardoner's castration, whether real or presumed, marks his transgression of the paternal law) is cut across by illicit yearnings for the Mother, represented by the Old Man, the Pardoner's *alter ego*, knocking his phallic staff on the ground and demanding re-entry into the maternal earth. The Pardoner's resistance to the institutional language of confession reveals what Patterson calls the 'scandal' in the Christian scheme of the sacrifice of the son being required to mollify the Father, though his need for the paternal absolution remains no less pressing in what is a complex narrative of yearning for 'oneness' with both Father and Mother. Patterson further reads this latter desire for the mother in Lacanian terms as that for an original identity and 'self-presence' before the entry into the (paternal) symbolic order constitutes the self-alienated subject; his insistence on the validity of this desire for an 'autonomous selfhood', as well as on the requirement to recognize defining institutional constraints, represents a necessary social engagement that Patterson canvasses throughout his book and that is further discussed in my Introduction, pp. 10–12.

. . .

* Reprinted from LEE PATTERSON, *Chaucer and the Subject of History* (London: Routledge, 1991), pp. 397–412, 418–21.

III

In the *Pardoner's Prologue and Tale* Chaucer's revision of his inherited materials is in the same inward and problematic direction as in these other texts [*Piers Plowman* and the Middle English religious lyrics Patterson has been discussing]. The one-dimensional monologue of allegory is deepened here not by functioning as the Pardoner's confession but by becoming one element in a larger sequence of involuntary self-exposure that is fulfilled only in the *Tale*; and the *Tale* is in turn transformed by the context of its telling from an exemplum about avarice into a psychological allegory that reveals the Pardoner's despair. The confession of despair, like that of Pruyde or Couetyse [in *Piers Plowman*], is a theoretical impossibility, and it is this paradox that requires these transformations of genre: the direct self-revelation of autobiography is distorted by strategies of manipulation and concealment, and the negatives of his condition are visible only in the displacements of fiction. It may be that sacramental healing is in fact brought no closer by the Pardoner's confession, but his act of speaking carries a spiritual significance and must be understood within a penitential context. Simply to write him off as an impenitent sinner, and to confine criticism to the task of categorizing and measuring his sinfulness, is to preempt understanding. Not that the desire for critical superiority over the Pardoner is not itself indicative of his significance. For in both his mutilation and in his willingness to imagine sufficiency in Oedipal terms, the Pardoner at once enacts masculinism's deepest fears and challenges a theological orthodoxy that is itself sustained by profoundly masculinist assumptions. However we seek to understand him, the Pardoner places upon our critical faculties, or at least those of the male reader, a sometimes intolerable strain.[1]

The ironic smile with which the God of Love accepts Faus Semblant's pledge of loyalty is Jean de Meun's [in the *Roman de la Rose*] perfunctory gesture toward the discontinuity between character and speech implicit in the paradox of the truthful hypocrite. But whereas Jean de Meun evaded the force of the paradox by simply alternating passages of hypocritical piety with those of candid self-revelation, Chaucer defines his character as a professional speaker and so places this discontinuity at the center of his discourse. Language is the means by which the Pardoner creates himself for others and for himself, whether it be the cocksure prattle with which ⌐e simultaneously disguises and reveals his eunuchry, or the witty ⌐d learned sermon, embellished with telling exempla, with which he ⌐blishes his authority before the 'lewed people'. The *Prologue*, for all its apparent candor, participates in this image making. For there he presents a theatricalized self-representation of evil so extravagant that it necessarily calls itself into question.

The ostensible purpose of the *Prologue* is to demonstrate that the Pardoner knows himself to be 'a ful vicious man' (459) motivated by an entirely 'yvel entencioun' (408). Tyrannizing the priest and his parishioners, and willfully undermining the penitential system of which he is an agent, the Pardoner appropriates and debases even the scriptural image of the dove by which medieval preaching was typically legitimized:

> Thanne peyne I me to strecche forth the nekke,
> And est and west upon the peple I bekke,
> As dooth a dowve sittynge on a berne.
>
> (395–97)

And throughout he insists upon the almost allegorical simplicity of his own motives – 'I preche of no thyng but for coveityse' (424) – and glories in his own hypocrisy: 'Thus kan I preche agayn that same vice / Which that I use, and that is avarice' (427–28). Delightedly wringing the last penny from a widow with starving children, he consigns the souls of his audience to an infernal black-berrying. 'Ho, ho, be-holde me!' said Belial, 'þe myȝte prynce of þe partys infernall', and the Pardoner's *Prologue* presents itself as an analogous display of self-delighting and unrepentant wickedness.[2] Always the rhetorician, he at once offends the censorious *gentils* and titillates the raucous lower elements (represented by Harry Bailly) by playing to the full the role of the deliberate sinner, the man who has chosen with open eyes the path to his own damnation. Hence he speaks in the uncompromising, and subject-less, tone of allegory and sounds much like Deguileville's Avarice, who tells *her* pilgrim-victim that 'I often go through the country-side showing false relics and objects to the simple people in order to hoodwink them out of their money'.[3] But rather than being created by the conventions of medieval allegory, the Pardoner himself exploits them. Simultaneously entertaining and horrifying his audience, he adopts allegorical excess as a strategy by which he can at once reveal and conceal himself. The allegorical figure speaks in order to be fully known, while the very extravagance of the Pardoner's revelations hides him from us.[4]

But of course his hyperbole betrays the more complicated self it seeks to conceal. Insisting early and often that his motives are brazenly simple (403–4, 423–24, 432–33, 461), he also claims – and repeats the claim – that he is doing good works:

But though myself by gilty in that synne,
Yet kan I maken oother folk to twynne
From avarice, and soore to repente.

(429–31)

For though myself be a ful vicious man,
A moral tale yet I yow telle kan.

(459–60)

What makes these hints persuasive is his own response to them,
for in both cases he hastily withdraws from these disturbing
complications to the comforting simplicity of an unqualified
avariciousness. 'But that is nat my principal entente', he insists, 'I
preche nothyng but for coveitise' (432–33), and he continues to claim
that his moral tale serves only as a device 'for to wynne' (461). And
in both these cases, when his own complexity might become visible
to himself and to his audience, he cuts off his line of thought with
a misdirected and defensive conclusion: 'Of this mateere it oghte
ynogh suffice' (434); 'Now hoold youre pees!' – although only he
has been speaking – 'my tale I wol bigynne' (462). These fugitive and
embarrassed self-defenses show the Pardoner acknowledging in his
spirit values he subverts in his working, a complication that occurs
again in the notorious benediction with which he closes his *Tale*. In
sum, he is by no means as unambiguously impenitent as he claims,
and his attempt to reduce himself to the simplicity of allegorical evil
itself witnesses to the painfully divided consciousness from which
he seeks to escape. By turns derisory and hesitant, vaunting and
awkwardly candid, the *Prologue* reveals in its very lack of clarity
a spirit in conflict.

Chaucer's representation of this self-division is derived from
medieval traditions of penitential theology and confessional writing.
Quite apart from the spiritual condition of despair that, as we shall
see, motivates the Pardoner's performance as a whole, the vaunting
confession of the *Prologue* is itself a conventional penitential form.
The *Prologue* is an instance of what in the *summae confessorum* is
called a *confessio ficti* – the confession, that is, of an imposter – and of
which a number of examples appear in vernacular literature.[5] Middle
English instances include Lady Meed's confession to the friar in *Piers
Plowman* and the Devil's confession with which Robert Mannyng
closes *Handlyng Synne*.[6] The most common appearance of the *confessio
ficti*, however, is in the Renart story, where Renart confesses no less
than five times in all; indeed, his habit of misusing the sacrament led
at least one cleric to label the perfunctory or uncontrite confession a
confessio renardi.[7] The instance closest to Chaucer's poem, and one

which he almost certainly knew, is Renart's confession to 'frere Huberz' the kite.[8] Desperately hungry, Renart lures the kite within striking distance by confessing, apparently truthfully, that he has in his gluttony devoured even Hubert's children. He begs the horrified kite to forgive him, and when the charitable Hubert leans forward to bestow a kiss of peace Renart gobbles him up. The parallels between this scene and the situation of Chaucer's Pardoner are intriguing: the confession as a trap, the extravagant sinfulness, the crucial role of the kiss of peace, and the ambiguity of both confessions – in neither case can we easily separate truth from fiction – argue for a relationship of influence. But whether this episode is a specific source for Chaucer or not, the analogies suggest that in revising the allegorical monologue Chaucer moved in the direction of the *confessio renardi*. 'ʒa, whanne þe fox prechyþ, kepe wel ʒore gees!' is a cautionary Middle English proverb that applies in the first instance to the 'lewed people'; but by giving his Pardoner a confessional prologue Chaucer brings it to bear as well upon the pilgrims – and upon the reader.[9]

There is a further difference as well. For the *confessio renardi* remains irrepressibly and unredeemably cynical: the narrator's only comment on Renart's betrayal of Frere Huberz is a laconic 'certes ci a mal pecheor / qui a mangé son confessor'.[10] But in his reaccenting of these narrative elements, Chaucer uses the penitential situation to create a character who is anxious and dependent. For not only does the trap in this instance close on the Pardoner himself, but the whole relationship between his real and his created selves is less controlled and deliberate. We have already seen how the *Prologue* is a theatricalized self-representation that reveals as it conceals a motivational complexity that yearns for a redemption it simultaneously disdains. This same ambiguity controls the *Tale*. Taken literally, as he recommends, it is an exemplum that means *radix malorum est cupiditas*; but read spiritually it is a moral allegory about the Pardoner himself, and it figures not avarice but despair. On the one hand, the rioters enact the Pardoner's life of self-damnation. Brazenly impenitent – 'And ech of hem at otheres synne lough' (476) – they are perverse *imitatores Dei* in action as well as symbol. 'Deeth shal be deed, if that they may hem hente!' (710) is their Christological claim; and as R. A. Shoaf points out, 'The cry of the prophet [Hosea], "O death, I will be thy death," exegesis consistently understands as the triumphant claim of Christ the Redeemer.'[11] They engage in the imitation of God symbolically as well: together a parodic Trinity – 'we thre been al ones' (696) – they enact as well a dark Eucharistic ritual as 'the yongeste of hem alle' (804) serves bread and poisoned wine.[12] And when, like the Pardoner, they issue from their tavern to misperform their divine mission, they receive their just desserts with terrifying efficiency.[13] In the guise of a story of three rioters, the *Tale* presents us with the facts of the Pardoner's case and the future that (he fears) awaits him. Thinking himself an Augustinian *venditor verborum*, the Pardoner is in fact a far more modern being, a Wordsworthian 'traveller whose tale is always of himself'.[14]

The penitential meaning of the Pardoner's history, with its tortuous inner complexities, is most powerfully expressed in the uncanny figure of the Old Man. Rather than the saintly wise man of the analogues, a philosopher or hermit or even Christ, the Pardoner presents a figure who accurately reflects his own irreducible contradictions. Like the Pardoner, the Old Man proffers advice both needful – 'Agayns an oold man, hoor upon his heed, / Ye sholde arise' (743–44) – and perilous: 'turne up this croked wey' (761). Also like the Pardoner, he knows the truth but is unable to use it. In the terms of the story, he knows where Death is to be found but cannot find it himself, while tropologically he has won through to a gentle wisdom that has done little to relieve his own suffering.[15] Hence he too offers a closing benediction – 'God save yow, that boghte agayn mankynde, / And yow amende!' (766–67) – that is in the event self-excluding. For the Old Man's fate is to remain ever unregenerate, whether this be expressed in the allegorical terms of exchanging age for youth or in the theological terms of exchanging the 'cheste' of his worldly goods for the 'heyre clowt' of penance.[16] As we should remember, he speaks with a voice traditional to the penitential lyric, that of the sinner whose repentance has come too late and whose wisdom is bought at the price of endless anguish. 'Deþ ich wilni mest, / Whi nis he me I-core?'[17] These are Maximian's words in his 'Regret', and it is precisely Maximianus's first elegy that Chaucer drew upon for this portrait and that directs us to the context of failed penance that helps to explain the Old Man. 'Mors est iam requies, vivere mea poena', says the speaker of Maximianus's original poem, and it is this rest that is now denied the Old Man, this punishment that he must now suffer.[18] Like the *quaestor* – the Latin term for a pardoner – whom he faithfully expresses, the Old Man is condemned to a life-in-death of Cain-like wandering, and in his fruitless penitential yearnings he has descended into the hell of despair. Living death, wandering, and sterility: these are the characteristics of despair, and they are characteristics shared by the Old Man and by his creator and *alter ego*, the Pardoner.[19]

The Pardoner's own body invites a similar exegesis. Robert Miller, in a widely influential reading, has suggested that we interpret the Pardoner's evident sterility as revealing him to be a *eunuchus non dei*. But this is a by no means common exegetical figure, and if indeed it is to be invoked here then this is, at least to my knowledge, its only vernacular appearance. What also militates against its relevance here is that there is in fact another, homiletically common image of sterility that is both linked to penance, and specifically to despair, and that finds a striking presence in the *Tale* itself. This is the *arbor infructuosa*. The *radix malorum* of the sermon appears in the *Tale* as the 'precious hoord' (775) the rioters find at the foot of an 'ook' (765), a tree that the exegetes interpret as a symbol of despair.[20] The Pardoner himself is like the fig tree of Matthew 21:18–21 that offers to the hungry Lord not fruit but foliage and is withered with his curse: according to the exegetes, the foliage shows that the tree glories in vain words while lacking the fruit of good works.[21] The Pardoner is one of those 'qui verba habent, et facta non habent', and his need is precisely for the 'fruit worthy of penance' (Matthew 3:8) that can alone save him from the fire of judgment.[22] 'For now the ax is placed to the root of the tree [*ad radicem arborem*]; therefore every tree that does not produce good fruit will be dug up and cast into the fire' (Matthew 3:10). Yet for all its judicial gravity, this sequence of biblical imagery includes a controlling message of mercy in the parable of the sterile fig tree in Luke 13:7–9. The *paterfamilias* commands that the tree be uprooted and destroyed, but the *cultor* advises that it be ditched and dunged and given one last chance; according to the exegetes the ditch is 'humilitas poenitentis' and the dung 'memoria peccatorum' and 'cordis luctus et lacrymarum'.[23] That 'an evil tree cannot bring forth good fruit' (Matthew 7:18) remains an inviolable principle, but as Augustine (among others) insists, each righteous Christian has been *made* a fruitful tree: 'Whoever therefore is today a good man, that is, a good tree, was found evil and has been made good.'[24] The *radix arboris*, the human will, can be changed by penance from *cupiditas* to *caritas*: 'so turn your eyes into yourself, descend into yourself, challenge yourself, appraise yourself, question yourself, and discover yourself: and what displeases you, destroy it; what pleases you, choose it and cultivate it.'[25]

The *Pardoner's Tale* contains an accurate account of the Pardoner's own spiritual condition, but it is one that he is himself apparently incapable of reading. His understanding of the spiritual life is as obstinately literal as that of the rioters, who set out on a journey to kill 'this false traytour Deeth' (699).[26] His sermon on the tavern vices conceives of sin in terms that are almost compulsively corporeal – the fall is ascribed not to disobedience but to gluttony – and his rhetoric throughout is pervaded with hyperbole pushed to the edge of personification: 'O wombe! O bely! O stynkyng cod, / Fulfilled of dong and of corrupcioun!' (534–35). Indeed, we are encouraged to understand his spiritual impasse as an effect of his own literalistic misreading of himself. As we have seen, contrition includes powerful at times overwhelming negations, its separate aspects traditionally termed *pudor, detestatio, dolor,* and *timor.* In self-evident ways each of these emotions is known to the Pardoner, but they derive not from spiritual self-inspection but from corporeal self-regard. Ashamed of a literal eunuchry, he hides behind a far more shameful spiritual sterility; fearing exposure to his companions, he mocks the judgment of God; his sorrow is not for 'the loss of heaven and his many offenses against the Creator' but simply *de ipso;* and his hatred is not for 'the vileness of sin' but for the vileness of his own body. In the *Parson's Tale* Chaucer quotes St Paul's famous lament, 'Allas, I caytyf man! who shal delivere me fro the prisoun of my caytyf body?'[27] In a sense that exceeds his comprehension, this is the meaning of the Pardoner's words. But only in the symbolic form of the 'resteless kaityf' is he able to acknowledge his condition. Deprived by what the exegetes would call his 'ariditas litterae' from understanding the spiritual meaning of his own discourse, the Pardoner enacts his confessional needs through a series of oblique displacements. The *Prologue* presents inflated self-advertisements and fugitive glimpses of a more genuine self; the *Tale* displaces into fiction the Pardoner's deepest self-understanding while hiding its meaning from the man who speaks. Finally, the offer of the relics comes as the fitting conclusion to this sequence, an elliptical and compact gesture that is as self-contradictory as the Pardoner's previous utterances. On the one hand, it asks for inclusion, either in the fellow feeling of a jest or the earnest respect due a 'suffisant pardoneer' (932); on the other hand, and especially in its taunting of the Host ('he is moost envoluped in synne' [942]), it solicits exclusion and punishment. The punishment that is then inflicted is painfully apt, for it brings into the open the physical source of the spiritual fruitlessness that only true confession can finally cure. In its full dimensions, then, as an invitation to be hurt and to be forgiven, this epilogue exactly fulfills the postconfessional part of penance: in its shaming of the Pardoner it provides – as the confessional handbooks advise – an appropriate punishment, and it serves to elicit a gesture of absolution: 'Anon they kiste and ryden forth hir weye' (968).[28]

IV

This interpretation of the *Pardoner's Prologue and Tale* is satisfyingly efficient: it accommodates a dauntingly complicated verbal performance to a stable structure of imagery and thought derived from the penitential system of which the Pardoner is an agent, and it xplains the Pardoner's own mutilation as a symbolic representation of his spiritual condition. But like all interpretations, it is in no sense simply a disinterested explication of meanings with which the text is endowed, an innocent reading out of that which the author has written in. On the contrary, it responds to certain interests and needs – needs that the text itself both solicits and, with characteristic self-awareness, dramatizes. The agency of dramatization is the contretemps between the Host and the Pardoner. We should remember that at the center of the Pardoner's performance is the gap between intention and language: not only a vicious man who can tell a moral tale, he is as well a speaker whose language serves simultaneously to conceal and expose him, at once to shroud his deepest spiritual needs and yet to enact them. Moreover, this is a gap that is, as we have seen, meaningful in terms familiar to both medieval and modern thought. On the one hand, it articulates the medieval understanding of sin as privation, a lack that the language of confession promises (perhaps overambitiously) to ameliorate. And on the other hand, it expresses the modern analysis of the difference between self-representation and self-presence as a rift or split endemic to a symbolic order that is itself the effect of a primal repression – a repression, moreover, that is both a disabling castration and the means by which the male subject is constituted.

Now the point for our purposes is that these two orders of understanding are brought together in the final, enigmatic exchange between Host and Pardoner, an exchange that reveals as well the interpreter's own implication within this linguistic economy. For one thing, it shows how the exegetical reading that the Pardoner's discourse elicits itself bespeaks the very need that motivates the Pardoner himself. When the Host is offered the relics, he responds with a comment that raises the issue not merely of the Pardoner's castration but of the linguistic instability that makes possible his verbal pyrotechnics:

> I wold I hadde thy coillons in myn hond
> In stide of relikes or of seintuarie.
> Lat kutte hem of, I wol thee helpe hem carie;
> They shul be shryned in an hogges toord!
>
> (952–55)

These lines are derived from a crucial passage in the *Roman de la Rose*, in which Raison justifies to the prudish lover her use of the word *coilles* to refer to the testicles that Jupiter cut off his father Saturn and threw into the sea.[29] Raison argues that whether she used the word *reliques* or *coilles* is a matter entirely of convention, and she demonstrates her point by saying that if we used the word *coilles* t refer to what we now call relics then we would adore *coilles* in church, and we would kiss them and enshrine them in gold and silver – a passage that so offended the scribes that it is excised from several of the manuscripts.[30] This scribal squeamishness is indicative of just how much is invested in the fiction of a natural or innocent signification, in the belief, for instance, that the phonetic image *coilles* bears a relationship to testicles that is more than merely arbitrary. For we habitually assume that the relation of words to things is not conventional but natural, that words like *reliques* are necessarily tied to certain things and cannot wander promiscuously from, for instance, sacred and venerated objects to genitals.[31] It is just this instinctive belief in a natural and innocent signification that Raison subverts in her equation of *coilles* and *reliques*. Moreover, by deriving her example from the scene of Saturn's castration she invokes the initial act of severance by which the golden age of natural innocence was separated from the fallen world of history. Because of the absence or lack of verbal sufficiency, meaning is now a function of a convention that can (presumably) be changed at will. Hence the success of the Pardoner's verbal pyrotechnics: a castrate himself, he deploys words that are by definition empty to mean whatever he wants.[32]

Now it is the exegetical reading of the Pardoner that promises an antidote to this castrated language. When read exegetically, his *Prologue and Tale* are an instance of what Roland Barthes in *S/Z*, itself a book about a book about castration, calls Replete Literature. Rather than 'the *nothingness* of castration, [in which] the envelope of things cannot be authenticated [and] the dilatory movement of the signifier cannot be stopped', we have in an exegetically read *Pardoner's Tale* a classic or readerly text, one that is 'like a cupboard where meanings are shelved, stacked, safeguarded (in this text, nothing is ever lost: meaning recuperates everything)'.[33] The endless deferral that characterizes writing is in the readerly text cut short by a single, authoritative hermeneutic code.[34] To the reader armed with the repertory of exegetical meanings, the deceptive veiling with which the Pardoner seeks to conceal his despairing condition serves only to proclaim it. Despite his efforts to speak the merely literal language of exemplum, both he and his *Tale* are controlled by the spiritual subtext of an allegory that signifies despair. In other words, exegetical reading is a way of rendering the Pardoner harmless.

That he needs to be disarmed is demonstrated both by the apparently endless production of forensic readings of the Pardoner and by the reaction of the Host.[35] The Host fears that the Pardoner will force him to submit to a humiliating ritual of scatological castration:

Thou woldest make me kisse thyn olde breech,
And swere it were a relyk of a seint,
Though it were with thy fundement depeint!

(948–50)

Alluding to the famous relic of St Thomas's breeches that were
awaiting the pilgrims at Canterbury, the Host in effect accuses the
Pardoner of trying to preempt the pilgrimage by substituting his
counterfeits for the true relics that urge them on their pilgrim way.[36]
Yet the language of his accusation, with its fascination with the
corporality that is itself so much a part of the Pardoner's own
discourse, shows how profoundly the Host's imagination has been
infiltrated by that which he here seeks to exorcise. In summoning up
a parodic representation of the true relic, saturated now not with the
healing power of sanctity but with bodily waste, he effaces, in a gesture
of infantile regressiveness, the goal of his own spiritual efforts. Barthes
is thus evidently right when he says that to the masculinist mind,
'Castration is contagious, it touches everything it approaches': the
compulsions of the Pardoner become those of his audience.[37] The Host's
parody unwittingly reveals how easy it is to imagine St Thomas's
holy breeches as fouled garments. Once the underwriting spiritual
presence has been called into question, is it relics we kiss or feces?

The exegetical reading seeks to restore that presence. It stabilizes
the letter with a spiritual truth that is anchored in institutional
orthodoxy and reasserts a norm of linguistic rectitude that chastens
the promiscuity of the letter. Yet in an important sense exegetics also
partakes of the very condition it seeks to amend. It is a hermeneutics
for a fallen world, and if it spiritually replenishes the letter it must
also dispense with distracting and even illicit meanings. Allegorical
reading is able to do its healing work only by first instituting a deep
cleavage between the letter and the spirit. In order to be redeemed
by spiritual significance, the letter must first be drained of histor
value: youth in the *Pardoner's Tale* is a condition not of chronolo
earliness but spiritual rebirth; the Old Man is not an old man b
spiritual despair; the rioters' oak tree is not a tree but an *arbor
infruttuosa*. And the Pardoner is not an individual member of t
human community but Chaucer's 'one lost soul'. Exegetics is a
hermeneutics of suspicion whose first step is an act of exclusio
cutting off, that necessarily renders the text it finally does recu
less than complete. And these are acts of repudiation that pro
precisely the fear of insufficiency exegetics is designed to ove

What the exegetically augmented *Pardoner's Tale* must exclu
expressed in the Old Man's famous self-description, a passag
however well known will bear repeating:

> Ne Deeth, allas, ne wol nat han my lyf,
> Thus walke I, lyk a restelees kaityf,
> And on the ground, which is my moodres gate,
> I knokke with my staf, bothe erly and late,
> And seye 'Leeve mooder, leet me in!
> Lo how I vanysshe, flessh, and blood, and skyn!
> Allas, when shul my bones been at reste?
> Mooder, with yow wolde I chaunge my cheste
> That in my chambre longe tyme hath be,
> Ye, for an heyre clowt to wrappe me!'
> But yet to me she wol nat do that grace,
> For which ful pale and welked is my face.

(727–38)

These lines articulate the desire for penitential conversion in terms that are unavoidably Oedipal, and they pose for the reader a central interpretive problem: what is the relationship between these two orders of understanding? On the one hand, the Old Man is expressing a desire that is fully comprehensible within the terms of penitential action: he wishes to exchange the chest of his worldly goods for the hair cloth of contrition.[38] And yet on the other hand, the act imagined here is a transaction conducted not with the Divine Father who sits in judgment but with the Mother Earth who is the chthonic, and unsanctified, source of life.[39] And when placed in this maternal context, these lines solicit another reading: the chest can be construed as the coffin that awaits the Old Man, and the hair clout as the swaddling clothes of infancy – one of the primary meanings of the Middle English *clowt* – and also perhaps as the even more primal genital hair within which can be found the physical origin from which he took his beginning.[40]

   The moment of fulfillment is thus imagined not as atonement with the Father but as reunion with the Mother, a return to primal oneness that the entrance into the fallen world of history has ruptured. And the confrontation with which the performance as a whole concludes provides the aetiology of this severance: presenting himself to the Host as 'a *suffisant* pardoneer' (832), the Pardoner is threatened with castration: 'Lat kutte hem of' (954). The claim of sufficiency – of self-sufficiency – transgresses a primal, paternal taboo, and the punishment consists in a maiming that undermines every effort at authenticity. Yet the dream persists, the phantasmic desire for a return to the Mother who will re-engorge the child and make him whole and will cancel the death that awaits him by reuniting him with the maternal source of all life. Thus the Oedipal reading of these lines stands in contrast, even in opposition, to their penitential meaning. On the one hand is the desire to atone with the Father through self-abasement and suffering (the chest of worldly goods, the clout of penance); on the other is the desire to escape from the world of fallen history into an imagined sufficiency that is provided (however illicitly) by the mother and denied (with brutal consequences) by the father.[41]

. . .

Certainly the kind of exegetical reading that the text as a whole solicits encourages us to understand [the Old Man's] Oedipal yearnings entirely in penitential terms, an understanding that passes upon them a harsh judgment. For within this interpretive category they represent an evasion of the severities of the penitential life, a reversionary movement that seeks to foreclose the possibility of spiritual conversion. Indeed, from the point of view of penitential (and, for that matter, psychoanalytic) orthodoxy, they mark his – and the Pardoner's – unregeneracy, the submission to a dark regressiveness that harks back to a dangerous, illicit origin. And it is precisely this transgression that is punished with the mutilation that makes the Old Man walk with a staff and that renders the Pardoner a gelding or a mare. But what makes me pause in assenting to this admittedly efficacious reading is its very power – its ability, that is, to appropriate the Pardoner to a scheme of understanding that the interpreter is able to deploy while remaining himself exempt. In other words the penitential reading dispenses with the embarrassment – the sense of interpretive transgression – that the Oedipal details themselves elicit. Is the staff really phallic? Are we right in thinking that the hair clout invokes the mother's pubic hair, at once identifying and concealing the orifice from which the child once issued and that the Old Man now seeks leave to re-enter? There is no definitive answer to these questions, but the fact of embarrassment shows that we have moved into that area of human experience in which the Oedipal drama takes place, a drama in which all male readers, at least, are implicated.

One of the things we have to acknowledge, then, is the authenticity of the Old Man's yearning. Against the religious assertion that rebirth can be achieved only through submission to the paternal law and a consequent penitential suffering, he posits a dream of maternal renewal, an end to the sufferings of age through the free gift of the maternal love. That this is only a dream is shown by the Old Man's helpless wandering, which marks it as not merely unattainable but illegitimate. Yet his sad wisdom, and the sheer imaginative force wit' which he is endowed (so that every reader of Chaucer, no matter

how casual, seems to remember him), invest him with an authority
that is not easily dismissed. So too does his presence in a tale that
has as its foil the *Physician's Tale*. For that is a tale, as we have seen,
in which the salvific value of childhood is powerfully if finally
ineffectively invoked. It is undone, moreover, by an incomprehending
adulthood: Virginia is sacrificed to her father's idea of sexual purity,
while the generic innocence of hagiography is demeaned at the hands
of the all-too-experienced Physician. It is in the context of paternal
violence, in other words, that the Old Man's desire for maternal love
must be placed. And so too should we understand the Pardoner's
desire for spiritual sufficiency as confronting both the Host's outraged
masculinism and the divinely authorized injunctions of penance
– injunctions that take as their enabling premise man's inevitable
sinfulness, that is, his spiritual insufficiency. In short, if Virginia is a
victim of paternal violance, so too are the Pardoner and his fictive
alter ego, the Old Man. And so too, he implies, are all who groan
under the burden of their inevitable and finally unavoidable sinfulness.
Just as in the *Physician's Tale* paternal norms of righteousness can be
satisfied only by the sacrifice of the innocent Virginia, so too for
Christianity as a whole paternal indignation can be mollified only by
the sacrifice of the only begotten son. This is the scandal to which the
Pardoner constantly reverts in his discourse – *Prologue and Tale* are
laced with allusions to the crucifixion and to its re-enactment in the
Mass, most explicitly in the denouement beneath the oak tree[42] – and
which, in his mutilation, he has taken upon himself. And it is a scandal
that he enacts but refuses to endorse.

In sum, the Pardoner's confession contains within it an anti-
confession. It is a penitential act that challenges the legitimacy of
the very penance it seeks to perform. In this sense the Pardoner's
deliberate mockery of the Church's penitential procedures should be
seen as not merely a theatrically exaggerated representation of evil
but as an oppositional political statement.[43] His *Prologue and Tale*
stage many of the issues central to the theological and ecclesiastical
debates of late fourteenth-century England. The legitimacy of
indulgences, relics, and pilgrimage; the definition of who can preach,
where, and to whom; the question whether the justification of
sins is best accomplished by a deeply felt contrition or by ritual
participation in the sacrament of penance; the relation of spiritual
office to individual virtue; and the validity of auricular confession:
these controversies, each of which is relevant to the Pardoner's
performance, are at the center of late-medieval religious debate.[44] In
one sense, the Pardoner's abuses serve to justify the criticism of an
ossified and empty formalism that the religious reformers of the time,
whether orthodox or Lollard, leveled against the established Church.

Yet insofar as the Pardoner presents himself as a deliberately extravagant instance of evil, he is himself mocking that formalism, is himself revealing the emptiness of the penitential procedures of which he is an agent.

Yet his criticism of religious formalism, unlike that of Langland or the Lollards, is not mounted in the name of a desire for a more intense spirituality, for a deeper, purer piety. On the contrary, the Pardoner speaks from the position of the victim, asking questions that are plaintive rather than accusatory. What kind of religious system is it that imposes upon its believers the spiritual torment he is forced to endure? Is the desire to be 'suffisant' really anything more than a desire to be free of that endlessly painful sense of lack that characterizes the human condition *per se*? And should such aspirations be punished with social and religious exclusion, a cutting off from the corporate body of Christendom? Even more profoundly, the Pardoner's discourse poses an opposition between two kinds of language. On the one hand is the institutional language of penance, with its 'exegetical edge' and its absolutist judgments; on the other is the language of mythography, with its ability to grant expression to illicit desires.[45] These are languages that yield two different Pardoners: on the one hand is Chaucer's one lost soul, the feminoid figure who has transgressed the paternal prohibition against sufficiency and been punished with castration; on the other is a man willing to dream of a sufficiency made possible by reunion with the original mother. In effect, the Pardoner's discourse is uneasily poised between a deforming institutional self-representation and a promise of authenticity, between Lacan's *parole vide* and *parole plein* – empty and full language. Perhaps a language of the self's deepest instincts, a discourse of self-presence, is only a dream – everything in contemporary thought conspires to make us think so. But perhaps also Chaucer had something to teach us when he not only imagined it but imagined it as written in the characters of myth.

In returning to the Theban matrix, Chaucer is recuperating and perhaps even redeeming an earlier obsession. The kind of earliness that Thebes represents to the Chaucerian imagination is invoked here in a form that marks it as both illicit and authentic, both fetal and genuine. Here Thebes represents a value that is not dissimilar to that embodied in the perfect earliness of Virginia. It is a phantasy of self-enclosure and self-presence, a perfect circularity. The world outside that circle is marked by time, change, and difference; and it is as well the world of language, in which words stand permanently at a distance from the things to which they refer. That this is a world which both the poet and the Pardoner manipulate to their benefit does not render it any less foreign, and together they gesture, in however oblique and even contradictory a fashion, to a moment not merely outside but before time, a moment of plenitude and fulfillment.

Notes

1. Criticism has generally stressed the Pardoner's spiritual hard-heartedness, and Kittredge's too memorable description of him as 'the one lost soul among the Canterbury pilgrims' has found support in the enormous number of critical accounts that seek to pass theological and other sorts of judgment upon him. For a recent and powerfully argued instance of this forensic criticism, see R. A. SHOAF, *Dante, Chaucer, and the Currency of the Word* (Norman: Pilgrim Books, 1983), pp. 211–27. As FELICITY CURRIE points out in 'Chaucer's Pardoner Again', *Leeds SE*, 4 (1970), 'What remains intriguing about the Pardoner is that he has elicited identical reactions from his fellow-pilgrims and from decades of critics. To all he is wicked and vile' (p. 11). In 'Chaucer's Idea of the Pardoner', *CR*, 14 (1979–80), BERYL ROWLAND says that 'current sympathy with the sexually maladjusted has not yet contributed a convincing defence of the Pardoner' (p. 142). My argument is not that the Pardoner's unusual circumstances solicit our sympathy but that they are themselves metaphorically representative, serving as the means by which he is able to typify both fourteenth-century penitential concerns and larger issues.

2. BELIAL, 'The Conversion of St Paul', in *Late Medieval Religious Plays of Bodleian MSS Digby 133 and E Museo 160*, ed. Donald C. Baker, John L. Murphy and Louis B. Hall, Jr, EETS OS 283 (Oxford: Oxford University Press, 1982), p. 15.

3. Souvanteffois par le pais
   Faulx sainctuaires et fainctiz
   Va moustrant a la simple gent
   Pour faussement tirer argent.

   GUILLAUME DEGUILEVILLE, *Le Pelerinage de lhomme* (Paris, 1511), fol. 70ᵛ; cf. *Canterbury Tales*, VI, 953, and I, 694–706. Lydgate's rewriting of these lines shows that he too was struck by the resemblance between Avarice and the Pardoner:

   som tyme by borows and by towns
   I walke about[en] with pardons,
   with reliks, and dedë bones,
   closyd vndar glase and stons:
   I shew them vndar sell and bull,
   and thus the pore people I pull,
   of ther sylvar I make them quite,
   in falsnes I ha so grete delyght.

   The Pilgrimage of the Life of Man, ed. F. J. Furnivall (London: Roxburghe Club, 1905), 484 (lines 18103–10).

4. For this sense of the Pardoner's *Prologue* as a deliberate put-on, see JAMES L. CALDERWOOD, 'Parody in *The Pardoner's Tale*', *ES*, 45 (1964): 302–9; and JOHN HALVERSON's excellent 'Chaucer's Pardoner and the Progress of Criticism', *CR*, 4 (1969–70), 184–202. This interpretation is close to the more familiar one that sees the Pardoner as an entirely self-conscious entertainer: for example, PAUL E. BEICHNER, C. S. C., 'Chaucer's Pardoner as Entertainer', *MS*, 25 (1963), 160–72; RALPH W. V. ELLIOTT, 'Our Host's "Triacle": Some

The Subject of Confession: The Pardoner and the Rhetoric of Penance

Observations on Chaucer's "Pardoner's Tale"', *REL*, 7 (1966), 67–8; and JOYCE E. PETERSON, 'With Feigned Flattery: The Pardoner as Vice', *CR*, 10 (1975–76), 326–36.

5. For the *confessio ficti* in the *summae*, see THOMAS N. TENTLER, *Sin and Confession on the Eve of the Reformation* (Princeton, NJ: Princeton University Press, 1977), 274–5, 279.

6. WILLIAM LANGLAND, *Piers Plowman: The B-Text*, ed. George Kane and E. Talbot Donaldson (London: Athlone Press, 1975), 3, 35–63; ROBERT MANNYING, *Handlyng Synne*, ed. F. J. Furnivall, EETS, OS 119, 123 (London: K. Paul, Trench and Trubner, 1901–3), 392–96.

7. T. F. CRANE, ed., *The Exempla . . . of Jacques de Vitry* (London: Folk-lore Society, 1890), 125: 'Hec est confessio vulpis, que solet in Francia appellari confessio renardi.' See JOHN BLOCK FRIEDMAN, 'Henryson, the Friars, and the *Confessio Reynardi*', *JEGP*, 66 (1967), 550–61; and J.-C. PAYEN, *Le Motif de repentir dans la litterature française medievale (des origines a 1230)* (Geneva: Droz 1968), 547–8 n. 65.

8. MARIO ROQUES, ed., *Le Roman de Renart*, Classiques Français du Moyen Age 88 (Paris: Champion, 1960), Branche XIV, 37–55. As Charles Muscatine has shown, the name of Chaucer's Friar Huberd is almost certainly taken from the *Roman de Renart* and most likely from this episode (*MLN* 70 [1955]: 169–72). See also JOHN C. JACOBS, trans., *The Fables of Odo of Cheriton* (Syracuse: University of Syracuse Press, 1985), pp. 95–6, for a very similar episode.

9. For the proverb, see MARK ECCLES, ed., *The Macro Plays*, EETS, OS 262 (London: Oxford University Press, 1969), 27; see also Friedman, 'Henryson', 553 n. 9, and G. G. SEDGEWICK, 'The Progress of Chaucer's Pardoner, 1880–1940', *MLQ*, 1 (1940), reprinted in Edward Wagenknecht, ed., *Chaucer: Modern Essays in Criticism* (New York: Oxford University Press, 1959), p. 130.

10. 'He is indeed a wicked sinner who eats his own confessor.'

11. SHOAF, *Dante, Chaucer, and the Currency of the Word*, p. 220, and p. 274 n. 18.

12. In the A text of *Piers Plowman* Langland says laymen argue about theology and 'telleth . . . of the trinite hou two slowen the thridde' (*Piers Plowman: The A-Text*, ed. George Kane (London: Athlone Press, 1960), 11, 38–40). On Christians as imitators of God, see Ephesians 5:1–4. In the later Middle Ages the injunction to be an *imitator Dei* was directed specifically to those who were, like the Pardoner, preachers. As one medieval writer said, 'Would that each preacher were to become such a diligent imitator of Jesus Christ, that he should preach not with the word alone but also with works' (HARRY CAPLAN, 'A Medieval Tractate on Preaching', in *Studies in Rhetoric and Public Speaking in Honor of James A. Winans* [New York: Century, 1925], p. 72). In fact, as ALFRED L. KELLOGG and LOUIS HASELMEYER point out, pardoners were forbidden by papal injunction from preaching ('Chaucer's Satire of the Pardoner', *PMLA*, 66 (1951), 255–57). On the Eucharistic parody, see ROBERT E. NICHOLS, Jr., 'The Pardoner's Ale and Cake', *PMLA*, 82 (1967), 498–504; and CLARENCE H. MILLER and ROBERTA B. BOSSE, 'Chaucer's Pardoner and the Mass', *CR*, 6 (1971–72), 171–84.

13. As Stephen Barney has well observed, the *Tale* shows how 'the world properly behaves *sub specie aeternitatis*, turning intangibles into tangibles and rendering justice at the end of time' ('An Evaluation of the *Pardoner's Tale*', in Dewey Faulkner, ed., *Twentieth-Century Interpretations of the* Pardoner's Tale [Englewood Cliffs, NJ: Prentice-Hall, 1973], p. 90).

14. *Prelude* 3, 198–99.

15. That the Old Man proffers the wisdom of age to the rioters is demonstrated by JOHN M. STEADMAN, 'Old Age and *Contemptus Mundi* in *The Pardoner's Tale'*, *MAE*, 33 (1964), 121–30.

16. ROBERT P. MILLER, 'Chaucer's Pardoner, the Scriptural Eunuch, and the *Pardoner's Tale'*, *Speculum*, 30 (1955), identifies the Old Man as the *vetus homo* of sin, the antithesis of the *novus homo* who has been reborn, and he points out the Old Man's thwarted penance: 'He desires "an heyre clowt to wrappe" himself in – i.e. the hair shirt of penance, and he wishes to be buried: for the Old Man must be crucified and buried that the New Man may live' (p. 197). Subsequent criticism has rightly argued that to restrict the Old Man to this exegetical significance is unnecessarily reductive; see, for example, the qualifications of Miller's reading offered by CHRISTOPHER DEAN, 'Salvation, Damnation, and the Role of the Old Man in the *Pardoner's Tale'*, *CR*, 3 (1968–69), 48 n. 28; and ALFRED DAVID, 'Criticism and the Old Man in Chaucer's *Pardoner's Tale'*, *CE*, 27 (1965), 39–44.

17. CARLETON BROWN, ed., *English Lyrics of the XIII Century* (Oxford: Clarendon Press, 1939), 99.

18. A. BAEHRENS, ed., *Poetae Latini Minores* (Leipzig: Teubner, 1883), 5:316.

19. For texts that make these connections, see the following: Gregory, *PL* 75:821–22, 829; Isidore, *PL* 83:617; Rabanus Maurus, *PL* 107:506–7, *PL* 113:99; THOMAS AQUINAS, *Summa Theologica*, ed. Piero Caramello, 3 vols (Rome: Marietti, 1952–53), II, 2, 20, 1; Bernard, *PL* 183:989; and especially Bonaventure, in A. C. PELTIER, ed., *Opera omnia* (Paris: Vivès, 1868), 13:455–56; see SUSAN SNYDER, 'The Left Hand of God: Despair in Medieval and Renaissance Tradition', *Studies in the Renaissance*, 12 (1965), 56–8. For instances in the vernacular, see RICHARD MORRIS, ed., *The Pricke of Conscience* (London: Asher, 1865), 7282–9, and Preface, xi; ROBERT HENRYSON, *Orpheus and Eurydice*, 310–16, 607–9, in Denton Fox, ed., *The Poems of Robert Henryson* (Oxford: Clarendon Press, 1981). Chaucer's own use of the language of despair is usually in a romantic context, a very common transference in medieval literature: *The Book of the Duchess*, 581–90; *Troilus and Criseyde* 4, 279–80; 1, 603–9; 2, 526–32; and see the 'Complaint Against Hope', KENNETH G. WILSON, ed., *University of Michigan Contributions in Modern Philology*, 21 (Ann Arbor: University of Michigan Press, 1957).

20. For the oak as 'duritia desperationis', see BERNARD F. HUPPÉ and D. W. ROBERTSON, JR., *Fruyt and Chaf: Studies in Chaucer's Allegories* (Princeton, NJ: Princeton University Press, 1963), p. 55; and CAROLYN P. COLLETTE, '"Ubi Peccaverant, Ibi Punirentur": The Oak Tree and the *Pardoner's Tale'*, *CR*, 19 (1984–85), 39–45.

21. Hilary of Poitiers, *PL* 9:1037; Drumarthus, *PL* 106:1434; Rabanus Maurus, *PL* 107:1044; Radbertus, *PL* 120:714.

22. Augustine, *PL* 37:1688; and see also *PL* 36:264 and, especially, 334: 'Vide in verbis numerositatem, et in factis sterilitatem'.

23. Augustine, *PL* 36:569, *PL* 36:1027, *PL* 38:467–70, *PL* 38:467–70, and *PL* 38:638–39; Gregory, *PL* 76:1229–30 and *PL* 79:51; Bruno of Segni, *PL* 165:402; Haymo, *PL* 118:698–99.

24. 'Quisquis igitur homo hodie bonus est, id est, arbor bona, mala inventa est et bona facta est' (*PL* 38:467); see also *PL* 34:1305–6.

25. 'Ut in semetipsum oculos convertat, in se descendat, se discutiat, se inspiciat, se quaerat, et se inveniat: et quod displicet, necet; quod placet, optet et plantet' (Augustine, *PL* 38:468).

26. The Pardoner's culpable literalism is a persistent theme in the criticism of the *Tale*: see, for example, A. LEIGH DeNEEF, 'Chaucer's *Pardoner's Tale* and the Irony of Misinterpretation', *JNT*, 3 (1974), 85–96; WARREN GINSBERG, 'Preaching and Avarice in *The Pardoner's Tale*', *Mediaevalia*, 2 (1976), 77–99.

27. Line 344, quoting Romans 7:24.

28. In the Mass, the Pax or kiss of peace is exchanged after the Fraction – the breaking of the bread that signifies both the act of sacrifice and the violation of community – and prior to communion: it is a way of restoring community before the act of communal eating (see JOHN BOSSY, 'The Mass as a Social Institution, 1200–1700', *Past and Present*, 100 [1983], 52). Discussions of penance almost always include the shame of exposure as part of the satisfaction for the sin; see AMÉDÉE TEETAERT, O. C., *Les Confessions aux laïques dans L'église latine depuis le VIIIe jusqu'au XIVe Siècles* (Paris: J. Gabalda, 1926), 277, 297, and *passim*. Also relevant here is the fact that the spiritual value of shame stems in part from its role in bringing the sinner to genuine contrition.

29. *Roman de la Rose*, ed. Daniel Poirion, (Paris: Garnier-Flammarion, 1974) lines 7064–152 (212–14). The relevance of this passage to the Pardoner's performance was first made clear to me by Carolyn Dinshaw in a paper delivered at the MLA in December 1984; and my reading of this passage is much indebted to her account and to that by R. HOWARD BLOCH, *Etymologies and Genealogies: A Literary Anthropology of the French Middle Ages* (Chicago: University of Chicago Press, 1983), pp. 137–41.

30. See the textual notes to lines 7120–21 in ERNEST LANGLOIS, ed., *Le Roman de la Rose*, SATF (Paris: Champion, 1921), 3:279.

31. Indeed, even Raison asserts the natural fitness of words and things – a fitness that her discourse as a whole serves to undermine – when she says that she was empowered by God to name things, and that she therefore named them 'proprement' (7093): everything has, apparently, a proper name – precisely the assumption that her discussion of *reliques* and *coilles* shows to be unwarranted.

32. As STEWART JUSTMAN ('Literal and Symbolic in the *Canterbury Tales*', *CR*, 14 [1979–80], 199–214) points out, 'Words are of a symbolic order, a quantum apart from lived experience. There is nothing objectionable in an immoral man's telling a moral tale, but that act clearly implies that words are disconnected from reality.... The Pardoner may ironically remind us of the purely symbolic, un-real character of words. As a professional talker, the Pardoner finds it easy enough to exploit the falsity inherent in language' (p. 207).

33. Trans. Richard Howard (New York: Hill and Wang, 1974), 122–3, 200–1.

34. Ibid., 75.

35. See above, note 1.

36. For the allusion to St Thomas's breeches, see DANIEL KNAPP, 'The Relic of a Saint: A Gloss on Chaucer's Pilgrimage', *ELH*, 39 (1972), 1–26.

37. ROLAND BARTHES, *S/Z*, trans. Richard Howard (New York: Hill and Wang, 1974), 198. As JOHN HALVERSON, 'The Progress of Chaucer's Pardoner', rightly says about the confrontation with the Host, 'It is not that the Pardoner is evil, but that he is somehow deadly' (p. 200). For a reading in terms of this deadliness, see DEREK PEARSALL, 'Chaucer's Pardoner: The Death of a Salesman', *CR*, 17 (1983–84), 358–65.

38. See Miller, 'Scriptural Eunuch', pp. 197–8.

39. For a fourteenth-century account of Mother Earth, see the gloss by Nicole Oresme to his translation of the pseudo-Aristotelian *Oeconomica*: 'Et selon ce, les poetes appellent la terre la grand mere, si comme Virgille, qui dit: Salve magna parens frugum saturnia tellus [*Georgics* II, 73]. Et Ovide dit que les os de la grant mere laquelle est la terre: Magna parens terra est; lapides in corpore terre ossa reor dici [*Metam.* I, 393]. Et en la Saincte Escripture est dit: Usque in diem sepulture in matrem omnium [*Ecclicus.* 40:1]. Et donques, aussi comme l'enfant est nourri du lait de sa mere, nature humaine est nourri des fruis de la terre et est chose naturele' (Nicole Oresme, *La Livre de Yconomique d'Aristote*, ed. and trans. Albert Douglas Menut, *Transactions of the American Philosophical Society*, NS, 47, part 5 [1957], 810). For pictorial representations, see Ilene H. Forsyth, 'Children in Early Medieval Art: Ninth through Twelfth Centuries', *Journal of Psychohistory*, 4 (1976–77), 48 and n. 38; see also 32, where Forsyth describes how the illustrator of the Utrecht Psalter illustrates Psalm 84:12 ('Truth shall spring out of the earth') with an image of a newborn babe held aloft by its mother.

40. For 'cheste' as coffin and 'clowt' as swaddling clothes, see *MED*, s.v. In *Le Regret de Maximian*, the speaker says, 'Ich wolde ich were on rest, / Wel lowe leid in a *chest*' (Carleton Brown, *English Lyrics of the XIIIth Century* (Oxford: Clarendon Press, 1939) p. 98 (lines 202–3). For 'clowt', see 'Song of the Husbandman': 'And at the londes ende lay a litell crom-balle, / And there on lay a littel childe lapped in *cloutes*, / And tweyne of tweie yeres olde opon another syde' (cited, Barbara A. Hanawalt, 'Conception Through Infancy in Medieval English Historical and Folklore Sources', *Folklore Forum*, 13 [1980], 141); and 'Lullay, lullay litel child', a lullaby to the Christ Child, in Brown, *Religious Lyrics of the XIVth Century*, 2nd edn (Oxford: Clarendon Press, 1952): 'Child, it is a weping dale þat þu art comen inne, / þi pore *clutes* it prouen wel, þi bed mad in þe binne' (83 [lines 13–14]).

41. Several pages are omitted here in which Patterson discusses medieval legends of Judas that treat him in Oedipal terms; that is as someone who has killed his father and committed incest with his mother before his encounter with Christ. Patterson also outlines the portrayal of Oedipus in Statius's *Thebaid*, before returning to the discussion of Chaucer's Old Man within this Oedipal framework.

42. On these allusions, see Rodney Delasanta, 'Sacrament and Sacrifice in the *Pardoner's Tale*', *AnM*, 14 (1973), 43–52.

43. See David Aers, *Chaucer, Langland and the Creative Imagination* (London: Routledge and Kegan Paul, 1980), pp. 89–106.

44. See R. N. Swanson, *Church and Society in Late Medieval England* (Oxford: Blackwell, 1989); Anne Hudson, *The Premature Reformation: Wycliffite Texts and Lollard History* (Oxford: Clarendon Press, 1988); and Margaret Aston, *Lollards and Reformers: Images and Literacy in Late Medieval Religion* (London: Hambledon Press, 1984).

45. For the 'exegetical edge' of the Pardoner's discourse, see H. Marshall Leicester, '"Synne Horrible": The Pardoner's Exegesis of His Tale, and Chaucer's', in *Acts of Interpretation: Essays in Medieval and Renaissance Literature in Honor of E. T. Donaldson*, ed. Mary J. Carruthers and Elizabeth D. Kirk (Norman: Pilgrim Books, 1982), pp. 25–50.

11 Aspects of Female Piety in the *Prioress's Tale**

Elizabeth Robertson

In this essay Robertson claims medieval female piety as a position of power, and not, as has been argued, one of submission to a patriarchal Christian system, insisting on the authenticity of the spiritual benefits it brings, as well as on (following Luce Irigaray) the opportunity it provides to escape a 'societally defined femininity'. The socially marginalized position occupied by women in fact enables a powerful identification with Christ (as outcast) himself, and in her reading of the *Prioress's Tale* Robertson sees a feminine spirituality (represented in the story of the young boy) triumphing over the official spirituality of the Church, within which at this time the offices of women like the Prioress were being increasingly subordinated to male control. For more on Robertson's essay, see my Introduction, p. 9.

My tasks in this essay are to set out some ways in which feminist theory might be fruitfully applied to Chaucer's religious tales and to illustrate this application through an analysis of the *Prioress's Tale*. There has been no feminist study of the religious tales as a group, and there have been only a few articles on *Melibee*, the *Second Nun's Tale*, the *Prioress's Tale* and the *Man of Law's Tale* that consider gender. Feminists have given most of their attention to the *Clerk's Tale*. None of the feminist studies of the latter tale consider its religious implications, and feminist work on the tales, especially those whose protagonists or tellers are women, has highlighted the social and political structures in the tales at the expense of the issues raised by their religious subject matter. This neglect of the religious both reflects some limitations inherent in recent feminist theory (if not in critical theory more generally) and also seriously distorts the real and pressing feminist issues raised by the tales. I shall argue here that feminist theory that takes into account the complexities of

* Reprinted from *Chaucer's Religious Tales*, ed. C. David Benson and Elizabeth Robertson (Cambridge: D. S. Brewer, 1990), pp. 145–60.

the relationship between women and religion can help us recognize that what appear in these tales to be extremes of female suffering and violence against women are actually representations of positions of power and strength.

Feminists may have misconstrued the religious tales in part because theory in its current state is not well equipped to confront them. At the moment, feminist theory is split between two opposing viewpoints – on the one hand, an ahistorical psychological essentialism which has at its basis an assumption that men and women's biological differences radically distinguish their perceptions and experiences of the world no matter what the cultural conditions of the sexes are, and, on the other hand, a non-absolutist and sometimes relativistic cultural materialism that assumes that gender is entirely a social construction only to be understood through consideration of the socio-political conditions surrounding the representation of gender. A third emerging position, and one that I would like to show can be usefully applied to Chaucer, is a non-essentialist psychological approach which tries to bring the psychological insight of essentialist readings together with the historical insights of the cultural materialist/new historicist readings.

Feminists ought to be interested in the religious tales because, with the exception of the *Parson's Tale*, every religious tale has a woman at its center as protagonist or as teller. Why should Chaucer so consistently choose women as the site of his investigation of the nature of religious values? I suggest that to Chaucer women and Christian spirituality occupy the same marginal space. While male characters, such as the male martyrs of the story of Saint Cecilia or the small boy of the *Prioress's Tale*, may also occupy a marginal position because of their faith, women are inherently marginal by virtue of their inferior status as the fourth estate in medieval society and their social condition in conjunction with their faith provides a clear alternative to patriarchal values.[1]

The idea that Chaucer's exploration of marginality in general might also suggest his simultaneous understanding of the oppression of women will disturb some feminists because such a position apparently glosses over the fact that in almost all the religious tales Chaucer repeatedly represents women who suffer. Critics commonly respond to this suffering by concluding that because women suffer, they are victims (and often, because they are such obvious victims, Chaucer must be parodying a society that would victimize women in this way). For example, in her excellent Marxist article 'Womanliness in the Man of Law's Tale,' Sheila Delany bases her interpretation of the tale on a definition of Constance as having 'masochistic qualities of extreme humility and silent endurance' (p. 36). She argues that 'her passivity is what orthodox Christianity of the period recommended as a response to the human condition' and that 'it is precisely in her sexual role that Constance's main virtue is best seen: the acceptance of fate and authority' (pp. 37, 40). Then, reading the tale within the context of the 1381 peasants' rebellion, Delany suggests that Chaucer espouses a conservative platform of passive acceptance by suggesting that in the face of political corruption we should follow Constance's mirroring of Mary. The peasants, in Delany's view, adopted Eve as their model of rebellion. Delany concludes by deploring the tale's reassertion of traditional hierarchical values.

Delany's conclusions underestimate Constance's power. Constance eludes definition either generically or allegorically, and such an ability to elude categorization or 'place' is, in fact, a mark of her power. Furthermore, her directionless power challenges the ruling secular powers that she encounters and ultimately triumphs. Whatever we conclude about Chaucer's notions of revolutionary potential, at least we can say that in this tale constancy and faith successfully undermine political hierarchies. What Delany has failed to acknowledge is that Constance holds spiritual power, a power that has a relationship with, but is not identical to, secular power. Constance gives up secular power for a reason, not for self-fulfillment or to satisfy men, but because of a belief in something outside of herself – a power for good. Certainly, the endurance and suffering in the tale disturb the reader – especially the feminist reader – as they should – but not because they victimize women but because society has victimized itself by neglecting these values.

David Aers, on the other hand, reads the *Second Nun's Tale* as evidence that Chaucer must be mocking a society that would victimize women. He views that tale as a parody of materialist magical Christianity and Cecilia as a parody of militant Christianity, an argument that again refuses to contend with the given ideology of the tale. This habit of labelling Chaucer's female characters as victims overlooks the fact that from a Christian perspective suffering leads to rewards, if not on earth, then certainly in heaven. Studies of the religious tales too often neglect the fact that women's endurance does in the end triumph. Richard Firth Green in a study of the *Legend of Good Women* makes a valuable suggestion that we first consider the suffering of innocent characters at face value to see what Chaucer is getting at through his portrayal of suffering. He urges us not to assume that women are victimized and therefore conclude that the tales must be parodic or socio-critical commentaries. We might fare better critically if we take as a caveat the desirability of considering the values represented by these women as the dominant values in the tales.

Chaucer's interest in marginality has affinities with the most extreme feminists, and, thus, an understanding of their theories can illuminate his texts. Hélène Cixous's theories and practice are especially useful. She reserves for herself 'the position of marginality, of maximum maneuvaribility' (Conley, p. 97).[2] Going beyond Derrida who 'pushes his work to the limit where logic vacillates, Cixous pushes her prose beyond that vacillation to define a "feminine border" in which outmoded male logic ceases to speak' (Conley, p. 97). Cixous describes female experience as a 'struggle to undermine the dominant phallogocentric logic, split open the closure of the binary opposition', that is the dominant male tradition (Moi, p. 108). Masculinity is characterized by the words 'proper, property, appropriate: signalling an emphasis on self-identity, self-aggrandizement and arrogative dominance', leading to a 'masculine obsession with classification, systemization and hierarchization' (Moi, p. 110). Cixous argues further that such 'female' experience is not limited to the female writer alone; rather it is a more general stance, a 'libidinal femininity which can be read in writing produced by a male or a female' (Moi, p. 108).

Chaucer, throughout his religious tales, challenges self-aggrandizement and classification. Like Cixous, Chaucer pushes his work to the borders thereby implicitly questioning a static hierarchical system. Like Cixous, Chaucer finds in the investigation of marginality a position of maximum maneuvaribility. Like Cixous, he threatens, disturbs, and unravels the assumption of the establishment, and, unlike the cultural materialist critic, refuses to outline his boundaries because to do so would validate the categories of the ruling hierarchy. And again like Cixous, Chaucer by design is often ambiguous about his position on anything, including his Christianity.

French feminist discussions of female mysticism such as those of Simone de Beauvoir, Luce Irigaray and Julia Kristeva can illuminate some of the power that can be identified in the coincidence of Christianity and femininity found in Chaucer. These theorists agree that mystical contemplation from the Middle Ages to the present has afforded women a powerful and distinctively different voice. Although these critics take different positions ranging from De Beauvoir's social criticism of female mysticism to the more essentialist positions of Irigaray and Kristeva, they nonetheless share some insights. They argue that the female mystic identifies with Christ as one who occupies a position of victimization analagous to her own. They suggest that female contemplation is conditioned by a female mystic's embrace of her marginal and subordinate position in society, an embrace that to some of these critics, paradoxically frees her from some of these social constraints. Finally, they argue, women, whether by nature or by experience, are particularly suited, first, for an empathy and identification with suffering and victimization, second, for an identification with and exploration of the emotional bonds of motherhood, and, third, for the expression of an erotic emotionalism.

De Beauvoir writes of female mystics, 'it is not a transcendence that they seek: it is the redemption of their femininity. . . . In the humiliation of God, she sees with wonder the dethronement of man; inert, passive, covered with wounds . . . she is overwhelmed to see that man, man-God, has assumed her role. She it is who is hanging on the tree . . . her forehead bleeds under the crown of thorns' (pp. 634–36). De Beauvoir thus suggests that women in particular will be drawn to the suffering of Christ. While it is true that affective piety in general does focus on the gruesome suffering of Christ, it is also true that such suffering has special meaning for the female viewer who is both inured to suffering in her own life and defined by Aristotelian medical theory as dominated by moisture, blood and tears, and by nature suited to suffering.[3] Whether or not Chaucer accepted such reductive views of women is unknown, but he could not fail to be aware that such was the medieval view of women. De Beauvoir, basing her argument on the premise that love itself is a symptom of women's subordination, focuses particularly on the social implications of the female mystical experience. A drawback to her work is that she sees Christianity only as an expression of oppression, and that she fails to situate the mystics she considers in their historical time and place. She leaves out entirely the power found in religion by those who practice it. Her work, therefore, is, in the end, secularly reductive.

While De Beauvoir ultimately deplores the mystic's acceptance of 'essential' feminine attributes, Irigaray suggests that the contemplation and acceptance of these features lead to a redemption of femininity. Such a transformation entails an hyperbolizing of the features that society considered to be essential to female nature. Allying the lips of Christ's wounds with female oral and genital lips, Irigaray argues that Christian mysticism allows a woman to outdo her sense of subordination and humiliation by identifying and sympathizing with the victimization and humility of Christ. This identification thus becomes the basis for the female mystic's exploration and perhaps transcendence of her societally defined femininity. To Irigaray, the acceptance of subordination is the very access to power for women. According to Toril Moi, Irigaray's point in her obscure essay, 'La Mystérique', is that 'the mystical experience is precisely an experience of the loss of subjecthood, of the disappearance of the subject/object opposition, it would seem to hold a particular appeal for women, whose very subjectivity is anyway being denied and repressed by patriarchal discourse. . . . The mystic's often self-inflicted abjection paradoxically opens up a place where pleasure can unfold' (pp. 136–37). Most of Chaucer's religious heroines represent an alternative power achieved in part through a denial of their subjecthood. The female mystic's transformation of the position of the oppressed into one of power suggested by Irigaray might, for example, be usefully applied to the experience of Constance or Griselda.

Kristeva's work on Mary, motherhood, and the nature of the feminine might open up further areas useful for the study of the religious tales. In her essay 'Stabat Mater,' Kristeva argues that mysticism is 'vouchsafed only to those who take "the maternal" upon themselves' (p. 100). While the maternal features in both male and female mystical writing, to Kristeva the contemplation of Mary offered women both authority and power, although the figure of Mary is both comforting and alienating to women for, as she writes, the 'uniqueness [of women] is achieved only by way of exacerbated masochism; an actual woman worthy of the feminine ideal embodied in inaccessible perfection by the Virgin could not be anything other than a nun or a martyr. . . . But there a bonus awaits her: the assurance of ecstasy' (p. 115). Surely, this passage could be applied to Griselda.

All three of these writers are limited because they ignore historical context. Kristeva, for example, fails to consider the different ways the figure of Mary operated for men and women and for both men and women during different periods, and, finally, that our own modern concepts of motherhood might differ markedly from those of the Middle Ages. Similarly, Margery Kempe's class and circumstances make her a very different mystic from the better educated Julian of Norwich. Nonetheless, the elements the French feminists explore – the exaggerations of the affective, the hyperbolic images of blood and tears and of suffering – are the very same features Chaucer explores in different ways in his religious tales. As feminists, we must respond to the questions of victimization, masochism, and suffering raised by the tales, but we should also put them into the context of the relationship between women and Christianity in Chaucer's own time.

I will argue that Chaucer uses female characters as a means to explore not the subordinate position of women in society, but rather the subordinate position of Christian values in society. Because Chaucer's primary concern in the religious tales seems to be to unsettle the notions of those in power who deny Christianity in general rather than those who represent an oppressive patriarchy, Chaucer cannot properly be said to have feminist political concerns. Yet often the oppression of women and society's neglect of Christian values coincide and Chaucer's interest in this coincidence shares the challenge of feminism. To understand Chaucer's feminism, then, as slippery and elusive as Chaucer is, we must come to terms with Chaucer's Christianity. We should bear in mind that Christianity itself has both radical and conservative potential, and furthermore that Christianity is inherently suspicious of earthly power and is often invoked to question the ruling hierarchy.

In addition, why not inquire whether those things that disturb feminists – such as the Prioress's apparent excesses, the extremes of Griselda's submissiveness and Constance's passivity – were also disturbing to Chaucer and his readers? If we start with the assumption (easily justifiable given Chaucer's constant disruption of genre and estate) that Chaucer deliberately intends to disturb, then we might see that it is this unsettling quality which shatters hierarchies and conventions and which forces us to reassess the nature of politics and social change in relationship to Christian self-knowledge. However, what disturbs modern readers might be quite different from what disturbs a medieval reader. Given the Christianity of the age, I suggest that what was most likely disturbing to the medieval reader was not the troubling representation of women in the religious tales, but rather the disturbing clash of the spiritual and secular worlds found within the tales, a conflict that encompasses some of the problems experienced by women in the tales.

It might be argued that a feminist analysis of the religious tales is anachronistic, yet such an analysis only brings to the fore aspects of femininity that were being discussed in the period. For example, there was much anxiety and debate about the nature and quintessential difference of women's speech. Medieval commentary generally viewed women's speech with distrust and criticized women for following in the footsteps of the garrulous Eve. Yet, as Sharon Farmer has recently argued, women's different persuasive power was also valued especially as a way to influence men to support the church. As she writes, 'clerical writers persistently emphasized the ability of women to use spoken language . . . to soften men's hearts' (p. 539). Chaucer, himself, celebrates the different kinds of persuasive power found in women's speech in a variety of his tales including the *Tale of Melibee* and the *Second Nun's Tale*, as Jane Cowgill argues.

In addition, we also know that women in the Church were rapidly losing position and authority. In Chaucer's day, for example, prioresses were very much subject to the authority of abbots and no longer had the right to conduct the sacraments without the aid of a priest. Such a context, as I shall consider later in this essay, might complicate our understanding of Chaucer's Prioress. In addition,

Chaucer's representation of women might well have been influenced by the prominent role women took historically in the affective movement. It would be illuminating to know who, if any, of the powerful female contemplatives of his day Chaucer knew, and how the court responded to them. It would also help to know more generally what debates beyond those of the Church fathers about virginity, motherhood, and female sexuality were current in Chaucer's time. Myriad questions surround these historical issues, and we may never know exactly what Chaucer's specific knowledge of female religious was, but much can be gained by a study of the historical context.

Most importantly, we should follow Charlotte Morse's advice and 'ask ourselves to address imaginatively and sympathetically the alterity of medieval and renaissance texts. Otherwise we endorse cultural solipsism' (p. 53). The virtues of patience and submission, constancy and faith are no longer valued in our culture, but they were Christian values. To espouse these values today seems to conflict with self-realization, but such an espousal was the key to self-realization within a Christian context. The fact that these varied women do exhibit power should not be neglected even if that power is conditioned by their Christianity. It is time that Christian feminism be given its due.

Let us turn now to the *Prioress's Tale* and consider the ways in which an historicized French feminist perspective might contribute to an understanding of the tale. The apparent contradiction between violence and sweetness in the *Prioress's Tale* has divided critics. For positive readings of the tale see, among others, Benson, Burlin, and Rodax. Critics who have been disturbed by both the violence and anti-semitism of the tale include Donaldson, Schoeck, and, from a Freudian perspective, Cohen. The latter group, uncomfortable with what it views as the work's extremes of both violence and humility, resolves its discomfort by viewing the tale as a satire of the teller. The former group, dismissing the poem's violence as conventional and underplaying the relationship of the teller to its tale, celebrates its sweet humility and praises it as Chaucer's successful experiment in sentimental affective piety. The two groups share a desire to resolve the discomfort raised by the tale. I propose, however, to show that discomfort is essential to the meaning of this tale.

Discomfort is in part aroused by the brutality of the story of the victimization of a small, innocent boy, but it is heightened and complicated when the story is told by a female speaker because the speaker herself shares the powerlessness of the protagonist in a process analogous to the mystic's identification with Christ as described by De Beauvoir, Irigaray, and Kristeva. Woman readers may be simultaneously drawn and repulsed by the story's mirror of their own weakness and powerlessness, while the male reader may be threatened by a feminine critique of authority. The uneasiness inspired by the *Prioress's Tale* can only be fully understood by viewing this tale not simply as an experiment in affective piety, but more specifically as Chaucer's deliberate experiment in *feminine* affective piety. Chaucer's tale is a construction of and commentary on the nature of a specifically female religious voice.

Women's identification with Mary and Christ's transformation of victimization and humiliation into power can be seen to be at the root of the conflicting brutality and humility of the *Prioress's Tale*. By adopting Mary's humility as her own, the Prioress is able to overcome her own sense of inferiority, and find her own voice. The tale both embodies and investigates the nature of the power of that voice, for the Prioress describes herself as speaking like a child in her Prologue and then tells a tale that is an explicit analysis of the nature and effects of childish voices. Her extreme humility, which has led some critics to view the tale as a satire of her religiosity, is in fact a crucial aspect of her claim to authority as a religious speaker. The situation of the small boy is analogous to her own, sharing with him as she does a status that limits the authority of her speech. It might be argued that the story of a small boy says little about the condition of women. Yet he seems an appropriate subject for a female speaker, for through that choice of subject she simultaneously gains the attention of male speakers who might be indifferent to the suffering of a female child (especially given the age's attitude to the undesirability of female children) and highlights the pathos in the suffering of the small and defenceless, that is of those like herself. Furthermore, at the literal level of the story, the boy's spirituality is feminine, originating as it does from both his mother and Mary. Finally, the violence of the tale, both in the story of the child and in the revenge taken against the Jews, raises troubling questions that in part can be answered if we view that imagery as expressions or perhaps displacements of the Prioress's sense of her own victimization and her rage at male authority for perpetrating that brutality.[4] The subduing of the Jews and the humbling of the monks illustrate the triumph of an alternative, intuitive faith, a triumph that might well be hoped for by the Prioress and her community of nuns. The tale, I claim, thus reflects Chaucer's consideration of the subordination of women in the religious life, particularly that of prioresses, as well as his exploration of the alternative voice women discover within the context of their relative powerlessness.

Turning now to the Prologue, which R. W. Hanning calls a 'glorification of helplessness', we see that by comparing herself to a child, the Prioress claims her own authority to speak despite her simultaneous acknowledgement of her own worthlessness (p. 589). There are several steps to this process. First, in the last stanza of her Prologue, the Prioress links herself with the child of the tale by comparing herself to an infant:

> My konnyng is so wayk, O blisful Queene,
> For to declare thy grete worthynesse
> That I ne may the weighte nat susteene;
> But as a child of twelf month oold, or lesse,
> That kan unnethes any word expresse,
> Right so fare I . . .

> (VII.481–86)

When we meet the child of the tale, we may be reminded of the Prologue's small child, especially when we consider the fact that Chaucer altered his sources to make the boy younger than he is in the sources. The Prioress, like a small child, is worthy to speak despite her humble station. The rhymes of 'worthynesse', 'lesse', and 'expresse' here bind together ideas of worth, speech, and size. She finds her worth, however, through the aid of Mary and her dependence on the Virgin is reinforced here by the insertion of the phrase 'O blisful Queene' in the middle of her discussion of her uneasiness about her own speech.

This women-child's speech is explicitly contrasted to male speech in the opening stanza:

> O Lord, oure Lord, thy name how merveillous,
> Is in this large world ysprad – quod she –
> For noght oonly thy laude precious
> Parfourned is by men of dignitee,
> But by the mouth of children thy bountee
> Parfourned is, for on the brest soukynge
> Somtyme shewen they thyn heriynge.

> (VII.453–59)

The Prioress here reminds us that children have the authority to speak despite the fact that men usually are the 'performers' of praise. Their speech, like women's, exists on the border described by Cixous where logic ceases to speak. It offers non-logical access to truth. The Prioress might be particularly concerned about the right to 'perform' praise of God, since as Caroline Bynum points out, from Innocent III's 1210 decree on, abbesses and prioresses were forbidden to exercise the clerical roles of preaching, blessing nuns and hearing confession ('Eucharistic Devotion', p. 179). Prioresses were thus often resentfully dependent on male intervention. The power to preach and praise was the sole responsibility of 'men of dignity'. In the stanza above, the Prioress also claims authority for children and, by implication, also for those like children – herself. The fact that 'quod she' is introduced here and in the tale itself, and that there are a number of instances where a narrative 'I' surfaces (513, 551, 572, 670 – a significant number given the shortness of the tale) highlights the centrality of the female speaking voice to the tale's meaning. Finally, the subsequent image of the child at the breast praising God evokes the image of the Christ-child at the breast of Mary, thus reinforcing the authority of the child or child-like speaker. Caroline Bynum has argued that medieval images of the Christ-child at the breast of Mary encouraged a new positive appreciation of the female breast in general (*Holy Feast*). This image thus enhances the idea of female power by alluding to Christ's dependence on Mary. While the child itself is weak and defenceless at the breast, nonetheless it gains power through the mother's milk he receives, a traditional icon for the word of God. The image therefore suggests the idea that the child's dependence on the female breast will lead to words of wisdom. That this image is directly relevant to the issue of speech is further suggested by the focus on the word 'mouth'.

In the Prologue's third stanza, the Prioress explores her identification with and dependence on Mary. Such a focus by a self-proclaimed humble speaker suggests the speaker's hope that her own humility may also prove to be a source of power and wisdom. The Prioress calls on Mary to help her speak.

O mooder Mayde, o Mayde Mooder free!
O bussh unbrent, brennynge in Moyses sighte,
That ravyshedest doun fro the Deitee,
Thurgh thyn humblesse, the Goost that in th'alighte,
Of whos vertu, whan he thyn herte lighte,
Conceyved was the Fadres sapience,
Help me to telle it in thy reverence!

(467–73)

The Prioress's identification with Mary in this passage further suggests that she too desires the inspiration of the Holy Spirit, an inspiration that will impregnate her with the power to speak. Such a sexualized view of a contemplative's relationship to Christ occurs in writing by men and women alike (e.g. John Donne), but, as I have argued elsewhere such images have different meaning for the male and female speaker.[5] Where the male speaker often adopts a 'feminine', that is passive, role, the female speaker often celebrates a literal marriage to Christ uniquely available to her as a woman.

In the next stanza, conventional forms of praise are compared to praise of children and women.

> Lady, thy bountee, thy magnificence,
> Thy vertu and thy grete humylitee
> Ther may no tonge expresse in no science;
> For somtyme, Lady, er men praye to thee,
> Thou goost biforn of thy benyngnytee,
> And getest us the lyght, of thy preyere,
> To gyden us unto thy Sone so deere.

(474–80)

Perhaps 'science' here has a more specific meaning than human learning as glossed by the editors of the *Riverside Chaucer*. It may refer more specifically to traditional knowledge most often learned by men in the monasteries and schools and rarely offered to women, even those in convents. Here, then, the Prioress indirectly claims the power to praise by stating that knowledge – 'science' – that is, the knowledge she is not likely to have but others around her might have, is not adequate to the task of praising Mary. Her intuitive knowledge, it is implied, may be sufficient, and, after all, her story is one in praise of Mary. In addition, this stanza lauds female praise in particular for we are told Mary's prayer finally preempts the prayers of men. Clearly this passage celebrates an alternative kind of prayer, one performed by women. Perhaps not only prayers but also tales 'performed' by a prioress, might also have a special status. Even though women can never be quite as powerful as Mary who was unique among women, nonetheless as women they are more able to model themselves upon her than are men. Finally, sometimes before men pray to Mary, we are told, Mary goes before and 'getest us the lyght, of thy preyere, / To gyden us unto thy Sone so deere'. If we consider the 'us' here as gender specific, then the relevance of Mary's support for the female speaker is strengthened: Women, because of their capacity to loose their subjecthood, as Irigaray would put it, with Mary's guidance, can circumvent male authority and be led directly to Christ by Mary.

In its form as well as in the images of the child's song within it, the tale that follows is offered in contrast to male 'science'. The Prioress's own rhyme royal poem in praise of Mary, with its echoes of the liturgy, parallels the child's song. That the Prioress privileges song over speech is suggested by her avoidance of the word 'speech', which only occurs twice in the tale, and by her emphasis on the

words 'sing', 'singing', and 'song' which occur eleven times in the
tale (Benson, p. 137). The tale raises questions about the nature of
song as characteristic of an alternative spirituality for the powerless,
a spirituality that is based on intuition and emotional devotion rather
than on argument. The Prioress not only celebrates the power of
song, but also herself speaks in a nearly song-like musical meter.

Song is presented as an alternative style for women and children,
that is for those who have less access both to theological training
and to Latin. The child is sent to school to gain traditional male
knowledge, to study 'swich manere doctrine as men used there'
(499), which we are told includes singing and reading, but the child's
song is contrasted to these kinds of learning. The child has another
teacher besides his schoolmaster, his mother. She taught him to say
the 'Ave Marie' whenever he saw a portrait of Mary (504–9) and her
training is particularly effective since, as we are told, he 'forgat it
naught' (511).

In school, the child's feminine aspect is apparent. He is
instinctively drawn to a song he overhears, the *Alma redemptoris*.
He does not know what it means, 'noght wiste he what this Latyn
was to seye' (523), but he determines to learn the song by Christmas
when he learns that it is in praise of Mary. That the boy's song is
subordinated to other kinds of learning in the eyes of his teachers is
suggested by the Prioress's statement that the small boy learned it
despite the possibility of being beaten for neglecting his primer.

Chaucer highlights the boy's similarity to women by raising the
issue of Latin literacy in this incident. He adds to his sources a scene
in which the child tries unsuccessfully to learn the meaning of the
words of the song from an older boy. His Latin illiteracy not only
illuminates the alternative inspiration of the child's song, but also
reflects the condition of Latin learning among women in nunneries.
Like a nun dependent on male authorities for translation into the
vernacular, a subject discussed by Bernard, the child also depends
on an older authority to construe the song and expound it in his
own 'langage' (526).

The fact that the older boy also does not know the meaning of
the words of the song stresses the alternative ways in which song
conveys meaning. Feminist theorists have argued that song is a mode
of expression particularly suited to the female speaker and others in
analogously powerless positions precisely because of its mysterious
power to effect change through the emotions rather than through
argument. The song about Mary offers the unschooled a source of
power that is realized through the heart rather than the mind: 'The
swetnesse his herte perced so / Of Cristes mooder that . . . / He kan
nat stynte of syngyng' (555–57). The rhymes of 'note', 'rote', and

'throte' in the stanza containing these lines imply that the child's speaking voice is identified with intuition, memorization, and song.

The child's song is set against Satan's words. Satan says, 'Is this to yow a thyng that is honest, / That swich a boy shal walken as hym lest / In youre despit, and synge in swich sentence, / Which is agayn youre lawes reverence?' (561–64). Although this is a corruption of logic, the force of persuasive reason that Satan represents is opposed to a superior truth that defies reason. That Chaucer was concerned to highlight the different persuasive power of Satan's language as opposed to the boy's song is suggested by the fact that Chaucer adds this passage to his sources.

The female power of song that allows the child to sing boldly and merrily is opposed by male authorities. We have already seen the schoolmaster's opposition and Satan's argumentative incitement of the Jews. The association of the Jews with corrupt male authority is supported by the fact that the Jews are 'sustened by a lord of that contree / For foule usure and lucre of vileynye' (490–91). As Hanning writes of this passage, 'the lord – the highest secular (and, we might add, masculine) authority – is implicated in the Jews' presence and therefore in their crime against an innocent helpless child' (p. 590). The revenge taken against the Jews at the end of the tale asserts the triumph of the unschooled voice and the punishment awaiting those who deny the authority of that voice. Thus, the anti-semitism of the tale may in part be a disguise for the Prioress's own criticism of male authority in general.

Both the violence and the pathos of these scenes are linked specifically to the assumption of power by seemingly powerless voices. The child dies by having its throat cut. That Chaucer's version markedly reduced the violence of the sources, as Florence Ridley points out, strengthens the focus of the tale on violence against speaking, since the violence is restricted to the image of the child's cut throat and excludes the dismemberment, crucifixion and the like found in the source. By focusing on the violence against the throat alone, the seat of the singing voice, Chaucer makes a stronger comment on the danger facing those who, like the child, choose an alternative style. The Prioress's limitation of the wound to the cut throat evokes the association of the wounds of Christ with female oral and genital lips made by Irigaray in her discussion of female piety. Thus, it has special resonance for women. There is a continuing circle of identification for the female contemplative speaker between her own speaking, the wounds of Christ, her femininity, and the cut throat of the child.

In addition, what to some may seem to be the Prioress's excessive delight in violence might more properly be identified as displaced rage against men. It should be remembered that men, whether Jewish or not, are not particularly favorably represented in the tale. That the Jews were chosen to be the particular enemies of this story may have been a reflection of the fact that the tale is told by a woman speaker, since, as Frank observes, the Jews in doctrine and in late medieval drama were represented as special enemies of Mary and therefore of all women.

The rage the story inspires against the Jews may also have served ulterior purposes for the female speaker. By presenting the violence as perpetrated by those the audience would not identify with and against whom the audience could be roused, the Prioress may have been able to stir the indignation of the audience against those who attack the defenseless, inadvertently bringing them around to her own cause. In other words, Chaucer may have been deliberate in his alignment of a disturbing anti-semitic tale with the female speaker. The anti-semitism of the tale itself raises larger questions of who is victimizing whom in society, but Chaucer, despite the fact that such anti-semitism was conventional in the period, may also have intended such ambiguity.

If we wished to extend this argument to include not only the Prioress of the prologues, but also the Prioress of the *General Prologue*, we might consider the fact that the *General Prologue* Prioress is also upset particularly by the violence of men. We are told: 'But sore wepte she if oon of hem were deed, / Or if men smoot it with a yerde smerte; / And al was conscience and tendre herte' (I.148–50).[6] It is consistent with medieval female physiology, according to which women are particularly linked by nature to blood and tears, that a woman would respond sympathetically to a bleeding animal, and further that the prologue's portrait should mention her tears twice (144, 148). This strengthens the impression of the speaker's female point of view.

The compassionate portrait of the mother heightens other issues of relevance for women. She is linked with Rachel and becomes an emblem of all women who are driven mad with grief. She further represents all those women who are told one thing by authorities (in this case, the Jews) but led to another by intuition and the aid of Mary. Her inner knowledge is here pitted against what authority tells her.

The representation of the dead child's inspired singing at the end of the *Prioress's Tale* firmly opposes male authority with female power. The grain underneath the child's tongue, put there by Mary, evokes the idea of nourishment, a topic that, as Bynum has shown us, had special meaning for women in the Middle Ages (*Holy Feast*). If we view the grain more specifically as a reference to the eucharist, this image would have even further resonance for medieval women. This sacrament was particularly important to female mystics who were, as Bynum tells us 'inspired, compelled, comforted and troubled by the eucharist to an extent found only in a few male writers of the period' ('Eucharistic Devotion', p. 182). Indeed, Bynum argues, 'the eucharistic miracle almost seems a female genre' (p. 182). Because women had been denied control of the sacrament, she explains, eucharistic ecstasy served as an alternative to priestly office and was 'a means by which women either claimed "clerical" power for themselves, or by-passed the power of males, or criticized male abuse of priestly authority' (p. 193). In the final scene of the tale, the Prioress, a woman who might particularly resent her convent's dependence on an abbot for the office of the sacrament, represents the administration of a motherly 'meal' with eucharistic effects by a woman – Mary.

The grain gives the child the power to speak with an authority that bypasses that of the male establishment. A power that originates from a woman, Mary, shames men. The abbot and his monks are subordinated to the child. The positive impression of the female power of the grain is reinforced by the ambiguous picture of the abbot's authority and role in the boy's case. The Prioress implicitly casts doubt on clerical authority in her comment about the abbot 'which that was an hooly man, / As monkes been – or elles oghte be' (VII.642–43). The Prioress again draws attention to the abbot's holiness further on when she says, 'This holy monk, this abbot, hym meene I' (VII.670), a comment that, within the context of the earlier remark again raises at the very least the question of his holiness. Having cast doubt on the abbot's holiness, she presents him as enacting the eucharist in reverse. He has the grain as wafer removed from under the tongue. The removal of the grain ceases song, just as the denial of the women's right to celebrate the eucharist was seen as an attempt to deny women access to God. Nonetheless, through a direct association with God, the child's song, like female mystics' eucharistic visions, will find its proper fulfillment in heaven. In addition, the ending of the tale reasserts the triumph of childish power, for the abbot and the rest of the monks fall to the ground 'wepynge, and herying Cristes mooder deere' (678). As Hanning writes of this passage, 'Masculine adult authority has been forced to its knees, taught to honor the heavenly mother by her oracle, the unlearned child' (p. 581).

It is important to recognize that the aspects of expression raised in the *Prioress's Tale* stem from a tradition specifically developed for and by women. Several critics including Frank, Collette, and Benson have argued that the tale must be viewed within the context of affective piety, but the affective piety of the *Prioress's Tale* forms part of a tradition specifically connected with women. The specifically feminine nature of affective piety deserves further consideration. For example, it is rarely mentioned that Anselm, often considered the father of affective piety, wrote for women; his prayers and meditations that focus especially on blood, tears, and compassion were written for Mathilda of Tuscany. Also, Ailred of Rievaulx, in the meditations on Christ's suffering that he provided for his sister, emphasized just those features of identification with suffering that French feminist critics have argued are essentially feminine and that we have seen present in the tale. Abelard, too, in his letters to Heloise, argues that it is woman's privilege to feel compassion for Christ since this was a woman's historical role in Christ's passion. In his emphasis on Heloise's peculiar capacity for both compassion and empathy, Abelard stresses those aspects of contemplation that are deemed to be both biblically and physiologically appropriate to women. These writers redeem femininity through recommending the acceptance of feminine attributes much as Irigaray does in 'La Mystérique', though the purposes for male writers might well differ from those intended by Irigaray.

Although it is unclear exactly what Chaucer himself may have known about feminine affective piety, he must have been aware of the emotional fervor of female meditation so prominent in late thirteenth- and fourteenth-century female mysticism in England and on the continent. He may well have observed the emotional intensity of female contemplatives in art, the drama, and in the Church. Margaret Miles has discussed the importance of paintings as a source for understanding the role of women in the Middle Ages. Mary Magdalene, for example, is often portrayed as clinging compassionately to the feet of Christ. Indeed, maudlin is a word often applied to the Prioress. In paintings and plays, the pathos of Mary's suffering was also often emphasized. Chaucer in addition may have observed women's emotionalism in their participation in church devotions such as the stations of the cross. The *Prioress's Tale* may well have been the result of his observation of women's role in meditation.

To conclude, it would be misleading to view the *Prioress's Tale* as a polemically feminist tale. It seems more likely that for Chaucer the attributes of women he investigates – willingness to endure suffering, capacity to lose subjecthood, sympathy with suffering – often coincide with Christian values that he wishes to evaluate or reassert. The *Prioress's Tale* allows him the opportunity to investigate the strengths of compassion and pity. Lowes's much quoted comment about the Prioress as an 'engagingly imperfect submergence of the feminine in the ecclesiastical' (p. 60) deserves restatement, for, on the contrary, the Prioress and her tale should be viewed instead as Chaucer's deliberate realization of the feminine in the ecclesiastical. Chaucer illuminates Christian values through the exploration of the feminine voice. The insight gained through a feminist analysis grants us access to the feminine in the text and thus resolves the very features that have puzzled and divided critics about this so vicious and so delicate a tale.[7]

Notes

1. Of course, gender is not the only area where Chaucer exhibits interest in marginality; he also explores it in his formal questioning of the nature of genre or medieval estates as well as in his social commentary.

2. I am using remarks of Verena Conley and Toril Moi here and below to summarize the positions of Cixous and Irigaray in part because the French feminists' own comments are exceedingly obscure when taken out of context and would muddy rather than clarify this discussion.

3. For an extended discussion of this theory see Robertson (1990).

4. R. W. Hanning made a similar argument in his discussion of the *General Prologue*'s portrait of the Prioress where he suggests that we see in her 'not only a heightened awareness of helplessness in others (even mice!) but also compulsive feelings of resentment and hate toward the oppressor. Such feelings at their most untutored might resemble the resentful paranoia of the child who believes he has been arbitrarily mistreated by a cruel adult world, the very feelings I believe exist beneath the naive piety of the Prioress' famous (or infamous) tale of the little child killed by Jews' (p. 589).

5. For a fuller discussion of this characteristic of female mystical texts see Robertson (1990).

6. As Hanning writes of the Prioress's portrait in the *General Prologue*, 'her treatment of her lapdogs, her sympathy for trapped mice, dead or bleeding, suggests an identification with small, helpless things, trapped and punished in a world of men who smite "with a yerde smerte"' (p. 588).

7. I would like to thank Gerda Norvig and Pamela Benson for their expert editorial assistance in the completion of this essay. I am grateful to Judith Ferster for her contribution to the development of these ideas.

Works cited

ABELARD, *Letters of Abelard and Eloise*, trans. Betty Radice (London: Penguin, 1973).

AERS, DAVID, 'Introduction', *Medieval Literature: Criticism, Ideology, and History* (New York: St Martins Press, 1986).

ANSELM, *Prayers and Meditations of Saint Anselm*, trans. Sister Benedicta Ward (London: Penguin, 1973).

BENSON, C. DAVID, *Chaucer's Drama of Style* (Chapel Hill: University of North Carolina Press, 1986).

BERNARD, *Saint Bernard of Clairvaux Seen through His Selected Letters*, trans. Bruno Scott James (Chicago: Regnery, 1953).

BRYAN, W. F. and GERMAINE DEMPSTER, eds, *Sources and Analogues of Chaucer's Canterbury Tales* (New York: Humanities Press, 1941).

BURLIN, ROBERT B., *Chaucerian Fiction* (Princeton, NJ: Princeton University Press, 1977).

BYNUM, CAROLINE, *Holy Feast and Holy Fast: The Significance of Food to Medieval Religious Women* (Berkeley: University of California Press, 1986).

BYNUM, CAROLINE, 'Women Mystics and Eucharistic Devotion in the Thirteenth Century', *Women's Studies*, 11 (1984), 179–214.

CIXOUS, HÉLÈNE and CATHERINE CLEMENT, *The Newly Born Woman*, trans. Betsy Wing (Minneapolis: University of Minnesota Press, 1987).

COHEN, MAURICE, 'Chaucer's Prioress and Her Tale: A Study of Anal Character and Anti-Semitism', *Psychoanalytic Quarterly*, 31 (1962), 231–49.

COLLETTE, CAROLYN, 'Sense and Sensibility in the Prioress' Tale', *ChauR*, 15 (1980), 138–50.

CONLEY, VERENA, 'Review of Hélène Cixous: Writing the Feminine', *Rocky Mountain Review*, 40. 1–2 (1986), 97.

COWGILL, JANE, 'Patterns of Feminine and Masculine Persuasion in the "Melibee" and the "Parson's Tale"', *Chaucer's Religious Tales*, ed. C. David Benson and Elizabeth Robertson (Cambridge: D. S. Brewer, 1990), 171–83.

DE BEAUVOIR, SIMONE, 'The Mystic', *The Second Sex*, trans. H. M. Parshley (1953; New York: Bantam Books, 1970).

DELANY, SHEILA, 'Womanliness in the Man of Law's Tale', *Writing Woman* (New York: Schocken Books, 1983).

DONALDSON, E. TALBOT, *Chaucer's Poetry* (New York: Ronald, 1958).

FARMER, SHARON, 'Persuasive Voices: Clerical Images of Medieval Wives', *Speculum*, 61 (1986), 517–43.

FRANK, ROBERT W. JR., 'Miracles of the Virgin, Medieval Anti-Semitism and the "Prioress's Tale"', *The Wisdom of Poetry: Essays in Early English Literature in Honor of Morton W. Bloomfield*, ed. Larry Benson and Siegfried Wenzel (Kalamazoo: Medieval Institute Publications, 1982), 177–88.

GREEN, RICHARD FIRTH, 'Chaucer's Victimized Women', *SAC*, 10 (1988), 3–22.

HANNING, ROBERT W., 'From Eva to Ave to Eglentyne and Alisoun: Chaucer's Insight into the Roles Women Play', *Signs*, 3 (1977), 580–99.

IRIGARAY, LUCE, 'La Mystérique', *Speculum de l'autre Femme* (Paris: Les Éditions de Minuit, 1974). *Speculum of the Other Women*, trans. Gillian C. Gill (Ithaca, NY: Cornell University Press, 1985), 191–202.

KRISTEVA, JULIA, 'Stabat Mater', *The Female Body in Western Culture*. ed. Susan Rubin Suleiman (Cambridge, MA: Harvard University Press, 1986), 99–118.

LOWES, JOHN LIVINGSTON, *Convention and Revolt in Poetry* (Boston, MA: Houghton Mifflin, 1919).

MILES, MARGARET, *Image as Insight: Visual Understanding in Western Culture and Secular Culture* (Boston: Beacon Books, 1961).

MOI, TORIL, *Sexual/Textual Politics* (London: Methuen, 1985).

207

MORSE, CHARLOTTE, 'The Exemplary Griselda', *SAC*, 7 (1985), 51–86.

RIDLEY, FLORENCE H., *The Prioress and the Critics*, University of California English Studies, 30 (Berkeley: University of California Press, 1965).

ROBERTSON, ELIZABETH, *Early English Devotional Prose and the Female Audience* (Knoxville: University of Tennessee Press, 1990).

RODAX, YVONNE, *The Real and the Ideal in the Novella* (Chapel Hill: University of North Carolina Press, 1968).

SCHOECK, RICHARD J., 'Chaucer's Prioress: Mercy and Tender Heart', rpt. *Chaucer Criticism: The Canterbury Tales I*, ed. Schoeck and Jerome Taylor (Notre Dame: University of Notre Dame Press, 1960), 239–55.

12 Signs and/as Origin: Chaucer's *Nun's Priest's Tale**

Britton J. Harwood

Harwood uses the work of Derrida to interpret the *Nun's Priest's Tale* as manifesting a Chaucerian anxiety that language is not a derivative of the 'things' it refers to but that it actually constitutes the 'reality' its users experience. Although Chaucer is ironic about the 'supplementarity' of language, and about the various ways in which it effaces what it seeks to present, and although his thinking is based on a standard medieval belief that signification is 'fallen' and subsidiary to an original 'truth', the divine Logos, that stands outside the signifying system, there is evidence in the Tale that language does in fact produce the origin that claims to produce it. Harwood posits a set of hierarchical (Christian) oppositions in the Tale which become similarly 'destabilized', and while Chaucer attempts to suppress his knowledge of the 'dangerous nature of signs', his Tale finally confesses 'a sign of an epoch to come'. For introductions to Derrida's work, see Jonathan Culler, *On Deconstruction: Theory and Criticism After Structuralism* (London: Routledge and Kegan Paul, 1983); Terry Eagleton, *Literary Theory: An Introduction* (Oxford: Blackwell, 1983), chapter 4; Christopher Norris, *Deconstruction: Theory and Practice*, rev. edn (London: Routledge, 1991); Robert Young, ed., *Untying the Text: A Poststructuralist Reader* (London: Routledge and Kegan Paul, 1981).

In the twelfth-century Flemish–Latin narrative *Isengrimus*, a rooster is encouraged by Reynard the fox to stretch his neck and close his eyes in order to sing his very best. After the rooster has been seized, Reynard boasts that he will devour the bird, allowing the victim to escape from his mouth (Yates, p. 121). This sequence of events – singing while not looking, then a self-defeating prophecy – is shared by three other analogues of the *Nun's Priest's Tale*: the *Roman de Renart* (*Sources and Analogues* 655, 657; Branch II, lines 347, 433–34),

* Reprinted from *Style*, 20 (1986), 189–202.

Reinhart Fuchs (*Sources and Analogues* 661; lines 133, 145–46), and an Anglo-Norman fable 'Del cok e del gupil' by Marie de France (p. 42). I mean to suggest here that the *Nun's Priest's Tale* is Chaucer's expansion of his perception that these two events are, in some essential way, the same event. When the cock sings with his eyes closed, whatever his voice might be referring to in the external world has disappeared. Because the word 'cock' passes through the throat of the fox, the thing it signifies will not.[1] The *signum datum*[2] displaces the referent. Because bird and fox delete the referent by essentially the same mistake, at the end of Chaucer's tale they do not really draw different morals (cf. Myers, p. 212). And their comic errors have come to exemplify the dangerous nature of signs for Chaucer.[3]

Chaucer altered the plot of his sources to show this same danger. In the *Roman de Renart*, hen and cock debate the truthfulness of the cock's dream, but it is the cock who denies it: 'Ja nel crerai . . . / Que j'aie mal por icest songe' (268–69). In *Le roman de Renart le Contrefait*, Pinte the hen rehearses the ugly consequences of cowardice, but then separates that from reasonable prudence – not setting sail during a storm, for instance, or being too stingy or spending too much: 'Tel couardie doit on avoir.' Far from disagreeing with this indeterminate counsel, the cock goes off to divert himself fatalistically and anxiously (*Le roman de Renart* lines 31369–448, 31459; cf. Pratt, pp. 431–33, 646–50, 656). Chaucer first of all removes the evenhandedness from the hen's advice: 'I kan nat love a coward,' she begins (2911). Thereafter, Chaucer gives the debate the sharpness it had in the *Roman*, but now with the *cock* arguing that his dream reliably predicts 'adversitee'. This change becomes pivotal for interpretation, since the cock's ultimate fearlessness (3176), which Chaucer retains from the *Roman*, must now result from something else than the contents of Chauntecleer's arguments.

Chaucer makes these revisions, I suggest, in order to assimilate the cause of the rooster's fearless descent to Chauntecleer's other errors. A good many readers believe that 'he fley doun fro the beem' (3171) because his desire for Pertelote subdued his better judgment; love, of a sort, cast out fear (Brody, p. 33; Owen, p. 138; David, pp. 230–1; Payne, p. 209; Dean, p. 8; Donaldson, p. 1107). By what process, however, did groaning and roaring turn into the insouciant, patronizing flattery with which Chauntecleer set Pertelote up to be trodden? To suggest that desire made him urbane and complimentary does not explain how he came to be desirous. In another sophisticated if not mock-heroic Middle English comedy, all the while Bercilak's wife flirts with Gawain, he is not in the mood. How does Chauntecleer move from anxiety to lubricity?

Surely, as a number of readers have already argued for somewhat
different reasons, the process has to do with the 184 lines in which
the cock shows how right he is to 'been agast' (2921).[4] As a guide for
interpreting this lengthy Chaucerian supplement, we may take a brief
one occurring later on, when the cock is walking with his wives in
the yard. Chauntecleer

> Caste up his eyen to the brighte sonne,
> That in the signe of Taurus hadde yronne
> Twenty degrees and oon, and somwhat moore,
> And knew by kynde, and by noon oother loore,
> That it was pryme, and crew with blisful stevene.
> 'The sonne,' he seyde, 'is clomben up on hevene
> Fourty degrees and oon, and moore ywis.'

> (3193–99)

Almost the first thing the narrator mentions about Chauntecleer is
that 'By nature he knew ech ascencioun / Of the equynoxial in thilke
toun' (2855–56). Every time the sun moves another fifteen degrees he
crows. On the one hand, the cock crows because of something in his
animal nature: John Steadman explains, in terms of medieval medical
theory, how the flow of choler was thought to account for this galline
regularity (237, 242–43). On the other hand, the cock expands his
crowing by giving the entirely denatured, scientific grounds on which
he crows. Time itself for the cock, since his crowing designates the
'houres equales' as 'a clokke or an abbey orlogge' does (2854), is
cultural and social, the natural or 'kyndely' referent, the 'houres
inequales', having been supplanted. Correlatively, his systematic
means for referring to time, explained by Chaucer in his *Treatise
on the Astrolabe* (2.3–4), substitutes for the natural, instinctual time-
telling of a rooster. Whatever he has 'by nature', 'by kynde', is
displaced at the moment he adds the knowledge drawn from culture.
To tell the time by saying 'The sonne . . . is clomben up on hevene /
Fourty degrees and oon . . .' designates the crowing only to replace it.
Accretion and substitute, language conceals the very thing it explains
and expands. An easy instance is the Priest's ironic request to overlook
any blame he may have cast on 'conseil of wommen'. He 'seyde it in
[his] game. / Rede auctours, where they trete of swich mateere . . .'
(3261–62). These authorities would not only endlessly add to the
Priest's misogynist lines (3256–59) but overthrow them, so far as the
Priest wishes to govern their interpretation by calling them a joke.
When 'sustres' is expanded with 'paramours' (2867), the addition
comically subverts 'sustres' by displacing any suggestion of
human kinship.

As Chauntecleer's articulation of the time supplements an instinctual sound, so his long case that many dreams foretell the future designates and dilates the groans and roars made in his sleep. Later in the *Tale*, Chaucer gives a prehistory for this process in the sounds that erupt once the fox has made off with Chauntecleer:

> This sely wydwe and eek hir doghtres two
> Herden thise hennes crie and maken wo,
> . . .
> And cryden, 'Out! harrow! and weylaway!
> Ha! ha! the fox!' and after hym they ran,
> . . .
> ...the verray hogges,
> So fered for the berkyng of the dogges
> And shoutyng of the men and wommen eeke,
> They ronne so hem thoughte hir herte breeke.
> They yolleden as feendes doon in helle;
> The dokes cryden as men wolde hem quelle.
> . . .
> So hydous was the noyse, a, *benedicitee!*
> Certes, he Jakke Straw and his meynee
> Ne made nevere shoutes half so shrille
> . . .
> Of bras they broghten bemes, and of box,
> Of horn, of boon, in whiche they blewe and powped,
> And therwithal they skriked and they howped.

(3375–400)

In this mêlée, pursuers and pursued feed endlessly back and forth into each other. The hogs and ducks, frightened by the barking and the shouting, contribute to the uproar in back of the fox. Likewise, articulate and inarticulate sounds, people and animals, become virtually inseparable: 'the fox' are words, and blasts from the horns are noises; the shrieks, however, like 'harrow! and weylaway!' are borderline cases. Pigs and people interchangeably 'yolleden' and 'skriked'. This scene of need situates language at its threshold, as if it had just emerged from animal sound, with need itself an origin for language. In the sense, then, that 'the more rational' a language is, 'the better it expresses need' (Derrida, *Grammatology*, p. 242), Chauntecleer's argument for the truthfulness of dreams 'expresses' his plight before the 'glowynge eyen tweye', expands and justifies the groaning,[5] supplements its deficient ability to control.

The articulateness giving language its clarity as needs multiply begins when two things are hinged in the differential relationship that brings signs into being: 'dremes been significaciouns / As wel of *joye* as of *tribulaciouns . . .'* (2979–90; emphasis added). Chauntecleer uses such a system when he articulates the 'adversitee' in store for him. 'Sweven' and 'dreme' are not alike, for dreams are veridical or not: they 'be somtyme – I sey nat alle – / Warnynge of thynges that shul after falle' (3131). Subdividing further, the cock, knowing that Pertelote has been generalizing from the *insomnium*,[6] acknowledges the last of the untruthful kinds according to Macrobius's science (the *visum*) by having the ill-fated voyager use it as his own description of dreams: 'swevenes been but vanytees and japes'.

> Men dreme alday of owles and of apes,
> And eek of many a maze therwithal.
>
> (3091–93)[7]

Then, with those who believe, or come to believe, in dreams, the cock canvasses the *oraculum* (3001–109), the *visio* (3110–21, 3141–48), and the *somnium* (3126–40). This system links the fox with other disasters that were 'forncast'. Chauntecleer affirms a lack – the ghastly otherness of the fox – by systematically filling it through a chain of mediations that produce the meaning of the very thing that they also displace.

Where the fox's boasting will let the object slip, so the cock's singing – the re-presentation of the instinctual cry – has substituted itself for an object that was there to be seen. As Chaucer had begun by tracing Chauntecleer, from his crenelated comb to the nails on his toes, so the cock outlines the beast: 'tipped was his tayl and bothe his eeris / With blak' (2903–4). And just as Chaucer counts on his audience letting the image of Chauntecleer slip during the survey of dreams, with the consequence that we laugh to be reminded that Pertelote's beauty partly consists in scarlet about her eyes, so the fearful image – the 'glowynge eyen' – has been effaced by the very elaboration which insists that this *res* is real.

In Chauntecleer's description of the fox, discourse aspires to the pictograph, 'an impossible sign, . . . giving the signified, indeed the thing, *in person*, immediately, closer to gesture or glance than to speech' (Derrida, *Grammatology*, p. 234). Writing as painting, while it attempts to procure and master the object, begins the inevitable process of its impoverishment. An outline introduces difference – and thereby in principle the whole of Chauntecleer's articulated dream system. The very gestures by which Chauntecleer attempts to seize the fox dispossess him of the fox. Within the voice of the cock, which first tries to trace, then substitutes a taxonomy for the tracing, 'the presence of the object already disappears. The self-presence of the voice and of the hearing-oneself-speak conceals the very thing that

213

visible space allows to be placed before us' (p. 240). Laughably,
the fox has been depleted by Chauntecleer's voice to the point of
disappearance; accordingly, later, lying among 'the wortes', he has
the quality of a discovery for the cock. Once signified, the fox takes
his place in Chauntecleer's argument within a sign system. The cock
idealizes the fox, as signification takes and removes its signifiers
from the external world. In idealizing the fox, the cock *repeats* him,
first as description, then as repetitive argument. Thus, writes Derrida,
'sensory exteriority . . . submits itself to my power of repetition, to
what thenceforward appears to me as my spontaneity and escapes
me less and less' (p. 166). On the one hand, the supplement holds the
fox, 'an absent presence', at a distance through its image 'and masters
it' (p. 155). On the other, through this articulation of a danger, the
cock becomes, comically, a self-presence, a plenitude that will not
allow itself to be described as 'replecciouns' (2923).

The image of the fox added by Chaucer to his sources is
erased by Chauntecleer's adding to it. Meanwhile, the object having
disappeared, yet another substitution occurs. In the emptied space,
the hen appears, a second divinely determined (3159) *res*, and the
cock names her beauty, traces it 'aboute' her eyes. This sort of oral
picto-hieroglyphics adds to the fearfulness of the fox once again, for
this gesture towards the object of desire will double the risk posed by
the eclipse of the fox. Yet as supplement, it substitutes for the first
object once again, deferring it, securing itself against it as 'mannes
joye and al his blis'.

These substitutions are funny because within Christian ontology they
inevitably have the character of displacing reality with appearance,
the immediacy of the uncreated Word with the mediation of
language, and so on. In a tradition ranging from Aristotle to Ockham
and beyond, spoken words signify concepts and things, while written
words merely signify spoken ones (William of Ockham, p. 50). The
privilege conferred upon the voice derives from the immediacy with
which, when I speak, I am present to myself. Beyond this, 'The word
heard outside', Augustine held, 'is the sign of the word which is
luminous within, which is more appropriately called a "word"'
(Markus, p. 77; translation of *De Trinitate* 15.11.1). Augustine takes
this *verbum mentis* as begotten 'by the knowledge which remains
in the mind' (*De Trinitate* 15.11.44–46). This immanent knowledge
of exterior objects is guaranteed by the Divine Word, the Interior
Teacher, who created both the knowledge and the objects themselves.
The divine ideas are both the principles of speculative knowledge
(the idea) and exemplars for the production of the external things
which are understood (Lonergan, pp. 356–57). The inner word,
signifying both, is itself spoken within (*intus dicitur*) by the Interior

Teacher. As this inner word, in no particular language, comes into relationship with the outer word, it retains its proximity to the divine Logos. The determination of the sign by the thing[8] is thus secured by the Word. The sign makes known the object that it signifies at the instant it makes itself known. As I am immediately present to myself in speech, the Logos suffers no division within itself when it creates the *res* for which it provides signs; for all things in their capacity as *vestigia Trinitatis* signify the Creator, who alone is a mere *res*.[9] Chauntecleer's dream makes immediate contact with the divine unity (3054–56). Although the cock correctly argues that his lot is 'adversitee', his dream predicts because the divine plenitude exists, full to overflowing, and is the ultimate signified of the objects that scare him into speech.[10] The transcendental signified anchors all signs and ultimately turns up, like the corpse from the bottom of the cart.

Signs nevertheless 'always seem to make an apparent, provisional, and derivative notch in the system of first and last presence. . . . The sign is always a sign of the Fall. Absence always relates to distancing from God' (Derrida, *Grammatology*, p. 283). Discourse, which within Christian metaphysics is derivative and determined, begins the descent from 'things that ben alle hole and absolut . . . into uttereste thinges . . . empty and withouten fruyt' (*Boece* 3, pr. 10). In this view, supplementation or signification befalls a presence, as metaphor comes to wear away a literal sense. For the Christian Chaucer all signification is regrettable, infecting the signified with absence. Ironically, in the fallen world insisted upon by the induction, all signs of God open the space between God and man still further. Each of Chauntecleer's supplements of his dream, seeking to recover and master the fullness of God's presence, divides the present yet again in articulation.[11] The spacing of any system (for instance, the line between 'a beest' and 'his contrarie' [3279–80]) is seen as the catastrophic rupture of an original plenitude. 'Whanne [everything that is] forletith to be oon, it moot nedys deien and corrumpen togidres' (*Boece* 3, pr. 11).

For Christian ontology, the supplement, in its dual nature of accretion and substitute, is always sinful, whether it supplements need with the images of passion, a 'sklendre' diet with food to repletion, the monochrome of the induction with the polychrome of the chickenyard, music (or crowing) with (scientific) words, the 'verray preeve' with 'argument', 'soothfastnesse' with flattery, the fact of providence with 'altercacioun' on where, within it, necessity and freedom divide, the cry of fear with *amplificatio* and 'compleynt', fruit with chaff, or tale with elaboration. 'Evil always has the form of representative alienation, of representation in its dispossessing aspect' (Derrida, *Grammatology*, p. 296). For Christian ontology, nevertheless, each unfortunate supplement folds back within the 'heighe blisse' to which it ultimately refers. Michel Foucault has written that 'the Classical age [that is, the seventeenth and eighteenth centuries] . . . separates us from a culture in which the signification of signs did not exist, because it was reabsorbed into the sovereignty of the Like' (p. 43). In Chauntecleer's humility at the end, Chaucer humbles the sign before the thing. The bird's determination to see rather than sing, the beast's vow to 'holde his pees' (3435) signal the retreat of the signifier.

This is the nature of signs and their origin that Chaucer advances in the *Tale*. Nevertheless, this view cannot simply dispose of signification from the outside, as it were. While not annulled thereby, it is *'inscribed* within a system which it no longer dominates' (Derrida, *Grammatology*, p. 243).[12] The distinction that would arbitrate between things and words is founded by words and subject to them. (In an analogous way, as Derrida points out, the philosophical distinction between literal and metaphoric is itself produced by the founding metaphors of philosophy. And any philosophical taxonomy of metaphor would always be short the metaphors that constitute philosophy itself [Derrida, 'White Mythology', pp. 18, 28].) Chaucer would imply an origin for words: while Chauntecleer as plenitude gets into difficulty, he had been forewarned by God – perhaps a projection of a similar fullness of the voice, the immediacy with which one hears oneself speak, the illusion that one has ceased to borrow signifiers from the outside, that there is no outside or that the outside is nothing. This origin, however, is designated by a system of signs that 'has no outside' (p. 234) either and situates 'a multitude of origins' (p. 217). In doing so and thus opening 'the play of presence and absence' (p. 163), the *Nun's Priest's Tale* 'describe[s]' what Chaucer 'does not wish to say' (p. 229).

That 'there is nothing outside the text' (Derrida, *Grammatology*, p. 158) is a possibility already latent in one strand of medieval sign theory itself. On the one hand, Augustine teaches that the sign is learned from the thing, not the thing from the sign (*De magistro*, 10.132–33). On the other hand, the meaning of a sign, he points out, comes only from other signs (3.39–46). In *De magistro*, then, the *res* privileged by Stoicism and scholasticism is pulled into play already, in which the *'representamen* functions only by giving rise to an *interpretant* that itself becomes a sign and so on to infinity' (Derrida, *Grammatology*, p. 49). Within sign systems, no transcendental signified anchors meaning. It arises, to the contrary, with the constitutive differences of the sign system itself: 'initially the concept is nothing, . . . only a value determined by its relations with other similar values . . .'; 'in language there are only differences *without positive terms.* Whether we take the signified or the signifier, language has neither ideas nor sounds that existed before the linguistic system, but only conceptual and phonic differences that have issued from the system' (Saussure, pp. 117, 120).

These differences that make meaning possible begin with the discrepancy between objective exteriority and the word. Both designating and constituting an origin that has always already disappeared, the word, or trace, synthesizes an irreducible heterogeneity. This originating difference is the site on which all signification takes place. In the *Tale*, as an emblem of this, we find that, after a corpse has been discovered at the bottom of the dung cart, a confession is disinterred from the conspirators by torture (3058–61). 'Mordre wol out', Chauntecleer insists. But is that the body or the confession? What but language – a confession, for example – can constitute a dead body as a murdered one? The idea of a murdered body has no existence independent of the signifiers that constitute it. (Nor does simply the idea of its being a body or any other idea.) The confession, or something like it, rather than coming after the discovery of the body, precedes it as its condition. Language fills a lack, brings the body to light, but supplants it: the real death is the one carried inside the supplement as its hollow.

Within Christian ontology it is intolerable that the origin of words is something they produce. Once one opposition is inverted and writing turns out to be natural, all the metaphysical distinctions that writing produces (substance/accident, existence/essence, matter/ form, and so on) become destabilized as well. Strikingly, while Chaucer wishes to determine the supplement as an evil lying outside the divine plenitude, the most interesting recent criticism of the *Tale* reads it as a play between antitheses that cannot be finally adjudicated (Muscatine, p. 239; Fish, pp. 223–28; Lenaghan, p. 305; Mann, pp. 275–76; Brady, p. 33). This play all derives, perhaps, from the drift of an origin into the game of supplementarity. *'In principio'*, for instance, *'Mulier est hominis confusio –'* (3163–64). This means, says the cock to the hen, that 'Womman is mannes joye and al his blis' (3166). Ordinarily, the Latin is understood to report an original event; the English (falsely) reports the Latin. But Chaucer himself gives us, in his way, the original scene, where Pertelote is no worse than an accessory. Moreover, if she *had* ruined Chauntecleer, she would have done so precisely as object of desire, 'joye' and 'solas' (3170) (cf. Owen, p. 137). The English not only destroys the Latin but gives the *sententia* of it, indicating the origin of the confusion. (The outside, the supplement, is not merely the outside.)

The story is decentered in part by Chaucer's setting it at the beginning, when 'Beestes and briddes koude speke and synge'

(2881). Placing it on a Friday (3341) soon after 'March, whan God first maked man' (3188), he insists upon it as re-enactment of the Fall. This fall is a beginning, however, that puts the beginning at a distance, in two directions. That is, it substitutes itself for the beginning. From the induction on, the postlapsarian state of the world is unmistakable. Chauntecleer has parents as the fox does, 'daun Russell' being well known as the son of Reynard. Nonetheless Chauntecleer's reascent postpones the fall. At the end of the *Tale*, the cock, as Ann Payne has pointed out, has triumphed 'in spite of his innocence. He is Adam Unfallen . . .' (p. 212). This fall designates the fall and splits it. Articulation, difference (between the fall as representer and the fall as represented, between the fall that is and the fall that has already been or has not yet happened) turn out to be originary.

The structure of Chaucer's own text reveals the structure of the supplement. His description of the poor widow exploits an opposition between need and sufficiency – slender meals as opposed to a sufficiency of the heart (2839). One sign of her contentment is her never needing 'a deel' of 'poynaunt sauce' (2834). But she requires no sauce to sustain her appetite through 'many a sklendre meel' because she is likely still hungry even when such meals are over. Her never needing a sauce is not only the patience coming after the meal but the good appetite that preceded it. Likewise the physical activity made possible by her not eating too much ('The goute lette hire nothyng for to daunce') is simultaneously what makes eating possible, as when she gives chase to the fox. These are additions to what they also precede.

The time of the text itself discloses this structure. Down in the yard, in the early morning following the night of his dream, Chauntecleer

> . . . fethered Pertelote twenty tyme,
> And trad hire eke as ofte, er it was pryme.
>
> (3177–78)

> Whan that the month in which the world bigan,
> That highte March, whan God first maked man,
> Was compleet, and passed were also,
> Syn March bigan, thritty dayes and two,
> Bifel that Chauntecleer in al his pryde,
> His sevene wyves walkynge by his syde,
> Caste up his eyen to the brighte sonne,
> That in the signe of Taurus hadde yronne
> Twenty degrees and oon, and somwhat moore,

And knew by kynde, and by noon oother loore,
That it was pryme. . . .

(3187–97)

Chauntecleer feathers Pertelote twenty times before it is 9 a.m.
Thirty-two days pass since the beginning of March, and it happens
('Bifel') that Chauntecleer, out walking, notices that it is 9 a.m. In this
passage, narrative time seems to follow the order of story time. A
few lines after the beginning of it, the narrative becomes for a short
space (3187–90) a summary, to use Gérard Genette's term (p. 95),
with narrative time much less than the thirty-odd days of story time.
But then, with Chauntecleer's calculation of the hour, narrative time
and story time return to a rough equivalence. This reading of the
relation between the two, however, is later disrupted: the text will
stipulate that Reynard appears in the yard the very morning
following the dream (3218, 3254–55). The time between the last of the
featherings and the crowing at prime, that is, may be only a moment;
and the text will stipulate that the summary was an analepsis – an
account of story time *before* the rooster dreamed of the fox.

As a consequence, the relation between the days and the moment
becomes undecidable. No doubt Chaucer meant what the later lines
signify: the fox had burst through the hedges 'the same nyght'. But
this small analepsis, even if it could succeed in revising the reader's
experience of the earlier lines, is inscribed within a text that it cannot
rewrite. By signifying a second idea of the duration between 'er it
was pryme' and 'pryme', the text makes of the thirty-odd days a
period that extends before and beyond the moment *as well as* a
period that splits it. 'Extends beyond' the moment ('pryme' will be
no longer the *terminus ad quem*) because the text also resignifies the
'thritty dayes and two' since the beginning of March ('syn March
bigan'). When Chaucer goes on to say that the sun has run twenty-
one degrees in Taurus, he places the discovery of the fox on *May* 3.
One supplement – the 'Whan that the month' amplification chaffing
the supplement of rhetoric – opens a lack within the moment.
Another – one that would make everything clear – creates an
exteriority that was already the lack.[13] In short, the moment is
hollowed out, but the space is simultaneously what lies outside the
moment, retention and protention.

In principio, as the *Tale* refers to and distances a beginning, it is
clearly not 'wommannes conseil' that brings the cock 'to wo' (3257).
The *Tale* adds to Genesis by inserting a fiction at the heart of it, just
as Chaucer, by reproducing his own narrative in summary, inserts
a fiction at the heart of that: 'My tale is of a cok . . . / That tok his
conseil of his wyf, with sorwe . . .' (3252–53). These sources are

displaced by the very accretions that depend upon them. Are Chauntecleer and Pertelote additions to the widow, as an egg or two supplement her diet (2845)? If so, their gorgeousness ends by banishing the original scene. Is she rather an expansion of *them*, the fatal supplement chosen by Adam-rooster and Eve-hen, and the hardness of her lot a pale sign of a lost paradise of 'blisful briddes' and 'fresshe floures' (3201–2)? Chauntecleer's explanation that he has just crowed because 'The sonne . . . is clomben up on hevene / Fourty degrees and oon, and moore ywis' (3198–99) is, for the narrator, one of the cock's comic supplements. No celestial point exists for the crowing to designate, however, until 'Fourty degrees and oon' has constituted it. What is represented as supplementary for the bird is the only way the hour can exist for the poet. Any notion of origin shifts irreducibly between the instinctual noise and the rational calculation. In the same way, the *Tale* threatens to show that Chauntecleer's groans when he dreams of the fox are not closer to an origin, an 'authorizing presence', than his singing, with the passionate image of Pertelote in mind.

Cry and song supplement each other in turn, just as the Latin antifeminist slogan and its English mistranslation take their value only from their differential relationships with each other. Women evidently deceive themselves about the historicity of 'Launcelot de Lake' (3212). A beast fable is a safe sign, for Chaucer, of the fictitiousness of the other 'book'. Just as safely, the invocation of fable posits an inner core of truth, for 'al that writen is, / To oure doctrine it is ywrite, ywis' (3441–42). This polarity between *littera* and sentence, like the opposition between history and God, reinscribes the polarization of signifier and transcendental signified. The 'book of Launcelot de Lake' may have something to do with women's truth, nevertheless. (It had something to do with Francesca's.) History for 'wommen' may be something that is performed rather than reported, and texts may be radically figurative, for they are confirmed in desire. In short, the *Tale* threatens to show that supplementation has, in the phrase Derrida owes to Heidegger, always already begun.

Chaucer is ironic about the sign, the supplement, but in his *Tale* it threatens to *produce* the origin. The multiple oppositions within the poem – 'confusio' and 'blis', constraint and 'large grace', necessity and free choice, one beast and 'his contrarie', the ship that goes down and the others that sail on, dung and gold, *domina* and housewife, game and earnest, letter and meaning, cockcrow and astronomical construction, the sun riveting the 'natural' bird and the metaphorical light in which the metaphorical bird comes to 'see' (3431; cf. Derrida, 'White Mythology', pp. 45, 69 and *Grammatology*, p. 285) – may remain hinged, with no ontologically privileged side able finally to reduce its opposite, for the reason that such doubling inheres in the sign itself.

Christian ontology would disguise such a threat, reduce the synthetic heterogeneity of the sign with the sovereignty of the Like, bleach the sign before the thing, as if to repair the broken hedges of the yard. Chaucer's *Tale* may nevertheless give, even as it suppresses, a sign of an epoch to come.

Notes

1. This ignores the modern principle that a sign links a sound with an idea rather than with an extramental thing and follows instead the notion of Scotus and Ockham that words signify directly the same as concepts signify (see Leff, p. 125). The actual taunt in Chaucer is 'I wol hym ete, in feith, and that anon' (3413). Chauntecleer suggests this language to the fox, who, of course, gets no farther than 'In feith, it shal be don' (3414).

2. As against the 'natural sign', like Peirce's icon or index. The terms are Augustine's, whose sign theory, in *De doctrina Christiana*, seems to have been fundamental for the Middle Ages (see Chydenius, pp. 5–7).

3. Like D. V. Harrington, I shall make no distinction between the Nun's Priest as narrator and Chaucer. Except at a very few points (e.g., 3260–61), the *Tale* seems an instance of what Donald R. Howard has called unimpersonated artistry (243 *et passim*). So far as a narrator can be distinguished from the implied author, he appears reliable. (However, see also Lenaghan, p. 307.) And I shall be referring to Chaucer's 'intention'. I do not understand deconstruction as denying that intentions can be read in texts. Derrida, for instance, reading 'the deep intention' of Rousseau's *Essay on the Origin of Languages* (*Grammatology*, p. 199), writes that 'Rousseau *wishes* [*voudrait*] to think of space as a simple outside', 'desires to separate' the principles of life and death, 'wishes to efface this *always-already*', 'would wish' the opposition between southern and northern in order to place a natural frontier between different types of languages'; 'Rousseau would like the absolute origin to be an absolute south' (*Grammatology*, pp. 201, 208, 216, 217). Such wishes are not psychological realities outside the text (p. 158) but particular organizations within it, inhabiting textual systems and subject to the play of supplementarity. (On the 'original absence of the subject of writing', see especially *Grammatology*, p. 69.)

4. 'Having mastered [Pertelote] in academic debate', Ian Bishop has written, 'he feels entitled to master her sexually' (p. 266). Cf. Pearsall, pp. 234–5. If we think Chauntecleer is courting Pertelote by debating her, then Chaucer's alteration of his sources is evidently pointless: that a lover is not to be intimidated by dreams seems as good a position for a lover to defend as the one Chaucer assigns to Chauntecleer.

5. Chaucer appears to have added Chauntecleer's groans to his sources as he did most of the details of the tumultuous chase (see Pratt, pp. 429, 430).

6. With Pertelote's diagnosis that 'humours been to habundant' (2935), that Chauntecleer is 'repleet of humours', compare Macrobius: 'Corporis, si temeto ingurgitatus aut distentus cibo vel abundantia praefocari se aestimet, vel gravantibus exonerari' (*In somnium Scipionis*, 2.9).

7. In view of the 'vanytees', 'japes', and 'many a maze', owls and apes probably exemplify the 'vagantes formas' of the *visum*; but see Rowland, pp. 322–5.

8. Cf. Maquart, p. 49: 'Le signe est mesuré par la chose signifiée et en dépend comme une chose moins importante dépend d'une plus importante' (p. 42). The sign is measured by the thing signified and depends upon it as a less important thing depends on a more important.

9. Cf. Chydenius, p. 9, who distinguishes this position of Augustine's in *De Trinitate* from his earlier one in *De doctrina Christiana*.

10. In a typical explanation of the prophetic image, Moses Maimonides held that the image came to man only after the agent intellect, the divine overflow, conveyed transcendent, unimaginable truth directly to man's own predisposed intellect and then, *via* the human intellect, symbolic images to the imagination. The prophetic imagination was understood as higher ('by heigh ymaginacioun forncast' [3217]) when God impressed images upon it in this way (Curry, p. 214; Bundy, pp. 168–71) or lower, when reason, having apprehended the unembodied truth, guided the *phantasia* in constructing earthly images to mirror it. (On the meaning of 'heigh' in Chaucer's line, however, see also Hamm, pp. 394–5.)

11. 'Language *adds itself* to presence and supplants it, defers it within the indestructible desire to rejoin it' (Derrida, *Grammatology*, p. 280).

12. '. . . The writer writes *in* a logic whose proper system, laws, and life his discourse by definition cannot dominate absolutely. He uses them only by letting himself, after a fashion and up to a point, be governed by the system. And the reading must always aim at a certain relationship, unperceived by the writer, between what he commands and what he does not command of the patterns of the language that he uses' (Derrida, *Grammatology*, p. 158).

13. The decentering of an authorial intention (about the time of the story) is not to be confused with a phenomenology of reading. Compare Derrida: 'the concept of the trace will never be merged with a phenomenology of writing' (*Grammatology*, p. 68). '. . . The supplement adds itself without adding anything to fill an emptiness which . . . begs to be replaced' (p. 292).

Works cited

Augustine, *De Trinitate*, ed. W. J. Mountain, 2 vols, Corpus Christianorum Series Latina 50–50A (Turnholt: Brepols, 1968).

Augustine, *De magistro*, ed. K.-D. Daur, Corpus Christianorum Series Latina 29 (Turnholt: Brepols, 1970).

Bishop, Ian, 'The *Nun's Priest's Tale* and the Liberal Arts', *Review of English Studies*, NS 30 (1979), 257–67.

Boece Brody, S. N., 'Truth and Fiction in the *Nun's Priest's Tale*', *Chaucer Review*, 14 (1979), 33–47.

Bundy, M. W., *The Theory of Imagination in Classical and Mediaeval Thought*, University of Illinois Studies in Language and Literature 12.2–3 (Urbana: University of Illinois Press, 1927).

Chaucer, Geoffrey, *The Works*, ed. F. N. Robinson, 2nd edn (Boston, MA: Houghton Mifflin, 1957).

Chydenius, Johan, *The Theory of Medieval Symbolism* (Helsingfors: Societas Scientiarum Fennica, 1960).

CURRY, WALTER C., *Chaucer and the Mediaeval Sciences*, 2nd edn (New York: Barnes & Noble, 1960).

DAVID, ALFRED, *The Strumpet Muse* (Bloomington and London: Indiana University Press, 1976).

DEAN, NANCY, 'Chaucerian Attitudes toward Joy with Particular Consideration of the *Nun's Priest's Tale*', *Medium AEvum*, 44 (1975), 1–13.

DERRIDA, JACQUES, *Of Grammatology*, trans. G. C. Spivak (1967; Baltimore and London: Johns Hopkins University Press, 1976).

DERRIDA, JACQUES, 'White Mythology: Metaphor in the Text of Philosophy', *New Literary History*, 6 (1971; 1974), 5–74.

DONALDSON, E. T., ed., *Chaucer's Poetry*, 2nd edn (New York: Ronald Press, 1975).

FISH, STANLEY, 'The Nun's Priest's Tale and Its Analogues', *College Language Association Journal*, 5 (1962), 223–8.

FOUCAULT, MICHEL, *The Order of Things: An Archaeology of the Human Sciences* (New York: Pantheon, 1970).

GENETTE, GÉRARD, *Narrative Discourse,* trans. J. E. Lewin (Ithaca, NY: Cornell University Press, 1980).

HAMM, V. M., 'Chaucer's "Heigh Ymaginacioun"', *Modern Language Notes*, 69 (1954), 394–5.

HARRINGTON, D. V., 'The Undramatic Character of Chaucer's Nun's Priest', *Discourse*, 8 (1965), 80–9.

HOWARD, DONALD R., *The Idea of the* Canterbury Tales (Berkeley: University of California Press, 1976).

LEFF, GORDON, *William of Ockham: The Metamorphosis of Scholastic Discourse* (Manchester: Manchester University Press, 1975).

LENAGHAN, R. T., 'The Nun's Priest's Fable', *PMLA*, 78 (1963), 300–7.

LONERGAN, BERNARD, 'The Concept of *Verbum* in the Writings of St Thomas Aquinas', *Theological Studies*, 7 (1946), 349–92; 8 (1947), 35–79; 10 (1949), 3–40.

MACROBIUS, AMBROSIUS THEODOSIUS, *In somnium Scipionis*, ed. James Willis (Leipzig: Teubner, 1963).

MANN, JILL, 'The *Speculum Stultorum* and the Nun's Priest's Tale', *Chaucer Review*, 9 (1975), 262–82.

MAQUART, F.-X., 'De la causalité du signe', *Revue Thomiste*, 32 (1927), 40–60.

MARIE DE FRANCE, *Fables*, ed. A. Ewert and R. C. Johnston (Oxford: Blackwell, 1942).

MARKUS, R. A., 'St Augustine on Signs', *Phronesis*, 2 (1957), 60–83.

MUSCATINE, CHARLES, *Chaucer and the French Tradition* (Berkeley and Los Angeles: University of California Press, 1957).

MYERS, D. E., 'Focus and "Moralite" in the *Nun's Priest's Tale*', *Chaucer Review*, 7 (1973), 210–20.

OWEN, CHARLES A., *Pilgrimage and Storytelling in the* Canterbury Tales: *The Dialectic of 'Ernest' and 'Game'* (Norman: University of Oklahoma Press, 1977).

PAYNE, F. A., 'Foreknowledge and Free Will: Three Theories in the *Nun's Priest's Tale*', *Chaucer Review*, 10 (1976), 201–19.

Chaucer: The Canterbury Tales

PEARSALL, DEREK, _The Canterbury Tales_ (London: George Allen & Unwin, 1985).

PRATT, R. A., 'Three Old French Sources of the Nonnes Preestes Tale', _Speculum_, 47 (1972), 422–44, 646–68.

Le roman de Renart le Contrefait, ed. Gaston Raynaud and Henri Lemaître (Paris: Champion, 1914).

ROWLAND, BERYL, ' "Owles and Apes" in Chaucer's _Nun's Priest's Tale_, 3092', _Mediaeval Studies_, 27 (1965), 322–35.

SAUSSURE, FERDINAND DE, _Course in General Linguistics_, trans. Wade Baskin (1915; New York: Philosophical Library, 1959).

Sources and Analogues of Chaucer's Canterbury Tales, ed. W. F. Bryan and Germaine Dempster (1941; New York: Humanities Press, 1958).

STEADMAN, J. M., 'Chauntecleer and Medieval Natural History', _Isis_, 50 (1959), 236–44.

WILLIAM OF OCKHAM, _Theory of Terms_, trans. M. J. Loux (Notre Dame and London: University of Notre Dame Press, 1974).

YATES, D. N., 'Chanticleer's Latin Ancestors', _Chaucer Review_, 18 (1983), 116–26.

13 From: A Mixed Commonwealth of Style*

Paul Strohm

Strohm's book sees Chaucer's work and Chaucer himself as 'deeply implicated' in the 'urgent social contests of the time'. By virtue of his connections both with the Court and with the increasingly powerful mercantile class, Chaucer was exposed with a peculiar intensity to what Strohm describes as the transition from feudalism to capitalism in the fourteenth century, and his work attempts to give a voice to different and competing social outlooks (from traditional hierarchical models based on domination to a new ethic of communal interaction). Strohm sees the *Canterbury Tales* as the climax of Chaucer's social thinking, reading the work as a 'project of representation' of the various social groupings and as a 'conciliation' between them, 'in the environment of lessened risk provided by a literary work'. For further discussion of this reading of the *Tales*, see my Introduction, pp. 15–17.

. . .

The contribution of the *Nun's Priest's Tale* to history lies not so much in its allusions as in its socially charged assumption that diverse levels of argumentative style, socially conditioned genres and forms, and kinds of utterance can inhabit the same literary space, cooperating for the profit (here defined as literary *solaas*) of all. The *Nun's Priest's Tale*, together with the *Canterbury Tales* as a whole, conveys the reassuring message that competing voices can colonize a literary space and can proliferate within it without provoking chaos or ultimate rupture. We have already encountered a similar proposition at a different cultural level, in those treatises on statecraft that argue for the accommodation of heterogeneity in the form of the natural state. Here the argument is made in the relatively more tractable form of literary discourse, but it is no less social in its implications.

* Reprinted from Paul Strohm, *Social Chaucer* (Cambridge, MA: Harvard University Press, 1989), pp. 166–72, 225–6.

The assertion that history is an absent cause of aesthetic form would seem to be safe indeed, if no acts of interpretation are to be based upon it and if the assertion itself is unsusceptible to proof. Yet the texts of the *Parliament of Fowls* and the *Canterbury Tales* do contain indications of the sense in which mixed style is proposed as an aesthetic figure for social heterogeneity. Chaucer's proposal of stylistic variety as a figure for social difference relies on a rhetorical and literary connection between social levels and levels of style already well established, and in fact regarded as self-evident, within medieval tradition.[1] Conceived within this supportive tradition, the texts of the *Parliament of Fowls* and the *Canterbury Tales* bear manifest indications of their own social encoding, with Chaucer himself insisting on the social basis of generic and stylistic choice. The respective styles of the higher and lower fowl in the *Parliament* are connected with the speakers' status as *gentils* and *cherls*. Even the often-obtuse narrator has no difficulty in identifying the tercels' plea as 'gentil' (485), and the tercelet does not hesitate to label the duck's words as those of a 'cherl', seasoned with the socially defined 'donghil' from which they came (596–97). The narrator of the *Canterbury Tales* makes the same connection at the outset, when he asks that his plain speech not be taken as evidence of 'vileynye' (I.726) – a word that, though sometimes used figuratively to attribute base behavior to the better born, retained most of its literal sense of peasant origins (of association through villeinage to the feudal agricultural unit or *vil*). This same connection is of course made in the 'cherles . . . manere' in which the Miller tells his tale (I.3169). Social perspective is, the narrator goes on to suggest, embodied not only in matters of style but in generic choice; he contrasts the 'cherles tale' of the Miller with other, more dignified forms that embrace 'gentillesse' (I.3179).

The social basis of generic preference is amply borne out in the pilgrims' own responses. Provoking the Miller's eruption in the first place was the special admiration of the 'gentils everichon' (I.3113) for the Knight's storial narration, and the Miller in turn wins the broader approbation of diverse 'folk' (I.3855). Chaucer likewise connects different genres to particular strata: a historical narrative with subthemes of conquest, tourney, and dynastic succession is assigned to the militaristic Knight; a comic tale with its celebration of the lower body to the carnivalesque Miller; a work of pseudo-hagiographical derring-do to the complacently pious Man of Law; and so on. Similarly, he assigns different forms of narrative with different presuppositions about human action in time to different sorts of pilgrims. Whatever their own ethical or spiritual character, more traditionally situated characters like the Knight, the Squire, the Monk, and the Prioress tend toward narrative punctuated by assertion of the atemporal and the transcendent. Representatives of lower or more recently emerged strata tend on the other hand to embrace temporality and causality, as in tales by the Miller, the Reeve, and the Shipman. These associations between social levels of tellers and the styles, genres, and forms of narrative are imaginary in nature. Fabliaux were really read by knights and esquires, popular romances were addressed to every level of society, love lyrics were preserved in monasteries, and miracles circulated in popular collections. Chaucer offers his conventionalized points of attachment not as serious assertions about the social basis of production and reception, but as fanciful recastings that playfully flaunt the social basis of taste even as they evade the task of specifying it in a detailed way. Playful or not, however, these recastings serve to alert their audience to an area of social implication, in which different textual features suggest differences in the social sphere. Even though the relations that Chaucer draws between the genres and styles of his tales and the social situation of his tellers are offered as frank stylizations, they still invite deeper questions about the social messages that aesthetic features may bear.

Chaucer's frequent allusions to the social basis of literary production and taste alert his audience to a project of representation and conciliation, in which style- and discourse-conflict are associated with class conflict in the environment of lessened risk provided by a literary work. The form of the *Canterbury Tales* permits the elaboration of vocal and stylistic difference, in an ultimately reassuring arena. Whatever the frictions among Chaucer's pilgrims, no blood is shed; although temporary alliances are formed, the pilgrim polity is not riven by self-interested faction; however overweening Harry Bailly's sway, tyrannicide need not occur. Such *quiting* as occurs is more likely within and between tales than between their tellers, as we observed in the case of the Miller, whose revolt was directed at the tale rather than the person of the Knight. The special property of literary language as the vehicle for socially based disagreement is that it permits highly contrastive voices to co-exist, while reassuring its audience that extreme stylistic discrepancies need not fracture the enterprise. The hospitality of Chaucer's 'framing fiction' to the varied styles and genres and forms in which his tellers express themselves, and to the ultimate irreconcilability of their voices, thus enables the perpetuation of a commonwealth of 'mixed style', with ultimately reassuring implications for the idea of the natural state as a socially heterogeneous body that recognizes the diverse interests and serves the collective good of all.

A special property of the *Canterbury Tales* is the extent to which its generic and stylistic variety is couched in polyvocality, in its embrace of separate and distinctive voices as a means of asserting social difference. Chaucer's poetry was always polyphonic, permitting the juxtaposition of separate themes and generic structures within the external form of a given work, but it becomes increasingly polyvocalic in its capacity to contain unreconciled voices as we move from the avian disputants of the *Parliament* to the distinctive and ultimately incompatible voices of Troilus and Pandarus and Criseyde to the yet fuller degree of autonomy assigned to the diverse Canterbury speakers. The Canterbury tales are richly polyphonic *and* polyvocalic, in the sense that, like medieval music, they pursue autonomous lines of development, and in the twentieth-century sense that they remain independent and unmerged. The principal theorist of this latter sense is of course Bakhtin, who argues that the precondition for true polyphony is that its voices are never subject to dialectical resolution, but remain unmerged in 'unceasing and irreconcilable quarrel'.[2] Chaucer critics have long appreciated the senses in which his commitment to autonomous voices inspires debate, though critics of an earlier day regarded the principal debates of the *Canterbury Tales* as subject to dialectical resolution.[3] In recent years critics have moved to embrace more fully the concept of Chaucer's polyphony, as defined both by medieval practice and modern theory, and his poetry is now characterized by such terms as 'contrastive', 'exploratory', a repository of 'partial truths', 'pluralistic', 'inconclusive', 'plurivalent', and 'disjunctive'.[4]

Rather than repeating the work of the many critics who have set out to demonstrate the polyphonic presuppositions of the *Canterbury Tales*,[5] I wish instead to pose a related question: in what sense is Chaucer's commitment to polyvocality *itself* a socially significant gesture? I have asserted that the stylistic and generic variety sustained by Chaucer's varied speakers is a figure for social variety, within the more conciliatory sphere of literary language, and Bakhtin's own description of polyphony in Dostoevsky's novels specifies the dynamics of this process. Bakhtin argues that Dostoevsky's polyphony is a refraction, through available literary possibilities, of the 'contradictory multi-leveledness' of his own society. He argues that, had Dostoevsky perceived multi-leveledness as residing only in the human spirit, he could have created an ultimately monologic novel that took as its subject the contradictory evolution of the human spirit; instead, since he found multi-leveledness in the objective social world, he brought it into his novels as an equivalent for irreducible social contradiction.[6] Bakhtin here points to the possibility of an ultimately monologic portrayal of diversity, as opposed to a portrayal of diversity that is polyphonic through and through and could not have been otherwise because of divisions in the author's experience of society. The *Canterbury Tales* is, I believe, polyphonic in this latter sense, and the polyphony is bound up in its identity as a social text.

One need not search far for instances of Bakhtin's monologic portrayal of diversity, in works by Chaucer's contemporaries and (though far less often) in his own works as well. Gower's *Confessio*, for example, gives us a series of narratives that reveal a new and upside-down world of discord in which each estate of society shirks its responsibilities and places its selfish interests before the common good. Yet the task of the poet, according to Gower, is to assert ultimate 'acord'. And Gower sets out authorially to achieve a hypothetical state of accord through a number of devices intended to constrain interpretation, including direct authorial commentary, narration by the single-voiced Genius, Genius's own extensive commentary, persuasive Latin headnotes to the books of the poem, and authorially composed Latin glosses, all intended to line up these vices 'arewe', to place them in their 'degrees', and to show their relation to an ideal standard of selfless love.[7]

Diversity is described in similarly monological fashion at various moments in Chaucer's own work, especially when he adopts the voices of limited tellers. Such a moment is that of Cambyuskan's feast in the *Squire's Tale*, where the 'prees' of folk swarm in to 'gauren' or gape at the magical gifts (V.189–90). Their conclusions are varied: 'Diverse folk diversely they demed; / As many heddes, as manye wittes ther been' (V.202–3). Some derive their views from 'old geestes' or the recitations of 'jogelours', others spout pseudo-science, others suppose the presence of magical art, and no opinion is clearly to be preferred to any other: 'thus jangle they, and demen, and devyse / Til that the kyng gan fro the bord aryse' (V.261–62). Still, as much as diversity is insisted upon, this discourse remains monologic. Its perspective is consistently controlled by the Squire, who conveys his scorn for the people and his disregard for their views by a variety of strategies, including their portrayal as an undifferentiated swarm of 'folk', aspersions about the authoritativeness of their knowledge (V.235), and their ignorance in seeking to judge 'thynges that been maad moore subtilly / Than they kan in hir lewednesse comprehende' (V.222–23). The Squire, knowing the tradition within which such marvels occur (romance, rather than 'gestes' or old science), knows how they are to be taken. The seeming diversity of the views he describes is thus undermined by the singlemindedness with which he dismisses them as objects of interest.

Such instances are rare in Chaucer's poetry, however, and his more ambitious attempts to recount illustrative narratives with a single voice show signs of authorial dissatisfaction with such limitation. Those *tragedies* told by the Monk in a spirit of 'diligence' (VII.1966) in order to illustrate his 'honestee' (VII.1967) constitute such a single-voiced collection within the boundaries of the *Canterbury Tales*. While the inner tone of the tragedies yields no irrefutable evidence of parody, Chaucer must be suspected of some irony in turning a currently fashionable international form over to the relentlessly monologic Monk.[8] Its own unvarying explanatory frame (that Fortune's wheel will 'out of joye brynge men to sorwe' – VII.2398), its stultifying reiteration of its own intentions ('Of Sampson now wol I namoore sayn' – VII.2090), and its ponderous admonitions ('Beth war . . .' – VII.2140) disclose the perils of monologicality. That Chaucer intended such a disclosure is confirmed by his textualization of a critique of the Monk's unvarying 'hevyness' and monotony in the responses of the Knight and the Host (VII.2767–805). The Monk 'clappeth lowde' (VII.2781) – rants on repetitively and without variation – and Harry Bailly's suggested solution lies in diversification: 'sey somwhat of huntyng, I yow preye' (VII.2805). The Monk of course refuses this invitation to variation, and it remains to the Nun's Priest with his mock-tragic disclosure of Fortune's reversal and rereversal to inaugurate that multiple disclosure in which, for Chaucer, ample treatment of a subject consists.

A more complex experiment with single-voiced narration occurs in the *Legend of Good Women*, where one narrator again sets out to recount a series of instances illustrative of established criteria. Here, however, Chaucer varies his inner tone, playfully experimenting at revealing the shortcomings of temporal narration ('wel coude I, if that me leste so, / Tellen al his doynge to and fro' – 2470–71) and at times stepping entirely outside his own narrative stance to address his audience directly ('Be war, ye wemen . . . / And trusteth, as in love, no man but me' – 2559–61). Sensitive critics have revealed the extent to which Chaucer in the *Legend* varies his narrative voice by deliberate textual play.[9] Yet were those early critics really so wrong when they took literally Chaucer's narrator's protestations that he is 'agroted herebyforn / To wryte of hem that ben in love forsworn' (2454–55)?[10] Whatever the inner play of the *Legend*'s text, it remains less representative of Chaucer's mature practice than the *Canterbury Tales*, in which a proliferation of narrators opens the possibility of independent centers of narrative authority, each with its own distinctive personal or social or generic identity.

Helen Cooper describes Chaucer's 'house of fiction' as one that offers vantages through various windows, each presenting a perspective peculiar to a particular genre and each with its own partial truth,[11] and her metaphor is apt in its emphasis on Chaucer's rejection of a single, univalent 'truth' and preference for truths embodied in multiple voices. This is not to say that the claims of different Canterbury narratives to validity go unchallenged. The Wife of Bath's inversion of traditional authority is promptly challenged by the Clerk's reassertion of the necessity for submissiveness, the Merchant's disenchanted account of an abuse of human trust is promptly challenged by the Franklin's assertion of human trustworthiness to do the right thing once freed of sterile agreements. But, just as no claims are permitted to stand unchallenged, so is no claim – however overidealized on the one hand or jaundiced on the other – presented to us as devoid of any truth at all. The polyphonic work is, as Bakhtin has reminded us, 'dialogic through and through',[12] and it is grounded not simply in a perverse human nature that refuses to recognize transcendent truth, but in an experience of a society constituted by various groups, each with its own version of reality.

Like Bakhtin's Dostoevsky, Chaucer may be viewed as having 'participated in the contradictory multi-leveledness of his own time',[13] and the form of his work as the expression of a socially determined view that presupposes irreconcilable difference. The form of the *Canterbury Tales* is not, of course, to be regarded as a direct reflection of a society riven by faction and socially based disagreement, but rather as a mediation of that view. 'Mediation' is here taken not in its most traditional Marxist sense, in which the contradictions inherent in a given situation are restated at different cultural levels with added concealment but without any progress toward resolution. Mediation is, rather, conceived in an alternative – though, I would argue, still Marxist – sense, as a positive social process, which does not simply restate intractable situations but restates them *in terms more amenable to resolution.*[14] The potential of this restatement for socially constructive resolution lies in the receptivity of Chaucer's chosen form to the language of conflict. The socially creative form of the *Canterbury Tales* permits a relatively untroubled contemplation of extreme difference, a degree of difference that could not be acknowledged in the social sphere without danger to the participants. The literary language of the *Canterbury Tales* is thus 'conciliatory' in the sense proposed by Macherey, in its ability to restate and to accommodate extremes of opinion as great as those of Chaucer's social reality, but to accommodate them 'avec moins de risque', undangerously.[15] This accommodation is, as Macherey would be quick to point out, imaginary, since it has no necessary effect on social reality. Yet, in its literary reproduction of a social reality that embraces varied social tendencies for the good of all, Chaucer's work itself becomes a social agent in the constructive possibilities it imagines and poses.

Notes

1. On the relation of style to different 'states of men' as exemplified by John of Garland, see JAMES J. MURPHY, *Rhetoric in the Middle Ages* (Berkeley: University of California Press, 1974), pp. 178–9. These presuppositions are examined in ERICH AUERBACH, *Literary Language and Its Public in Late Latin Antiquity and in the Middle Ages* (New York: Pantheon Books, 1965).

2. M. BAKHTIN, *Problems of Dostoevsky's Poetics* (Minnesota: University of Minnesota Press, 1984), p. 30. Bakhtin would restrict total polyvocality, in which 'every thought' is represented as 'the position of a personality' (p. 9) to the capitalist era (pp. 20–1), and he may be correct in this most rigorous application of his term. But, even while recognizing that many passages of the *Canterbury Tales* bear meanings that cannot be attributed to their imaginary speakers, I would nevertheless argue for the general applicability of his concept to works by Chaucer, Langland, and other pre-nineteenth-century authors.

3. Especially in the influential formulation of G. L. Kittredge, who believed the *Franklin's Tale* to propose a solution with which 'the whole debate has been brought to a satisfactory conclusion'. G. L. KITTREDGE, 'Chaucer's Discussion of Marriage', *MP* (1911–1912), 467.

4. See HELEN COOPER, *The Structure of the Canterbury Tales* (London: Duckworth, 1983), pp. 54–5; LARRY SKLUTE, *Virtue of Necessity: Inconclusiveness and Narrative Form in Chaucer's Poetry* (Columbus: Ohio State University Press, 1984), pp. 3–12; JESSE M. GELLRICH, *The Idea of the Book in the Middle Ages* (Ithaca, NY: Cornell University Press, 1985), pp. 213–14.

5. For example, those critics listed in the previous note, together with DAVID A. LAWTON, *Chaucer's Narrators* (Cambridge: D. S. Brewer, 1985), and PAUL STROHM, 'Form and Social Statement in *Confessio Amantis* and the *Canterbury Tales*', *SAC*, 1 (1979), 17–40.

6. BAKHTIN, *Dostoevsky's Poetics*, p. 27.

7. These observations are developed at greater length in STROHM, 'Form and Social Statement', 26–30.

8. RENATE HAAS, 'Chaucer's *Monk's Tale*: An Ingenious Criticism of Early Humanist Conceptions of Tragedy', *Humanistica Lovaniensia*, 36 (1987), 44–70.

9. Especially LISA J. KISER, *Telling Classical Tales: Chaucer and the Legend of Good Women* (Ithaca, NY: Cornell University Press, 1983).

10. H. C. GODDARD, 'Chaucer's Legend of Good Women', part 2, *JEGP*, 8 (1909), 47–111. The entire subject of Chaucer's boredom with his task is surveyed by ROBERT WORTH FRANK, JR., *Chaucer and the Legend of Good Women* (Cambridge, MA: Harvard University Press, 1972), pp. 189–210.

11. COOPER, *Structure*, p. 55.

12. BAKHTIN, *Dostoevsky's Poetics*, p. 40.

13. Ibid., p. 27.

14. As in CLAUDE LÉVI-STRAUSS, 'The Structural Study of Myth', *Structural Anthropology* (New York: Anchor Books, 1967), esp. pp. 217–27.

15. ETIENNE BALIBAR and PIERRE MACHEREY, 'On Literature as an Ideological Form', in *Untying the Text: A Post-Structuralist Reader*, ed. Robert Young (London: Routledge and Kegan Paul, n.d.).

Notes on Authors

CAROLYN P. COLLETTE is Professor of English Language and Literature on the Alumnae Foundation at Mount Holyoke College. She is the author of several articles on medieval literature and on literary theory, and, with Richard A. Johnson, of *Common Ground: A Guide to Personal, Professional, and Public Writing* (1993).

CAROLYN DINSHAW teaches at the University of California at Berkeley. She is the author of *Chaucer and the Text: Two Views of the Author* (1988), *Chaucer's Sexual Poetics* (1989) and *Getting Medieval: Sexualities and Communities, Pre- and Post-Modern* (forthcoming).

ELAINE TUTTLE HANSEN is Professor of English at Haverford College, and author of *The Solomon Complex: Reading Wisdom in Old English Poetry* (1988), *Chaucer and the Fictions of Gender* (1992) and *Mother Without Child: Contemporary Fiction and the Crisis of Motherhood* (1997).

BRITTON J. HARWOOD is Professor of English at Miami University, Ohio. He has written many articles on medieval literature as well as *'Piers Plowman' and the Problem of Belief* (1992). He is editor, with Gillian Overing, of *Class, Gender, and Early English Literature: Intersections* (1994) and with James Creech et al. of *A Community at Loose Ends* (1991).

PEGGY KNAPP is Professor of English at Carnegie Mellon University. She founded and for many years edited the annual book series *Assays: Critical Approaches to Medieval and Renaissance Texts*. She is the author of *Chaucer and the Social Contest* (1990) and *Time-Bound Words* (forthcoming), a study of changes in language and society between Chaucer's England and Shakespeare's. She has also written extensively on Renaissance and contemporary authors.

H. MARSHALL LEICESTER, JR is Professor of English Literature and Fellow of Cowell College, at the University of California, Santa Cruz. He is the author of *The Disenchanted Self: Representing the Subject in the*

'Canterbury Tales' (1990), and of articles on Chaucer, medieval literature, opera and film.

ARTHUR LINDLEY is Senior Lecturer in English at the National University of Singapore. He is the author of *Hyperion and the Hobbyhorse* (1996), a study of Bakhtinian Carnival and Augustinian Theology in Chaucer, the *Gawain*-Poet, Marlowe and Shakespeare. His work on literature and on film has also appeared in many journals.

LEE PATTERSON is F. W. Hilles Professor of English at Yale University. He is the author of *Negotiating the Past: The Historical Understanding of Medieval Literature* (1987) and of *Chaucer and the Subject of History* (1991), plus numerous essays dealing with literature in its historical context.

ELIZABETH ROBERTSON is Associate Professor of English at the University of Colorado at Boulder. She is the author of several articles on medieval literature and of *Early English Devotional Prose and the Female Audience* (1990). She also co-edited with C. David Benson *Chaucer's Religious Tales* (1990) and was a founding editor of the *Medieval Feminist Newsletter*.

MARCELLA RYAN was a tutor in Early English at Sydney University until her early death in 1991. She authored several articles including the one in this volume.

MARK A. SHERMAN is Assistant Professor of English at Rhode Island School of Design. He is the author of several articles on medieval literature and co-author, with Dorothy F. Donnelly, of *Augustine's 'De Civitate Dei': An Annotated Bibliography of Modern Criticism* (1991).

JOHN STEPHENS is Associate Professor in English at Macquarie University. Among his many publications are *Literature, Language and Change: From Chaucer to the Present* (1990, co-written with Ruth Waterhouse), *Language and Ideology in Children's Fiction* (1992), *Reading the Signs: Sense and Significance in Written Texts* (1992) and *Retelling Stories, Framing Culture: Traditional Story and Metanarratives in Children's Literature* (1998, co-written with Robyn McCallum).

PAUL STROHM is, since 1998, J. R. R. Tolkien Professor of Medieval English Language and Literature at the University of Oxford, and author of *Social Chaucer* (1989), *Hochon's Arrow: The Social Imagination of Fourteenth-Century Texts* (1992) and *England's Empty Throne: Usurpation and the Language of Legitimation* (1998).

Further Reading

Items listed here, many of which are referred to in my Introduction, are confined to those which discuss the relation between modern reading practices and medieval texts, or which use approaches to Chaucer that draw on (for example) deconstructive, psychoanalytic, gender-based, Marxist or Bakhtinian theories.

1. General

AERS, DAVID ed., *Medieval Literature: Criticism, Ideology and History* (New York: St Martin's Press, 1986).

BLOCH, R. HOWARD and STEPHEN G. NICHOLS, eds, *Medievalism and the Modernist Temper* (Baltimore, MD: Johns Hopkins University Press, 1996).

BROWNLEE, MARINA S., KEVIN BROWNLEE and STEPHEN G. NICHOLS, eds, *The New Medievalism* (Baltimore, MD: Johns Hopkins University Press, 1991).

DELANY, SHEILA, *Medieval Literary Politics: Shapes of Ideology* (Manchester: Manchester University Press, 1990).

EVANS, RUTH and LESLEY JOHNSON, eds, *Feminist Readings in Middle English Literature: The Wife of Bath and All Her Sect* (London: Routledge, 1994).

FINKE, LAURIE A. and MARTIN B. SHICHTMAN, eds, *Medieval Texts and Contemporary Readers* (Ithaca, NY: Cornell University Press, 1987).

MIDDLETON, ANNE, 'Medieval Studies', in *Redrawing the Boundaries: The Transformation of English and American Literary Studies*, ed. Stephen Greenblatt and Giles Gunn (New York: MLA, 1992), pp. 12–40.

PATTERSON, LEE, *Negotiating the Past: The Historical Understanding of Medieval Literature* (Madison: University of Wisconsin Press, 1987).

PATTERSON, LEE, 'On the Margin: Postmodernism, Ironic History, and Medieval Studies', *Speculum*, 65 (1990), 87–108.

PATTERSON, LEE, 'Critical Historicism and Medieval Studies', Introduction to *Literary Practice and Social Change in Britain, 1380–1530*, ed. Lee Patterson (Berkeley: University of California Press, 1990), pp. 1–14.

SCHICHTMAN, MARTIN B., ed., *Medieval Literature and Contemporary Theory, a Symposium*, in *Philological Quarterly*, 67 (1988), 403–80.

SHOAF, R. A., 'Medieval Studies after Derrida after Heidegger', in *Sign, Sentence, Discourse: Language in Medieval Thought and Literature*, ed. Julian N. Wasserman and Lois Roney (New York: Syracuse University Press, 1989), pp. 9–30.

TRIGG, STEPHANIE, ed. and introd., *Medieval English Poetry*, Longman Critical Readers (London: Longman, 1993).

2. General Chaucer Criticism

AERS, DAVID, *Chaucer, Langland and the Creative Imagination* (London: Routledge and Kegan Paul, 1980).

AERS, DAVID, *Chaucer*, Harvester New Readings (Brighton: Harvester, 1986).

AERS, DAVID, 'Medievalists and Deconstruction: *An Exemplum*', in *From Medieval to Medievalism*, ed. John Simons (London: Macmillan, 1992), pp. 24–40.

Further Reading

ANDREAS, JAMES R., '"Wordes Betwene": The Rhetoric of the Canterbury Links', *Chaucer Review*, 29 (1994), 45–64.

BLOOMFIELD, MORTON W., 'Contemporary Literary Theory and Chaucer', in *New Perspectives in Chaucer Criticism* (Norman, OK: Pilgrim Books, 1981), pp. 23–35.

BOOKER, M. KEITH, 'Postmodernism in Medieval England: Chaucer, Pynchon, Joyce, and the Poetics of Fission', *Exemplaria*, 2 (1990), 563–94.

BURGER, GLENN, 'Queer Chaucer', *English Studies in Canada*, 20 (1994), 153–70.

BURTON, T. L., '"Al Is for to Selle": Chaucer, Marx, and the "New Historicism"', *Southern Review: Literary and Interdisciplinary Essays*, 20 (1987), 192–8.

COOK, JON, 'Carnival and the *Canterbury Tales*: "Only equals may laugh" (Herzen)', in *Medieval Literature: Criticism, Ideology and History*, ed. David Aers (New York: St Martin's Press, 1986), pp. 169–91.

DIAMOND, ARLYN, 'Chaucer's Women and Women's Chaucer', in *The Authority of Experience: Essays in Feminist Criticism*, ed. Arlyn Diamond and Lee R. Edwards (Amherst: University of Massachusetts Press, 1977), pp. 60–83.

DINSHAW, CAROLYN, *Chaucer's Sexual Poetics* (Madison: University of Wisconsin Press, 1989).

DINSHAW, CAROLYN, 'Chaucer's Queer Touches/A Queer Touches Chaucer', *Exemplaria*, 7 (1995), 75–92.

FERSTER, JUDITH, *Chaucer on Interpretation* (Cambridge: Cambridge University Press, 1985).

GANIM, JOHN M., *Chaucerian Theatricality* (Princeton, NJ: Princeton University Press, 1990).

HAHN, THOMAS, 'The Premodern Text and the Postmodern Reader', *Exemplaria*, 2 (1990), 1–21.

HANSEN, ELAINE TUTTLE, *Chaucer and the Fictions of Gender* (Berkeley: University of California Press, 1992).

JORDAN, ROBERT, M., *Chaucer's Poetics and the Modern Reader* (Berkeley: University of California Press, 1987).

JOST, JEAN E., ed., *Chaucer's Humor: Critical Essays* (New York: Garland, 1994).

KAHN, VICTORIA, 'Intention, Interpretation, and the Limits of Meaning: A Response to A. C. Spearing and H. Marshall Leicester, Jr.', *Exemplaria*, 2 (1990), 279–85.

KENDRICK, LAURA, *Chaucerian Play: Comedy and Control in the Canterbury Tales* (Berkeley: University of California Press, 1988).

KNAPP, PEGGY, 'Deconstructing the *Canterbury Tales*: Pro', *Studies in the Age of Chaucer Proceedings*, 2 (1987), 73–81.

KNAPP, PEGGY, *Chaucer and the Social Contest* (London: Routledge, 1990).

KNIGHT, STEPHEN, *Geoffrey Chaucer*, Rereading Literature (Oxford: Blackwell, 1986).

LAWLER, TRAUGOTT, 'Deconstructing the *Canterbury Tales*: Con', *Studies in the Age of Chaucer Proceedings*, 2 (1987), 83–91.

LEICESTER, H. MARSHALL, Jr, *The Disenchanted Self: Representing the Subject in the Canterbury Tales* (Berkeley: University of California Press, 1990).

MANN, JILL, *Geoffrey Chaucer*, Harvester Feminist Readings (Hemel Hempstead: Harvester, 1991).

MARTIN, PRISCILLA, *Chaucer's Women: Nuns, Wives and Amazons* (London: Macmillan, 1990).

PATTERSON, LEE, *Chaucer and the Subject of History* (London: Routledge, 1991).

PORTNOY, PHYLLIS, 'Beyond the Gothic Cathedral: Post-modern Reflections on the *Canterbury Tales*', *Chaucer Review*, 28 (1994), 279–92.

Reconceiving Chaucer: Literary Theory and Historical Interpretation, ed. Thomas Hahn, special issue of *Exemplaria*, 2, 1 (1990).

STROHM, PAUL, *Social Chaucer* (Cambridge, MA: Harvard University Press, 1989).

TAYLOr, ANDREW, 'Chaucer Our Derridean Contemporary?', *Exemplaria*, 5 (1993), 471–86.

Chaucer: The Canterbury Tales

WALKER, FAYE, 'Making Trouble: Postmodern Theory With/In Chaucer Studies', *Style*, 26 (1992), 577–92.

WYNNE-DAVIES, MARION, ' "He Conquered Al the Regne of Femenye": Feminist Criticism of Chaucer', *Critical Survey*, 4 (1992), 107–13.

3. Criticism on Individual Tales

ANDREAS, JAMES, ' "Newe Science" from "Olde Bokes": A Bakhtinian Approach to the "Summoner's Tale"', *Chaucer Review*, 25 (1990), 138–51.

BURGER, GLENN, 'Kissing the Pardoner', *PMLA*, 107 (1992), 1142–56.

CRAMER, PATRICIA, 'Lordship, Bondage, and the Erotic: The Psychological Bases of Chaucer's "Clerk's Tale"', *Journal of English and Germanic Philology*, 89 (1990), 491–511.

DELANY, SHEILA, 'Slaying Python: Marriage and Misogyny in a Chaucerian Text', in *Writing Woman: Women Writers and Women in Literature, Medieval to Modern* (New York: Schocken, 1983), pp. 47–75.

ENGLE, LARS, 'Bakhtin, Chaucer, and Anti-Essentialist Humanism', *Exemplaria*, 1 (1989), 489–97.

ENGLE, LARS, 'Chaucer, Bakhtin, and Griselda', *Exemplaria*, 1 (1989), 429–59.

HARWOOD, BRITTON J., 'The "Nether Ye" and Its Antithesis: A Structuralist Reading of the "Miller's Tale"', *Annuale Medievale*, 21 (1981), 5–30.

KRUGER, STEVEN F., 'Claiming the Pardoner: Toward a Gay Reading of Chaucer's "Pardoner's Tale"', *Exemplaria*, 6 (1994), 115–39.

LEICESTER, H. MARSHALL, Jr, 'Newer Currents in Psychoanalytic Criticism and the Difference "It" Makes: Gender and Desire in the "Miller's Tale"', *Journal of English Literary History*, 61 (1994), 473–99.

LOCHRIE, KARMA, 'Women's "Pryvetees" and Fabliau Politics in the "Miller's Tale"', *Exemplaria*, 6 (1994), 287–304.

McCLELLAN, WILLIAM, 'Bakhtin's Theory of Dialogic Discourse, Medieval Rhetorical Theory, and the Multi-Voiced Structure of the "Clerk's Tale"', *Exemplaria*, 1 (1989), 461–89.

McCLELLAN, WILLIAM, 'Lars Engle – "Chaucer, Bakhtin, and Griselda": A Response', *Exemplaria*, 1 (1089), 499–506.

NELLES, WILLIAM, 'The Narrating of Chaucer's "Merchant's Tale"', in *Semiotics 1986*, ed. John Deely and Jonathan Evans (New York: University Press of America, 1987), pp. 15–23.

STOCK, LORRAINE K., ' "Making it" in the "Merchant's Tale": Chaucer's Signs of January's Fall', *Semiotica*, 63 (1987), 171–83.

Index